The Historical Foundations of Grotius' Analysis of Delict

Legal History Library

VOLUME 24

Studies in the History of Private Law

VOLUME 13

The titles published in this series are listed at *brill.com/shpl*

The Historical Foundations of Grotius' Analysis of Delict

By

Joe Sampson

BRILL
NIJHOFF

LEIDEN | BOSTON

Cover illustration: Frontispiece of Hugo Grotius' De Jure Belli ac Pacis. By W. de Breen, engraving - Peace Palace Library, The Hague, Public Domain.

Library of Congress Cataloging-in-Publication Data

Names: Sampson, Joe, author.
Title: The historical foundations of Grotius' analysis of delict / Joe Sampson.
Description: Boston : Brill, 2018. | Series: Legal history library ; volume 24 | Includes bibliographical references and index.
Identifiers: LCCN 2017041673 | ISBN 9789004344365 (hardback : alk. paper)
Subjects: LCSH: Grotius, Hugo, 1583-1645. | Torts–History.
Classification: LCC KZ2093 .S26 2017 | DDC 346.03–dc23
LC record available at https://lccn.loc.gov/2017041673

Typeface for the Latin, Greek, and Cyrillic scripts: "Brill". See and download: brill.com/brill-typeface.

ISSN 1874-1793
ISBN 978-90-04-34436-5 (hardback)
ISBN 978-90-04-34437-2 (e-book)

This book is printed on acid-free paper and produced in a sustainable manner.

Contents

Preface

This book seeks to cast light on the intellectual origins of a generalised conception of liability for wrongdoing. It takes as its focus the writings of Hugo Grotius, principally on natural law but also on Dutch law, as an early and influential proponent of such a model of delict. But it is really a book about those who came before Grotius. Faced with centuries of material to comb through, and three years within which to turn it into a doctoral thesis, a filter of sorts was needed to differentiate the essential from the inessential. Trying to explain a single author's account of a doctrinal development proved highly effective at this, but inevitably leaves the resulting work feeling incomplete. For instance, the chapters that make up Part III of this book describe various developments within successive generations of Thomist authors, especially in the late sixteenth century. Absent from the list is Luis de Molina, a monumentally important figure in the history of Thomism's juridification. The absence of Molina from this work should not be seen as indicative of an absence of material relevant to delict in his written corpus. Quite the opposite is true. There is a huge amount of sophisticated thinking about delict contained in his writings, much of which runs directly counter to the approaches of the Thomists examined in this book. But there is no evidence of Grotius being influenced in the slightest by Molina's analysis of delict, and so any reference to him was cut from this work. The result is an account of Thomism that explains the origins of Grotius' account of delict, but which cannot claim to be representative of all that was said by Thomist authors in relation to delict before Grotius.

Working on this project has also called into question the utility of the concept of tradition. Two central tranches of sources are explored in this book, which can broadly be identified as civilian and Thomist in origin. The unity of the latter category is largely secured by the shared source material of each author dealt with under the heading of Thomism. Each and every one of them was writing a commentary on Thomas Aquinas' *Summa Theologiae*. The format of their commentaries might have undergone changes over time, with an overall shift from a *quasetio*-by-*quaestio* analytical scaffolding erected around Aquinas' text to a freestanding commentary. But the overall function of their writings was consistently explication. The merits of grouping together the various authors examined in Part II of this book as 'The Civil Law' are less obvious. It is commonplace to think in terms of the glossators and the commentators, together the *mos italicus* who are to be contrasted with the *mos gallicus*, separate again from the decretists and decretalists of canon law scholarship, and so on. But the examination of delict in these various fora, especially in the late

Middle Ages and the sixteenth century, left the author questioning the utility of the concept of tradition once one moves beyond making fairly elementary generalisations about sources and methodology. Do they have any place in a detailed studied of doctrinal development? Or are they a necessary means of systematising the bulk of material available to historians of medieval and early modern private law? This is a theme touched upon in Chapter 10, which briefly explores the extent to which Thomism and Romanist scholarship interacted before Grotius, but deserves further attention.

The overall picture that emerges in this work is a curious one. Delict, one of the main sources of obligations, was neglected by those who wrote on the *Corpus Iuris Civilis* after a very early point in the revival of Romanist scholarship in the Middle Ages. Signs of life were sought out across a wide range of sources and over a number of centuries, but few were found. Within commentaries on the *Summa Theologiae*, on the other hand, wrongdoing flourished. This book's principal argument is that the formulation of delict found within Grotius' writings is primarily, though not quite entirely, Thomist in origin. Though some civilian facets can be identified, these elements had already been incorporated into Thomist doctrine before Grotius. Of particular importance is the work of Leonardus Lessius, whose *De Iustitia et Iure* bears a striking resemblance to Grotius' account of delict in *De Jure Belli ac Pacis*. Such a claim is not to be made lightly. It is hoped that by examining the development of the central features of the Thomist account of liability for wrongdoing, showing how closely they correspond to Grotius' formulation of delictual liability, and showing the absence of any parallel formulation in the civilian literature the reader will be convinced that the similarities between Thomism and Grotius are more than mere correspondence, but evidence of a direct influence of the former on the latter.

For the purposes of this book Grotius' formulation of liability for wrongdoing is divided into three essential elements. Firstly, the use of rights (both natural and civil) to identify the interests protected by delict. Secondly, the use of a single fault standard that applies regardless of the interest infringed. Thirdly, the use of a single remedy with a restorative focus as the principal form of redress offered in cases of wrongdoing. These three elements are not a complete statement of Grotius' account of delict, but taken together form the general principle of delictual liability that lies at the heart of his work on the topic. There is an awkward tension between this general principle and Grotius' own enumeration of specific forms of wrongdoing, which do not neatly adhere to the general principle in all cases. But it is the general formulation that influenced later generations, and on which this book will focus. It will be argued that all three of these elements have clear roots in the Thomist literature. Though the language of natural rights had precursors outside of Thomism as well as within, the precise list of natural rights suggests a Thomist link. The language used to describe fault, *culpa*, might feel civilian, but was also used widely in Thomist texts. The manner in which it is deployed as a single fault standard that captures every species of wrongdoing is distinctly Thomist, with no comparable usage in civilian sources. Finally, Grotius' remedy, *restitutio*, is characteristically Thomist. From Aquinas onwards *restitutio* was at the core of the Thomist approach not just to delict, but to private law generally. It is quite unlike anything the civil law explored in relation to delict, and so it is difficult to see anything other than a direct Thomist influence on Grotius' analysis of delict.

Acknowledgements

This book is the direct result of doctoral research carried out in the University of Cambridge between 2012 and 2015. During the course of my PhD, in my pre-doctoral years in Cambridge, and the years since submitting I have incurred innumerable debts to both institutions and individuals. My PhD years were generously supported by the Arts and Humanities Research Council, and my earlier studies by my *alma mater*, Trinity College, which also proved to be the ideal starting point for a legal education. More than the College itself, it was the kindness of its Law Fellows while I was an undergraduate—Catherine Barnard, Kevin Gray, Louise Merrett and Jo Miles—that encouraged me to pursue the somewhat esoteric path that has led to this work. Whether they would want to be credited with such, I am not sure. On the other hand, I am certain that my doctoral supervisor, David Ibbetson, would happily take ownership of my conversion to legal history and Roman law. He likes to joke that he is responsible for all the law I know, a joke with more than a hint of truth to it. Nevertheless, I am not so unfair as to make him take a share of the errors to be found in this book. Thanks are also owed to my examiners, Boudewijn Sirks and Mark Godfrey, who strongly encouraged the speedy dissemination of my research in this form, and to the anonymous reviewers who looked over the manuscript. All made insightful comments—most commonly about my misidentification of Roman medical practice, and the differences between syringes and enemas—that only improved the final work. The final stages of the conversion from thesis to monograph were completed in the idyllic environment of Selwyn College, Cambridge, whose support for the sort of research contained in these pages is greatly appreciated. The debts to individuals are myriad, and any attempt to recreate the list would only result in thoughtless omissions. As such, I will address my thanks in the abstract: to the friends and family who have seen me through the last five years, you have my heartfelt thanks.

Joe Sampson
March 2017
Selwyn College, Cambridge

PART I

Introduction

Introduction

Why is Grotius' theory of delict worth discussing, and why is it a topic that requires further academic study? Few would deny the central place of Grotius in the history of private law in Western Europe, so one might reasonably ask what could possibly be left to say about such a monumental figure. These are the questions that are explored in the first chapter of this work, arguing that the existing literature has not adequately explored Grotius' delictual thought in relation to both the civil law and Thomist traditions. The second chapter then provides the framework for this book through a brief sketch of Grotius' delictual thought, drawing on his natural law and Dutch law treatments of the topic. Its goal is to identify the distinguishing features of Grotius' delictual thought, in order to provide focus to the explorations of the civil law and Thomist literature that make up the bulk of this work.

CHAPTER 1

The Place of Grotius in European Private Law

It has long been recognised that the writings of Hugo Grotius represent a turning point in the history of European private law. A pioneer of a natural law interpretation of the law of obligations, it is not uncommon to find terms like 'watershed' describing his most influential work, *De Jure Belli ac Pacis*.[1] The literature on the history of delict in Europe is vast, but invariably Grotius features in a prominent position, separating medieval exegesis from the theoretical inquiries of early modern scholars.[2] Before Grotius stood the imposing commentaries of the medieval commentators, after Grotius the lucid treatises of Pufendorf, Woolf and their natural law brethren. Within delict in particular, Grotius has been credited with introducing the first general formulation of liability for wrongdoing. At heart this is a statement of delictual principle: that the blameworthy infliction of loss must be restored.[3] The distillation of all of delict down to just three ideas—fault, loss and remedy—is a remarkable departure from the convoluted scholarship of earlier centuries.

Grotius' influence within delict can be felt in many modern regimes. A direct link can be drawn between his *De Jure Belli ac Pacis* and Article 1382 of the *Code civil des Français* through Jean Domat (1625–1696) and the

1 E.g. Pietro Cerami, '*La responsabilità extracontrattuale dalla compilazione di Giustiniano ad Ugo Grozio*' in *La responsabilità civile da atto illecito nella prospettiva storico-comparatistica*, ed. Letizia Vacca (Turin: G. Giappichelli, 1995), 103: '[the treatise] *rappresenta nella storia della responsabilità civile lo spartiacque fra esperienza postgiustinianea ed esperienza precodicistica*'; Nils Jansen, 'Duties and rights in negligence: a comparative and historical perspective on the European law of extracontractual liability' (2004) 24 *Oxford Journal of Legal Studies* 443.

2 A survey can be found in the footnotes of Robert Feenstra, 'Grotius' doctrine of liability for negligence: its origin and its influence in civil law countries until modern codifications' in *Negligence: The Comparative Legal History of the Law of Torts*, ed. Eltjo J.H. Schrage (Berlin: Duncker & Humblot, 2001), 129, 130 n.2–3. A handful of works deserve singling out for their influence on Anglophone scholarship: Giovanni Rotondi, '*Dalla* lex Aquilia *all'art. 1151 Cod. Civ: ricerche storico-dogmatiche*' in Giovanni Rotondi, *Scritti Giuridici* (Pavia: Tipografia e legatoria cooperativa, 1922), 465; Frederick H. Lawson & Basil Markesinis, *Tortious Liability for Unintentional Harm*, 2 volumes (Cambridge: Cambridge University Press, 1982); and Reinhard Zimmermann, *The Law of Obligations: Roman Foundations of the Civilian Tradition* (Oxford: Clarendon, 1990).

3 Grotius, *De Jure Belli ac Pacis* (hereafter 'DJBAP'), 2.17.1.

 | DOI 10.1163/9789004344372_002

eighteenth-century jurist Robert Pothier (1699–1772).[4] As will be seen in due course, Grotius' formulation of delict rests on the enumeration of specific rights and a single notion of blameworthiness that applies across the full spectrum of wrongdoing. Whenever one of the specific rights is infringed through blameworthy conduct, an obligation to repair the loss inflicted is imposed. Pothier takes this generalised form of delict a step further, removing even the need for a specific right to be infringed.[5] This was carried forward into the French Code, with the key term '*dommage*' left undefined.[6] Grotius' treatment therefore represents an important first step towards the remarkably general French formulation of delict. A less direct though nevertheless cogent link has been drawn between Grotius and later German law, reliant on the influence of successive natural lawyers.[7]

In recent decades the nature of Grotius' influence has been re-examined. Rather than his own personal genius, the prevailing view is that the colossal injection of new ideas that his works gave private law scholarship had its origins in Aristotelianism, as constructed by Thomist theologians in the second half of the sixteenth century.[8] The authors who will be referred to as the Thomists in this work are known in the literature by many names, such as the neo-scholastics, early scholastics and the School of Salamanca. But the name Thomist reflects their unique approach to legal questions. They were theologians who wrote not on matters of law directly but on the legal dimensions of the theology and ethics of St Thomas Aquinas. Grotius was not alone in being affected by this peculiar source for legal innovation. Many authors of the so-called 'northern natural law school' were similarly influenced by the Thomist approach to law.[9] But Grotius, as the first and most influential of their

4 See generally Feenstra, 'Grotius' doctrine of liability for negligence', 167–170.

5 Robert J. Pothier, *Traité des obligations, selon les regles tant du for de la conscience, que de for extérieur* (Paris: Chez Debure, 1768), para. 116: '*On appelle* délit, *le fait par lequel une personne, par dol ou malignité, cause du domage ou quelque tort à quelqu'un*'.

6 The assumption that Pothier's formulation of delict influenced Article 1382 is often made but rarely analysed. Putting aside the near-identical content, it is easy to see Pothier's treatise being used in the drafting stages of the codification process, even if the final text omits any references to its intellectual origins. However, there still appears to be room for doubt: Eric Descheemaeker, *The Division of Wrongs: A Historical Comparative Study* (Oxford: Oxford University Press, 2009), 118ff.

7 Feenstra, 'Grotius' doctrine of liability for negligence', 160–166.

8 James Gordley, *Foundations of Private Law: Property, Tort, Contract, Unjust Enrichment* (Oxford: Oxford University Press, 2006), 14.

9 James Gordley, *The Jurists: A Critical History* (Oxford: Oxford University Press, 2013), chapter 5.

number, deserves special attention. Whatever merits the Thomist approach to legal questions had of its own, its adoption by such a wide range of authors was in part due to its prior integration into Grotius' natural law.[10]

A natural response might be to ask why one would look for a lawyer's inspiration in the works of theologians. The reasons behind the theologians' interest in law are many and varied, but chief among them is the correspondence between a just society and a spiritually fulfilling life that recurs in Aristotelian thought, and by extension theologies built upon Aristotelian foundations.[11] The perfect formulation of legal rules and principles was a central aspect to the theologians' work, providing the rationale for a detailed exploration of legal doctrine according to higher principles rather than practical concerns. The use of legal sources by theologians has a long history, but the authors who supposedly influenced Grotius were clustered in the second half of the sixteenth century, working primarily in Spain.[12]

The re-evaluation of Grotius' work in light of Thomist thought has been effected piecemeal through individual strands of legal doctrine. The pioneer of the field was Robert Feenstra, who first toyed with a possible link between Thomism and Grotius' thought in the late 1950s.[13] He revisited the topic in relation to the law of unjust enrichment in a contribution to a volume of collected essays on the Thomist approach to legal doctrine.[14] The theme of this

10 It is interesting to note that although Grotius considered Aquinas an essential read for any man of learning, his own knowledge of the *Summa Theologiae* was heavily derived from sixteenth-century Thomist authors. His reading of the *secunda secundae* in particular was somewhat patchy, according to a recent analysis of his working library: Martine Van Ittersum, 'The working methods of Hugo Grotius: which sources did he use and how did he use them in his early writings on natural law theory?' in *Reassessing Legal Humanism and its Claims*, eds Paul Du Plessis & John Cairns (Edinburgh, 2015), 179–190.

11 For a broader overview of the theological context that enabled the Thomists to become quasi-jurists, see Wim Decock, *Theologians and Contract Law: The Moral Transformation of the Ius Commune (ca. 1500–1650)* (Leiden: Brill, 2013), 22–43.

12 On why this might be the case, see below, 120.

13 Robert Feenstra, '*Théories sur la responsabilité civile en cas d'homicide et en cas de lésion corporelle avant Grotius*', in *Etudes d'histoire du droit privé offertes á Pierre Petot* (Paris: Librairie Générale de droit et de jurisprudence, 1959), 157–171. Although this re-examination began in earnest in the 1950s, it had earlier roots, e.g. Karl Weinzierl, *Die Restitutionslehre der Frühscholastik* (Munich: Verlag Max Hueber, 1936).

14 Robert Feenstra, '*L'influence de la scolastique espagnole sur Grotius en droit privé: quelques expériences dans des questions de fond et de forme, concernant notamment les doctrines de l'erreur et de l'enrichissement sans cause*', in *La Seconda Scolastica nella Formazione del Diritto Privato Moderno*, ed. Paolo Grossi (Milan: Giuffrè, 1973), 377.

volume, capturing the excitement with which the academic community received the possibility of an entirely new tradition within European legal history, was what modern doctrinal scholars might learn from this esoteric group of churchmen. Consequently, questions of history were downplayed. For example, Hans Thieme's essay saw an immediate link between the Thomists and Grotius, but was more concerned with comparisons between modern French law and scholasticism.[15]

It was not until the early 1990s that studies were dedicated to the influence of Thomism on entire branches of private law. At the heart of the Thomist approach to private law is the concept of *restitutio*, and so it is perhaps not surprising that an early focus was unjust enrichment.[16] However, contract was also represented from the start.[17] By contrast, delict was neglected. The reasons for this are unclear. The second edition of Grotius' *De Jure Belli ac Pacis*, published in 1631, contains Grotius' own attribution of authority. The side notes of his treatment of delict are filled with the names of Thomists before all others. Nevertheless, early explorations of any possible links between Thomism and later delict were cautious.[18] Feenstra, the giant of the field, explored Grotius' delictual thinking twice. Both of these dedicated studies came late in his career, although early considerations of the Thomist approach to unjust enrichment and its influence on Grotius unavoidably touched on delictual topics. His first study focused narrowly on Grotius' treatment of wrongs to the person.[19] Though it recognised the possibility of a significant Thomist influence on Grotius' delictual thinking, it was too narrow a piece and too focused on Grotius' influence on later thought to make

15 Hans Thieme, '*Qu'est ce-que nous, les juristes, devons á la seconde scolastique espagnole?*' in *La Seconda Scolastica nella Formazione del Diritto Privato Moderno*, ed. Paolo Grossi, (Milan: Giuffrè, 1973), 7.

16 Gero Dolezalek, 'The moral theologians' doctrine of restitution and its juridification in the sixteenth and seventeenth centuries' (1992) Acta Juridica 104; Jan Hallebeek, *The Concept of Unjust Enrichment in Late Scholasticism* (Nijmegen: GNI, 1996). Significant groundwork had been laid in a PhD thesis: Nufer, *Über die Restitutionslehre der spanischen Spätscholastiker und ihre Ausstrahlung auf die Folgzeit* (privately published Munich, 1969).

17 James Gordley, *The Philosophical Origins of Modern Contract Doctrine* (Oxford, 1991). It continues to be explored in ever more detail: Decock, *Theologians and Contract Law*.

18 E.g. Arthur Von Mehren and James Gordley, *The Civil Law System: An Introduction to the Comparative Study of Law* (Boston: Little, Brown & Co., 1977), 572.

19 Robert Feenstra, '*Das Deliktsrecht bei Grotius, insbesondere der Schadenseratz bei Tötung und Körperverletzung*' in *Das römisch-holländische Recht*, eds Robert Feenstra & Reinhard Zimmermann (Berlin: Duncker & Humblot, 1992), 429.

any general conclusions about the intellectual origins of Grotius' approach to wrongdoing.

Feensta's second article, though it was also written with an eye to the future direction of European private law, provided a wider study of Grotius' delictual thought.[20] He concluded that the relevant chapter of *De Jure Belli ac Pacis* represented 'a fortunate synthesis of the doctrines of contemporary moral theology and Donellus' systematical approach of the Roman law'.[21] He claimed that the use of natural rights was unmistakably taken from Donellus, and so provided Grotius with a partially civilian basis.[22] By contrast, the language of inequality and *restitutio* is undoubtedly Thomist in origin.[23] For Feenstra, Grotius' brilliance lies in the way he reconciled these two traditions, all the while making it appear as if Thomist doctrine and contemporary civilian learning were in harmony.[24]

The topic was further explored in a series of wide-ranging surveys of the history of private law by James Gordley, who first examined the influence of Thomism on private law in relation to contract.[25] His first study of delictual doctrine focused not on Grotius, but on the Aristotelian tradition generally.[26] The occasional reference to Grotius is made, but only to show consonance with a conclusion made by a Thomist.[27] The language of 'the Aristotelian tradition' was adopted to facilitate a discussion of the then-novel theories of Ernest Weinrib, among others.[28] Though historical material is explored, it is primarily for the purpose of leveraging arguments against modern scholars advancing ancient views. Two more detailed studies of the history of delict on either side of Grotius followed.[29] But both volumes, though impressive in scope, are limited by their methodology. The first, *Foundations of Private Law*, advances an

20 Feenstra, 'Grotius' doctrine of liability for negligence', 129.

21 Ibid., 171

22 Ibid., 143.

23 Ibid., 133–134.

24 Ibid., 143.

25 Gordley, *The Philosophical Origins of Modern Contract Doctrine.*

26 James Gordley, 'Tort law in the Aristotelian tradition' in *Philosophical Foundations of Tort Law*, ed. David G. Owen (Oxford: Oxford University Press, 1995), 131.

27 E.g. Ibid., 135.

28 Chiefly Ernest J. Weinrib, *The Idea of Private Law* (Cambridge, Mass.: Harvard University Press, 1995), but also Ernest J. Weinrib, 'The special morality of tort law' (1989) 34 McGill Law Journal 403 and Ernest J. Weinrib, 'Liberty, Community and Corrective Justice' (1988) 1 Canadian Journal of Law and Jurisprudence 3.

29 On delict: Gordley, *Foundations of Private Law,* 159–284; regular references to delict are made throughout Gordley, *The Jurists.*

almost Whiggish account of the history of private law as a whole in Europe. The focus flits constantly between centuries, jurisdictions and even continents.[30] The project is clear: to show how individual problems of legal doctrine have been solved by different groups of scholars across time and space.[31] But whatever the gains it makes as a work of comparative law come at the expense of historical rigour. As a whole, the work lacks a sensitivity to the different contexts in which conceptual language is used, and is often content to take the concurrence of a given term within traditions as evidence of a shared understanding of the concept behind the word.[32] Moreover, its sheer scope prohibits any detailed analysis of small questions of influence—it must be content to address general questions of trends in scholarship, lest it balloon well past its relatively modest 450 pages.

Gordley's second survey shows a similar preoccupation with the idea of tradition.[33] Gordley's interest in legal traditions can be traced back to the start of his career.[34] Armed with the accumulated learning of two decades spent mostly researching questions of doctrine, he has in recent years returned to the theme. The result, *The Jurists*, is a work of remarkable scope. But a consequence of the sheer scale of his work is the need for compartmentalisation. Scholars are grouped together by perceived commonalities. Everyone who might be termed a medieval civilian, whether writing in the twelfth or the fifteenth century, whether discussing the *Corpus Iuris Civilis* or *Corpus Iuris Canonici*, is to be found in a single chapter.[35] So too for anyone who might be called a humanist.[36]

This manner of grouping could easily be forgiven. After all, when dealing with two millennia of scholarship, the material needs to be organised somehow. But Gordley's chosen taxonomy has an unfortunate effect on his analysis. The individual is subordinated to his assigned tradition, with little allowance made for individual thought or methodology. Instead the language of 'program' prevails.[37] As will be argued in due course, the humanists were a remarkably

30 For a work on foundational doctrines, twentieth-century American law features in a disproportionately large number of footnotes.

31 Hence extended sections are dedicated to topics as niche as water rights (Gordley, *The Jurists*, 103–129).

32 A particularly noteworthy example, to be discussed in due course, is the meaning of the word *negligentia* in different legal systems and theology. See below, pages 155–156.

33 Gordley, *The Jurists*, in which each chapter is dedicated to a tradition.

34 His first book was von Mehren and Gordley, *The Civil Law Tradition*.

35 Gordley, *The Jurists*, chapter 2.

36 Ibid., chapter 4.

37 E.g. recurring references to 'the humanist program' in Gordley, *The Jurists*, chapter 4.

disparate group of scholars, running the gamut from uninterested in anything other than the earliest days of Roman law and society to innovators of contemporary doctrine. To speak of humanists in the abstract as a school of scholars with a shared goal and methodology misses this nuance. The same problems recur in relation to the Thomists, a group of authors defined by their shared identity as jurists and theologians. But some authors were far closer to being theologians than others, and this is reflected in the way in which they formulated their doctrines.

Both these works, though sometimes lacking in historical rigour, should be praised for their breadth.[38] Important to this work is Gordley's general conclusion that the writings of the Thomists were largely responsible for many of the doctrinal revolutions found in seventeenth-century natural law and beyond. Like Feenstra, Gordley argues that this was achieved through a synthesis of Roman and Thomist doctrine. Unlike Feenstra, he attributes this synthesis not to Grotius, but to the Thomists themselves.[39] As it stands this is an incomplete argument. A conclusion has been reached: Thomist doctrine as formulated in the last days of the Second Scholastic is largely responsible for the content of the natural law theorists. But the reasoning by which this conclusion has been reached is too reliant on a mere correspondence between the overall shapes of delict in the writings of the Thomists and early natural lawyers. More needs to be done for a claim of direct influence to be viable.

Recent steps in this direction have been taken by Nils Jansen.[40] Returning to the *Restitutionslehre* of the Thomists, he has argued that the significance of this doctrine to later delictual scholarship has been overlooked in favour of unjust enrichment. The Thomist *restitutio*, as an inherently bifurcated concept, provides the foundations for both categories of obligation. He methodically shows how the Thomist *restitutio ratione acceptionis* developed in the sixteenth century, and went on to influence the likes of Grotius and Stair. But the question of influence is again incomplete. Jansen's study focuses exclusively on Thomist doctrine. There is no opportunity to discuss the possible influence

38 Indeed, this was a feature of *The Jurists* that has been singled out for specific praise. E.g. Katharina I. Schmidt, 'Review', (2015) 33 Law and History Review 467 describes the scope of Gordley's work as 'a welcome change of course'.

39 Gordley, *The Jurists*, 82. He argues that this was their very goal: 'The project of the late scholastics was to synthesize Roman and canon law with the moral philosophy of Aquinas and Aristotle'.

40 Nils Jansen, *Theologie, Philosophie und Jurisprudenz in der spätscholastischen Lehre von der Restitution* (Tübingen: Mohr Siebeck, 2013).

of civilian ideas of wrongdoing, except insofar as they were assimilated into Thomist doctrine.

This work seeks to strike a middle path between the approaches adopted by recent scholarship. The question it seeks to answer is simple: from where did Grotius pluck his ideas about delict? The literature seems united in identifying two possible pools of ideas: civil law, as formulated by humanist scholars, and Thomism. But was Feenstra right to suggest that he borrowed from both in similar proportions? Or should we prefer Gordley's suggestion that any Roman law that ended up in Grotius' natural law treatise was the product of prior assimilation by the Thomists? It is only by looking at the way in which delictual questions were answered by both civil lawyers and Thomists in the sixteenth century that we can hope to arrive at an answer.

CHAPTER 2

Grotius' Formulation of Delict

This work purports to look at delict in a range of intellectual contexts across the span of several centuries. It is a project that requires focus. This can only be attained by approaching the treatment of delict in both the civil law and Thomism with the knowledge of how Grotius deals with such liability, so that the correct strands of doctrine and thought can be identified and examined. This in turn risks putting the cart before the horse by identifying factors with a particularly civilian or Thomist bent. The purpose of this chapter is to give a brief overview of the entirety of Grotius' delictual thinking at a descriptive level, without passing any comment on its likely influences.

Grotius deals with delict in two distinct contexts: natural law and Dutch law. The former was by far the more influential outside of the Netherlands and its legal descendants, and when scholars talk about the influence of Grotius on an area of legal thought it is these works, and in particular *De Jure Belli ac Pacis*, that they have in mind. But Grotius' writings on Dutch law should not be neglected. Written at roughly the same time as *De Jure Belli ac Pacis*, his *Inleidinge tot de Hollandsche Rechtsgeleerdheid* provides many comparative insights into Grotius' delictual thinking. This chapter will consider both works, albeit with an overall emphasis on the more influential natural law formulation of delict. It will look first at how delictual liability is formulated in each, before considering commonalities between the two works and the degree to which the *Inleidinge* might help clarify some of the central concepts of Grotius' natural law formulation of delict.

The General Definition

Grotius' natural law theory recognises three sources of obligation: *pactus, maleficium* and *lex*.[1] Delict maps on to the second of these, though the term is not used by Grotius. The chapter on delict is brief, comprising just twenty-two paragraphs. These can be divided into a general statement of principle and a series of more detailed descriptions of individual wrongs. He begins with the general:

1 DJBAP, 2.17.1.

 | DOI 10.1163/9789004344372_003

> Maleficium hic appellamus culpam omnem, sive in faciendo, sive in non faciendo, pugnantem cum eo quod aut homines communiter, aut pro ratione certae qualitatis facere debet. Ex tali culpa obligatio naturaliter oritur, si damnum datum est, nempe ut id resarciatur.[2]

Simplicity itself: anyone who blameworthily causes loss, whether by act or omission, is naturally bound to repair it. From this we can extract three essential elements of delictual liability: fault, harm and remediation. But for fault, these are immediately given more concrete definitions. From there, he goes on to consider a series of individual wrongs: homicide, violence, adultery, rape, theft, robbery, contractual duress and deceit, vicarious liability and defamation. Each of these elements requires further consideration.

Remediation

The verb used to connote remediation in the general definition of delict is *resarciatur*, from *resarcire*. Its noun form is provided by the short title given to the definition at the chapter's outset: *restitutio*.[3] The term is not defined in relation to delict, though the word itself has connotations of restoration. Insights as to its possible meaning can be gleaned from the delictual remedy offered in Grotius' treatise on Dutch law: *weder-evening* (literally 're-equalisation').[4] In the *Inleidinge* this remedy arises solely in a delictual context. Delict (*misdaed*) is the term used for inequalities caused inimically by another, giving rise to two obligations: the obligation to suffer punishment (*straf*), and the obligation to redress the inequality caused. It is in the latter context that *weder-evening* arises. Elsewhere in the treatise the term 'compensation' (*vergoeding*) is used, such as in the case of a man consuming another's food.[5] It is *vergoeding* that is used in the passage that is generally seen as Grotius' general enrichment action.[6] Delict is clearly

2 Ibid., 2.17.1: 'Here the name of crime or misdemeanour [*maleficium*] is applied to every act of commission or neglect repugnant to the duties required of all men, either from their common nature or particular calling. For such offences naturally create an obligation to repair the loss or injury that has been sustained'

3 Ibid., 2.17.1: '*Culpam obligare ad restitutionem damni*'.

4 Grotius, *Inleiding tot de Hollandsche rechts-geleertheyd* (hereafter '*Inleidinge*'), 3.32.

5 Ibid., 3.1.15. *Vergoeding* is also the remedial term used in modern Dutch tort law, e.g. Burgerlijk Wetboek Book 6 Article 162.

6 *Inleidinge*, 3.30.18; e.g. Hallebeek, *The Concept of Unjust Enrichment in Late Scholasticism*, 90.

something apart, with a different remedial construct serving a different remedial purpose.

Weder-evening is discussed in the following terms:

> A man is bound to make compensation as soon as he can and so far as he can; therefore, since one who has killed another cannot give back the life which he has taken, he must give back what he can to those who have suffered from the man's death. A man is bound also to compensate another not only for taking from him or injuring what belonged to him, but also for depriving him of what he was likely to get: subject, however, to the consideration that uncertain and future advantages are not worth so much as what is certain and present.[7]

That *weder-evening* is a remedy distinct from straightforward monetary compensation is made readily apparent by the examples that follow:

> Defamation is 'compensated' by speaking honourably of the man who has been defamed untruthfully and unlawfully. Injury, as springing from contempt, is compensated by humiliation and tributes of respect.[8]

> 'Compensation' must be made in respect of ownership, complete or incomplete; also in respect of possession, unless it is quite notorious that the possessor who has been deprived was not the owner, but someone else was: in which case the offender is bound by lawful means to help the true owner to come by his own.[9]

---

7 *Inleidinge*, 3.32.16: '*Tot de weder-evening is iemand ghehouden soo haest de selve ken gechieden, ende voor soo veel die ken gheschieden. Daerom alsoo een doodslagher het leven niet en kan wedergheven, zoo moet hy weder-gheven dat hy kan, aen die ghenen de door des overledens dood zijn verkort: men is oock niet alleen schuldig te vergoeden de ontneeming ofte verachtering van 't gunt iemand hadde, maer oock van 't gunt hy gheschapen was te krijgen: doch opzicht daer op zijnde ghenoen, dat onzeecker ende toekomend goed niet soo veel waerd en is, als het zekere ende tegenwoordige*'.

8 Ibid., 3.32.17: '*Lastering werd verevent met eerlick spreecken van de gene die buiten waerheid onwettelick is gelastert. Hoon als spruitende uit verachting werd werevent door nederigheid ende eerbieding*'.

9 Ibid., 3.32.18: '*Men is schldig weder-evening te doen van eigendom volle ofte ghebreckelicke: oock van bezit, uitgenomen als kennelick is dat den bezitter, dien iet is benommen, geen eigenaer en is, maer een ander, in welken ghevalle den misdadige gehouden is door wettelicke middelen den rechten eigenaer aen het sijne te helpen*'.

With *weder-evening* the precise effects of the wrongdoing are identified and expunged. This is most clear in the case of defamation, for which the remedy does not simply attach a monetary figure to the plaintiff's reputation but seeks to undo the harm through countermeasures. *Weder-evening* is an obligation under natural law, while punishment is the right of sovereigns and a matter of civil law.[10] As such, we have to restore any inequalities we wrongfully cause immediately, while any punishment must only be suffered pursuant to a judicial order to that effect.[11]

Weder-evening is a remedy that is established *in solidum*.[12] Though a great many people can be required to make amends for their participation in wrongdoing, whether through command, consent or permission, the full restoration of the wrongdoing by any one wrongdoer frees his comrades from any obligation.[13] Overcompensation is straightforwardly impermissible, an outcome that ought to be obvious from the English translation of *weder-evening* as re-equalisation. To tip the balance of wealth too far in the claimant's favour is to create a fresh injustice. Finally, *weder-evening* is a general remedy. It has already been seen how it applies to damaged reputations as well as the paradigm case of financial harm.[14] But it also applies to injuries to life and limb, albeit in a limited capacity. The wrongful killer must make every possible step to undo the harm he has inflicted on those affected by the death of his victim, by fulfilling the deceased's financial commitments to his family and others.[15] As a remedy it looks not only to the actual loss inflicted but also any consequential failure to make a gain, though such gains are valued at a lower rate as they become increasingly speculative

The *Inleidinge* explicitly refers to natural law having a remedy akin to *weder-evening*.[16] That this should be understood as referring to *restitutio* as a similarly restorative remedy can be seen through the paragraph in *De Jure Belli ac Pacis* dealing with defamation. In relation to wrongs to *fama* and *honor*, Grotius writes:

10 Ibid., 3.32.7.

11 Ibid., 3.32.9.

12 Ibid., 3.32.15.

13 Ibid., 3.32.13, 15.

14 Should there be any doubt about the remedy's proper application to property: *Inleidinge*, 3.32.18. Interestingly the obligation to restore applies to displaced possession as well as displaced ownership.

15 Ibid., 3.32.16.

16 Ibid., 3.32.11.

> huic damni [*i.e. wrongs to* fama] reparatio quae fit culpae confessione, exhibitione honoris, testimonio innocentiae, et per ea quae his similia sunt: quanquam et pecunia tale damnum rependi poterit, si laesus velit, quia pecunia communis est rerum utilium mensura.[17]

The remedy is firmly focused on the precise harm inflicted, and seeks to undo its deleterious effects not through compensation but through countermeasures. A similar idea can be seen in his consideration of homicide, in which Grotius tries to show how a person's life might be 'restored' in a meaningful way.[18]

The word *restitutio* appears outside of Grotius' analysis of delict in 2.17. However, its usages invariably coincide with wrongdoing in one form or another. This can be seen at multiple instances where Grotius discusses unjust wars, viewing a failure to make *restitutio* as a barrier to salvation.[19] Like *wederevening*, *restitutio* is a remedy that arises specifically in response to injustice. And, as in the *Inleidinge*, it must be differentiated from punishment. As with *restitutio*, it is the law of nature that decides when a punishment ought to be imposed. However, the law of nature goes no further than this: it emphatically does not detail either the content of punishment, nor does it ascribe the right to punish to any individual.[20] These are matters for positive law. Punishment fulfils the useful end of correcting bad habits (undeniably important for anyone who subscribes to Aristotelian morality), but it is not something that can be given structure or content by natural law. This delineation of *restitutio* and *poena* is the final point of correspondence between Grotius' two delictual remedies. In every material way the two are the same: a general and restorative mechanism that serves to correct injustices.

The Harm Element

The term used to denote the effect of the wrong, *damnum*, is the first ingredient of liability to be defined:

17 DJBAP, 2.17.22: 'Such loss can be repaired by confessing to the wrong, by displays of honour, by attesting to the wronged party's innocence, and through similar methods; and in some situations such loss can be restored monetarily, at the wronged party's election, since money is the common measure of all things'.

18 Ibid., 2.17.13. This has a clear parallel in *Inleidinge*, 3.32.16.

19 E.g. DJBAP, 3.10; Ibid., 2.22.

20 Ibid., 2.20.3.

> Damnum forte a demendo dictum, est τό ελάτιον, cum quis minus habet suo, sive illud suum ipsi competit ex mera natura, sive accedente facto humano, puta dominio, aut pacto, sive ex lege. Natura homini suum est vita, non quidem ad pedendum, sed ad custodiendum, corpus, membra, fama, honor, actiones propriae.[21]

The principal division is between natural and civil rights. The former number six: *vita, corpus, membra, fama, honor* and *actiones propriae*.[22] Civil rights are by their very nature impossible to define in the abstract, though it is they that provide a basis for the protection of property rights in natural law. The meaning of *vita* is clear; the duality of *corpus* and *membra* less so. It is not a distinction that resurfaces elsewhere in the chapter. Similarly obtuse is the need for two personality interests in *fama* and *honor*. Grotius appears to have anticipated that their inclusion in a list of natural rights might meet incredulity. At the very close of the chapter, he repeats himself. This is noteworthy in a natural law work—an otherwise elegant and lucid statement of principle unmarred by needless tautology. Nevertheless, he says:

> Sed damnum, ut diximus, etiam adversus honorem et famam datur, puta verberibus, contumeliis, maledictis, calumniis, irrisu, aliisque similibus modis. In quibus non minus quam in furto atque aliis criminibus vitiositas actus ab effectu discernenda est.[23]

This passage reaffirms the pair of personality interests as protected rights, though it casts no light on the difference between the two. The tetchiness

21 Ibid., 2.17.2: 'By loss is meant a diminution of what one possesses, whether it be a right derived to him purely from the law of nature, or from the addition of human authority, that is from the law of property, contract or civil law. God has given life to man, not to destroy, but to preserve it; assigning to him for this purpose a right to the free enjoyment of [his body and limbs], reputation, [honour,]and the control over his own actions' (author's addition in square brackets; translation originally offers 'personal liberty' for *corpus* and *membra* and omits *honor*).

22 Cf the division of rights in the *Inleidinge*, 2.1.42 and 3.33.1: life (*leven*), body (*lichaam*), freedom (*vryheid*), reputation (*eer*) and property (*goederen*). The first four are said to be inalienable. Grotius' natural formulation omits property, which is a civil right, and introduces pairs of right in place of *lichaam* and *eer*.

23 DJBAP 2.17.22: 'But loss, as we have said, can be caused even as against honour and reputation, such as through blows, contumelies, curses, slander, mockery, and similar methods. The effects of these wrongs must be discerned, no less than in theft and other such vicious crimes'.

of Grotius' injection of his own voice in '*ut diximus*' seems to suggest that he anticipated hostility or disbelief in reaction to his inclusion of such interests within the general definition of delict. The final natural right, *actiones propriae*, is an idea akin to autonomy. It refers to a person's ability to make his own decisions, free from fear or deceit.[24] In the *Inleidinge* the natural rights are replaced with 'inalienable' rights: *leven* (life), *lichaam* (body), *vryheid* (autonomy or freedom) and *eer* (reputation).[25] The phrase '*ander niet zouden konnen toebehooren*' ('which cannot belong to another') is translated into Latin as '*inalienabiles*' in the margin.[26] When this list of rights resurfaces in a delictual context, property (*goederen*) is added to the list, though this is obviously not an inalienable right.[27] There is clearly a degree of overlap between the two groups of rights, with *vita* and *leven*, and *actiones propriae* and *vryheid* aligning neatly. The immediately noteworthy difference is the duplication of interests in the body and personality in natural law: *corpus* and *membra* together are reduced to just *lichaam*, and *fama* and *honor* become *eer*. The need for this duplication is something that can only be understood by looking into prior legal thought.

In addition to the six natural rights, Grotius' conception of delict is capable of dealing with the diminution of civil rights (i.e. rights positively conferred within a given legal regime, and not available through nature alone), including property. Property is said to include not only physical things, but also their fruits.[28] A claim for fruits needs to make some allowance for the cost and expenses involved in harvesting them, or else the claim would tip the scales too far in the favour of the claimant, who would effectively be enriched by free labour. Hypothetical losses, or the lost hope of an imminent gain, prove more difficult. These too are recoverable, but only in proportion to the likelihood of the gain being obtained.[29] The example given is of a sown field that is damaged, wherein damages are scaled according to the likelihood of a good harvest.

The exploration of individual wrongs sometimes appears inconsistent with the general principle that the blameworthy diminution of a right grants a remedy. This can be seen with the wrong against life, *homicidia*. Life (*vita*) is a natural right, and so any blameworthy diminution of life ought to result in *restitutio*. It is not clear whether *vita* is a binary right (i.e. something that one

24 Ibid., 2.17.17; see Gustaaf van Nifterik, 'Hugo Grotius on "slavery"' in *Grotius and the Stoa*, eds Hans W. Blom and Laurens C. Winkel (Assen: van Gorcum, 2004), 235.

25 *Inleidinge*, 2.1.42.

26 Ibid., 2.1.42.

27 Ibid., 3.33.1.

28 DJBAP, 2.17.4.

29 Ibid., 2.17.5.

either has or lacks) or whether a remedy might be available for lessening a person's lifespan. The wrong itself is undefined, a conscious departure from his account of the same wrong in Dutch law.[30] But Grotius' account of *homicidia* raises even more fundamental issues than the quality of *vita* as a natural right:

> Homicida injustus tenetur solvere impensas si quae factae sunt in medicos, et iis quos occisus alere ex officio solebat, puta parentibus, uxoribus, liberis dare tantum quantum illa spes alimentorum, ratione habita aetatis occisi, valebat ... Vitae autem in libero homine aestimatio non sit. Secus in servo qui vendi potuit.[31]

This denial of a remedy that addresses the loss of life itself can be explained in two ways. The first explanation uses the language of rights, and is provided in Grotius' initial enumeration of rights.[32] Though we have a natural right in our lives, it is only a right of guardianship. Implicit in such reasoning is the view that a delictual claim can only be brought to aspects of ownership, and that any of the other five rights that is given a full remedy ought to be thought of as a dimension of ownership. But in this passage Grotius takes a different approach. He argues that life itself is not something that can be given a value. Rather, delictual actions brought after a homicide seek to replicate the value of the deceased to their family.[33] It follows that where a person without a family dies, there is no obligation to restore, although there would still be a *poena*.[34] This might seem a trivial point, given the absence of a claimant to demand *restitutio*. However, it shows that it is not the mere diminution of life that generates an action, but the consequential financial loss. Thus there are two distinct

30 The *Inleidinge* delineates between assassinations and other homicides, knowing and unknowing homicides, homicides born of anger or passion, homicides resulting from a fight and homicides caused through neglect: *Inleidinge*, 3.33.5. All of these varieties are bound together by the notion that the simple causing of death through fault (*schuld*) is sufficient for a remedy. It is this sentiment that is carried forward into natural law.

31 DJBAP, 2.17.13: 'The case of excusable homicide may be alleged as one, wherein the person, who has committed it, is bound to [pay what is owed to doctors and to] make every reasonable compensation to the family, dependents and connections of the deceased party, in proportion to the loss, which they have sustained from his death ... [However, the life of a freeman cannot be assigned a value, or else they could be sold as a slave] (author's translation; original translation omitted reference to *medicos* and final two clauses).

32 Ibid., 2.17.2.

33 The *Inleidinge* would also allow funeral expenses: 3.33.3.

34 *Poenae* are aspects of positive law not natural law, and so no punishment for *homicida* can be formulated in the abstract.

aspects of Grotius' views on homicide that need to be identified in his source material: on the one hand, life as a natural right which if interfered with generates an action for damages; on the other, life as something beyond monetary valuation.

The same limitations arise in the remediation of *mutilatio*:

> Qui mutilavit similiter tenebitur ad impensas et ad aestimationem eius, quod iam qui mutilatus est minus poterit lucrari. Sed sicut ibi vitae, ita et hic cicatrices in libero homine aestimatio non sit.[35]

Once again we are confronted with a remedy limited to expenses, the core interest being beyond the scope of financial valuation.[36] It is also curious how neither *membrum* nor *corpus* are mentioned in the text. Instead Grotius focuses on the types of wound: dismemberment and scarring. That mutilation is an affront to the one of these interests is common sense, but the connection is proven by the *Inleidinge*, which deals with four types of injury to the body (*lichaam*): maiming (*afgeslagen*), fracture (*verminkt*), bloodshed (*gebloedritst*) and any other harm (*anderszins gekrenkt*).[37] The only ambiguity is whether *lichaam* is taken as a translation of *corpus* or *membrum*.

Two further wrongs are then discussed that by their location are presumably diminutions of *corpus* or *membra*.[38] The first is adultery that begets a child. Here the adulterous couple must ensure the adulteress' husband bears no cost for the child's upbringing. They must also make *restitutio* to any legitimate children whose inheritance is diminished by the illegitimate child's existence. The second situation concerns an entirely different type of wrong, intercourse with a virgin procured by force or deceit. Here the wrongdoer must make *restitutio* to the value of her damaged marriage prospects. Moreover, if he enticed her through promises of marriage, Grotius would have the wrongdoer live up to his word. Again, *corpus* and *membra* are entirely absent within the text. In this

35 DJBAP, 2.17.14: 'Upon the same principle the person, who has maimed or mutilated another, will be bound to make him a compensation, proportionably to the means of subsistence which he is deprived of by such a calamity'.

36 Paralleled in *Inleidinge*, 3.34.1.

37 Ibid., 3.34.1.

38 The right violated is not mentioned. In the *Inleidinge*, such wrongs are affronts to *vryheid*, which is far closer to the *actiones propriae* of natural law. Moreover, the text mentions *vis* and *fraus*, which are wrongs against *actiones propriae*. The text however follows on the heels of Grotius' discussions of *homicida* and *mutilatio*, while wrongs to *actiones propriae* are not discussed until two texts later, separated by *furtum*.

context the wrong seems anomalous. Whether it is better understood as an affront to the victim's *actiones propriae* will be considered in relation to that right. So far as *corpus* and *membra* are concerned, as with *vita*, it will be necessary to explore both the abstract natural rights found in the definitional portion of Grotius' analysis, and the list of specific wrongs given as representing breaches of those natural rights in the meat of the text.

Wrongs to *fama* and *honor* receive the most consistent treatment across the chapter. Under the general principle, any diminution of either natural right ought to generate an obligation to restore, and this is precisely what Grotius says at the very end of the chapter:

> Sed damnum, ut diximus, etiam adversus honorem et famam datur, puta verberibus, contumeliis, maledictis, calumniis, irrisu, aliisque similibus modis. In quibus non minus quam in furto atque aliis criminibus vitiositas actus ab effectu discernenda est. Nam illi poena respondet, huic damni reparatio quae fit culpae confessione, exhibitione honoris, testimonio innocentiae, et per ea quae his similia sunt: quanquam et pecunia tale damnum rependi poterit, si laesus velit, quia pecunia communis est rerum utilium mensura.[39]

Immediately noteworthy is the lack of a single nominate wrong like *homicidia* or *mutiliatio*. Rather, *fama* and *honor* can be hurt in a multitude of ways, from physical blows (*verberibus*) to mockery (*irrisu*). The focus on the harmed interests is necessary to unite this disparate range of conduct. Similarly important is the way in which the remedy of *restitutio* is adapted to the unusual nature of personality interests. Money is not the most effective means of restoring a damaged reputation. To 'restore' the harm caused, it is better to issue a public retraction, or to sing the victim's praises in order to improve his public image. Money can still be a viable remedy, at the election of the victim, given its status as a 'common measure'. But it is not the remedy of first recourse. Thus there are three aspects of Grotius' treatment of harm to personality interests that require focus: the duality of *honor* and *fama*, the

39 DJBAP, 2.17.22: 'But loss, as we have said, can be caused even as against honour and reputation, such as through blows, contumelies, curses, slander, mockery, and similar methods. The effects of these wrongs must be discerned, no less than in theft and other such vicious crimes. Such loss can be repaired by confessing to the wrong, by displays of honour, by attesting to the wronged party's innocence, and through similar methods; and in some situations such loss can be restored monetarily, at the wronged party's election, since money is the common measure of all things'.

wide range of conduct that can constitute a wrong, and the literally restorative nature of the remedy. By contrast, the *Inleidinge* considers only one personality interest: *eer*. This is defined as the opinions others hold about us, and so is closer to reputation (*fama*) than honour (*honor*).[40] Such wrongs occur 'either verbally or in writing, in presence or absence, in secret or in public'.[41] Though a wide range of conduct is again captured by the wrong, the focus is entirely on words. Physical violence is solely an affront to the body, and not to *eer*.

The wrongs attached to the final natural right, *actiones propriae*, arise within a contractual context.[42] To compel a person to make a promise through duress (*metus*) or deceit (*dolus*) is to deny them autonomy, and a man is naturally entitled to make his own decisions. A further wrong is grouped together with *metus* and *dolus*: '*qui id ex officio facere tenebantur facere noluerunt nisi pecunia accepta*'.[43] The link with *actiones propriae* is clear enough: someone who refuses to act in accordance with his duty is not fulfilling 'his' actions. But it is interesting to note that the right of *actiones propriae* can be used not only for interference with a person's capacity to act as an individual, but also to compel them to act as they ought to. This is very different from Grotius' treatment of wrongs to freedom (*vryheid*) in Dutch law.[44] Such wrongs are linked to the Roman delict of *iniuria*. *Dolus* and *metus* are seen as distinctly contractual doctrines, and dealt with in that context rather than as aspects of delict.[45] The category of wrongs to *vryheid* is used to group together any wrong that does not hurt another identifiable right. This includes rape, which harms not only the victim's body but her marriage prospects. Marriage prospects are too intangible a right to be considered elsewhere, and so compensation for them is seen as a dimension of *iniuria*.[46] The same logic grants a remedy for deflowering a virgin.[47] This wrong arises in Grotius' discussion of natural law in a context indicative of bodily harm, though the precise right infringed is left unsaid. Given the same focus on the harm done to the victim's marriage prospects, perhaps this too is best understood as an affront to her *actiones*

40 *Inleidinge*, 3.36.1.

41 Ibid., 3.36.2: '*Hierdoor worden verbonden alle, die mondeling of schriftelyk, in 't bywezen, of in 't afwezen, in 't heimelyk of in 't openbaar...*'.

42 DJBAP, 2.17.17.

43 Ibid., 2.17.17.

44 *Inleidinge*, 3.35.1.

45 Ibid., 3.48.

46 Ibid., 3.35.7.

47 Ibid., 3.35.8.

propriae. The physicality of the wrong might explain its location within the treatment.[48]

The final group of nominate wrongs does not concern a natural right. Instead they protect property rights. N o model of delict, natural or otherwise, would be complete without a mention of theft and robbery. Neither offence is defined beyond the term '*rem subtractam*', which suggests literal asportation.[49] Instead Grotius concentrates on the remedy. A *fur* or *raptor* must restore that which he has taken away, as well as accounting for any fruits or lost gains. Where the property has been destroyed, he must return a value '*non summam, non infimam, sed mediam*'.[50] According to whose estimation is left unsaid. Two further groups of wrongs are then included by extension. From theft, Grotius moves on to leaving taxes unpaid, which is viewed as akin to theft from the state. He then includes judges who pass unjust sentences, witnesses who give false testimony and accusers who make false accusations as a related type of wrong. It is difficult to think of these classes of defendants as thieves or robbers. Their inclusion in this context likely reflects their anomalous nature. They are grouped together as wrongs that occur in the courtroom or a similarly official context, and cannot be formulated in the abstract as a wrong to any of the six natural rights. Thus they are included with the sole group of wrongs that affect civil rights. In order to make the group work as a whole, it was necessary to bridge theft and wrongs that occur in an official context through the equally anomalous 'official' theft that is the non-payment of taxes. It is a messy solution that would only be adopted if Grotius was convinced the 'official' wrongs were worth including.[51]

Responsibility

A plurality of fault concepts pepper Grotius' natural law analysis of delict. The title of the chapter is '*de damno per iniuriam dato*'. The language of *iniuria* is immediately replaced by *maleficium*, which is then replaced by *culpa*:

48 After all, the ordering of the wrongs is far from systematic. Wrongs to *fama* and *honor* are separated from the main treatment of the forms of wrongdoing, and theft is thrown into the mix.

49 DJBAP, 2.17.16; cf *Inleidinge*, which under '*misdaad tegen goed*' considers spoiling (*goed-verderving*), stealing (*goed-beneming*) and damaging (*goed-verergering*) – Inleidinge, 3.37.1.

50 Ibid., 2.17.16.

51 The incongruous nature of this grouping is given away by the paragraph's short title: '*de fure, raptore et aliis*'.

> Maleficium hic appellamus culpam omnem, sive in faciendo, sive in non faciendo, pugnantem cum eo quod aut homines communiter, aut pro ratione certae qualitatis facere debent.[52]

These terms appear to be used interchangeably, without technical content. A glimpse into Grotius' understanding of *maleficium* is provided by the *Inleidinge*, the marginalia of which connotes *misdaad* with *maleficium*.[53] But the definition of *misdaad* is equally expansive: it is doing, or allowing to be done, that which is either unlawful by its inherent character, or under a specific prohibition.[54] This is very similar to the definition of *maleficium* in *De Jure Belli ac Pacis*, the only difference being a predictable switch from the standards of humanity inherent in a natural legal order ('*quod aut homines communiter, aut pro ratione certae qualitatis facere debent*') to those of a grounded legal system.[55] A further idea appears much deeper in Grotius' natural law analysis: voluntariness. He first considers the effects of fraud and deceit on a contract, and argues that such behaviour grounds a claim in delict as an unwarranted infringement of a person's right to control their own behaviour (*actiones propriae*). But then he considers what happens if a person is compelled through threats or deceit because he placed himself in a situation where this *ought* to happen:

> At qui causam dedit cur vim pati, aut metu cogi debeat habet quod sibi imputet. Nam involuntarium ex voluntario ortum habens moraliter pro voluntario habetur.[56]

The somewhat bizarre scenario envisaged in the first sentence is unimportant.[57] More significant is the implication of the second sentence: the act performed under compulsion, though involuntary itself, stems from a voluntary

52 Ibid., 2.17.1: 'Here the name of crime or misdemeanour [*maleficium*] is applied to every act of commission or neglect repugnant to the duties required of all men, either from their common nature or particular calling'.

53 *Inleidinge*. 3.32.3.

54 Ibid., 3.32.3: '*misdaad is een doen of laten, zynde uit zichzelve, of door eenige wet ongeoorloofd*'.

55 DJBAP, 2.17.1.

56 Ibid., 2.17.18: 'When a person has himself been the occasion of the fraud or violence, the consequences are imputable to his own conduct. For where a voluntary act gives rise to involuntary consequences, those consequences, considered in a moral light, are to be deemed the fruits growing out of the exercise of a free will'.

57 The level of obligation implied by *debeat* is troubling. When *ought* someone be compelled to act by fear or deceit? It might be dealing with the situation in which a person places

choice. This is sufficient for responsibility for it to be imputed to him. This imputation is achieved without any recourse to the language of *iniuria*, *maleficium* or *culpa*. From this plurality of concepts it would appear that fault is a loosely bordered concept within Grotius' analysis of delict. Nevertheless, it plays an utterly central role. The obligation to restore arises principally '*ex tali culpa*', though an additional ingredient is required in loss.[58] Indeed, a recent commentator suggested that the emphasis that Grotius places on *culpa* makes his model of delict one justified by 'the violation of first order duties of behaviour' rather than the infringement of right.[59] This seems a step too far: though the obligation arises '*ex tali culpa*', it also arises only where loss (soon after defined as the diminution of a right) has been inflicted. The underlying rationale for delictual liability is the coincidence of *culpa* and *damnum*. As such, it is surprising that no guidance is given on how *culpa* is to be understood

Grotius' loose formulation of fault was supported by a more robust model of causation. Grotius relies on a distinction between primary and secondary causes (*primario* and *secundario*) as applied to both acts and omissions. The combination of these two sets of considerations results in a matrix that maps out the different ways in which a person can contribute to harm without being the actual wrongdoer. The language of principals and accessories is sometimes mapped onto this distinction, but this is misleading.[60] Everything described as either *primario* or *secundario* operates in addition to the principal wrongdoer. Both categories would be thought of as accessorial liability in modern parlance.

> Primario qui iubet, qui consensum requisitum adhibet, qui adiuvat, qui receptum praestat, aut qui alio modo in ipso crimine participat.[61]
> Secundario, qui consilium dat, laudat, assentatur.[62]

themselves in a situation in which such coercion or deception is likely, but that does not explain the use of *debeat*.

58 DJBAP, 2.17.1.

59 Jansen, 'The idea of legal responsibility' (2014) 34 OJLS 221, 230, relying on the statement of delict's essence in DJBAP, 2.17.1: '*ex tali culpa* (not from infringement of an individual right, or *damnum*, or inequality) obligatio *naturaliter oritur si damnum datum est, nempe ut id resarciatur*'.

60 E.g. the English translation used in Hugo Grotius, *The Rights of War and Peace*, ed. Richard Tuck, from edition by Jean Barbeyrac (Indianapolis: Liberty Fund, 2005).

61 DJBAP, 2.17.6: 'Firstly, those who order, gives consent that is needed, helps, harbours or in such a way participated in the crime itself'.

62 Ibid., 2.17.7: 'Secondarily, those who give advice, praise or assent'.

> Non faciendo item primario aut secundario: primario, qui cum ex iure proprie dicto debeat vetare praecepto, aut opem ferre ei cui fit iniuria, id non facit.[63]
> Secundario, qui aut non dissuadet cum debeat, aut factum reticet quod notum facere debebat[64]

These ten possible causal contributions operate alongside the person who actually causes the harm ('*damnum dat*').[65] If any of these possibilities proves to be a 'true' cause of the loss ('*vera causa*'), meaning it contributed to the loss either in whole or in part, their authors too are liable to make *restitutio*.[66] The language of *restitutio* means that the amount the claimant can obtain is capped at the actual loss covered that the law recognises as recoverable. In the first instance it is the responsibility of the principal wrongdoer to restore the loss he has caused, but insofar as he is unable to fulfil that obligation the liability falls on any ancillary causes, first primary then, where the primary is incapable of discharging his obligation, secondary.[67]

Separate from these considerations is a further passage on noxal liability insofar as it applies to harm done by animals and slaves.[68] The argument against liability on the part of the owner where his slave or animal causes harm is founded upon the example of a ship that collides with another ship. In this scenario, the liability to make *restitutio* arises only in the presence of fault. So too for animals and slaves—where property harms property, liability on the part of the owner arises only in the presence of personal fault. This is perfectly consistent with the individualistic notion of fault just seen. The only quirk comes in how damages are to be calculated in the case of the ships colliding: given the difficulties in proving fault in the wake of a collision, damages are to be split across the parties involved. This is expressly not a rule of natural law, but '*multorum populorum legibus, ut et nostra*'.[69] If it is not a rule of natural law, it ought to have no bearing

63 Ibid., 2.17.8. 'Omissions are also divided into primary and secondary causes. Firstly, those who by virtue of their position ought to order against the commission of the wrong and does not do so'.

64 Ibid., 2.17.9 'Secondarily, those who fail to dissuade the commission of the wrong or stay silent when they ought to disclose what they know of the wrong'.

65 Ibid., 2.17.6. The same list appears in Inleidinge, 3.32.13-14. Any such causal factor is bound by natural law to make *weder-evening*, and that liability exists *in solidum*: *Inleidinge*, 3.32.15.

66 Ibid., 2.17.10.

67 Ibid., 2.17.11.

68 Ibid., 2.17.21.

69 Ibid., 2.17.21.

on the ordinary case wherein one person's property harms another's. These cases ought to be decidable according to the principles just outlined.

Conclusion

There is a great deal of overlap between Grotius' natural law and Dutch law formulations of delict, but the two are not without their differences. Both analyses place remediation at the fore, the lynchpin that holds delict together. In both the remedy is restorative, seeking to give the victim what he has lost so far as it is possible. Both cap compensation at that level, refusing to allow delictual liability to lead to enrichment. Both accept that monetary compensation might not be the best form for a remedy to take, and consequently place significant emphasis on the restoration of a damaged reputation through countermeasures. Indeed, the *weder-evening* of Dutch law is defined through comparison with the natural law *restitutio*. In both function and operation Grotius' delictual remedies are identical. This consonance also underpins both analyses' treatment of responsibility. In both the term *maleficium* (again, the Dutch term *misdaad* is defined by reference to the Latin) is given the same expansive definition of doing what one ought not to do, or failing to do what one must. The only difference between the two is the relevant standard against which conduct is measured: the lofty sense of human community in *De Jure Belli ac Pacis* and the positive legal obligations of the *Inleidinge*. Both allocate responsibility through a more elaborate model of causal contributions, using the same multifaceted analysis to determine whether a person is liable based not on their fault, but the role they played in causing the harm.

It is in the third element—harm—that differences can be seen. Both models of delict use the language of rights, but their precise nature and enumeration differs. In natural law there are six natural rights (*vita, corpus, membra, fama, honor, actiones propriae*) while in Dutch law there are just four inalienable rights (life (*leven*), body (*lichaam*), autonomy (*vryheid*) and reputation (*eer*)) alongside property (*goederen*). In natural law there are two sets of natural rights relating to the body and personality interests, while there is just one for each in Dutch law. However, both frameworks are comfortable dealing with the same range of wrongdoing.

Spanning just twenty-two short paragraphs, there is a remarkable volume to Grotius' natural law analysis of delict. At its core is an elegant maxim: anyone who blameworthily causes another loss must restore that loss.[70]

70 Ibid. 2.17.1.

It is this passage that provides the three pillars of Grotius' delictual thought. Firstly, responsibility through blameworthiness, a term that is conceptualised loosely but capable of accommodating a wide variety of causal contributions. Secondly, loss, defined as the diminution of any right a person has, whether naturally or under a system of positive law. Thirdly, a restorative remedy that seeks simply to place the victim in the position they were in prior to the harm occurring. Each of these three elements is distinctive, unlike much of what is found in the mainstream of prior delictual scholarship. This model of clarity is subject to a number of addenda through Grotius' exploration of individual wrongs. The blameworthy infringement of *vita*, although a natural right, is not in itself grounds for a claim for *restitutio*. Such a claim will only exist for any financial loss consequent on the death. But these contortions can only be examined at the end of this work, when the civil and Thomist approaches to delict have been fully analysed. For present purposes it is sufficient to arm ourselves with knowledge of what is uniquely Grotian about the model of delict advanced in *De Jure Belli ac Pacis*, and to this end three elements have been identified: an all-encompassing notion of loss in damnum, a universal fault standard couched in the language of blameworthiness, and a single remedy with a restorative focus.

PART II

The Civil Law

The Civil Law

This section explores the development of delict within the Civil Law across three chapters. The overall picture that emerges is one of neglect and fragmentation. The Roman foundations of delict were uneven. The initial division between delict and criminal law was a schism that underpins much of the later history of delict, and would prove an insurmountable barrier to the harmonisation of delict even into the seventeenth century. Those rights that were subject to the law delict were rigorously defended, but in a manner that defies systematisation. An inevitable by-product of the law of actions is a pluralistic approach to wrongdoing, with a variety of fault standards and inconsistent remedies protecting similar rights across the spectrum of delict, the result of historical patchwork and piecemeal doctrine. Moreover, those wrongs that were addressed by the criminal law, including the most serious forms of personal injury, were forever isolated from questions of compensation.

The popularity of civil law scholarship across Europe for most of the past millennium necessitates an extremely broad perspective in its dealings with much of the material across the next three chapters. Chapter three will take the Corpus Iuris Civilis as its basis, exploring the building blocks of delict laid down in antiquity. Chapter four will then attempt to paint in broad strokes the contours of delictual development from the rediscovery of the Corpus Iuris Civilis to the end of the fifteenth century. As will be seen in due course, this is a story that peters out quickly. In the twelfth century delict provoked great academic interest, but soon came to be seen as a subject for canonists and dedicated criminal lawyers. Its subject matter divided, the later glossators and commentators neglected delict is a source of obligations. By extension, this meant that the question of compensatory remedies arising from wrongdoing went largely unstudied. Chapter five will pick up the story in the sixteenth century, and explore the degree to which delictual scholarship was revived under the mos italicus and mos gallicus immediately before Grotius. It will be argued that but for a handful of pivotal characters, chief among them Donellus, delict fared little better in the sixteenth century than it had in the Middle Ages.

There is a colossal amount that can be said about the history of wrongdoing in medieval and early modern Europe. To maintain focus, these chapters will focus on the information that might have influenced Grotius. Firstly, they will focus primarily on wrongdoing as a source of obligation—on delict and not crime. Some attention will have to be given to the treatment of criminal law so as to be able to see the complete picture of wrongdoing at a given point in time, but the precise formulation of individual crimes is not of interest.

Secondly, they will look for trends towards generalisation and harmonisation. This means concentrating on the structure of wrongdoing over the detail of how they are applied. They will be searching for harmonised fault standards and remedies, and a drift towards basing liability on the results rather than specific patterns of conduct. In most of these foci they will be disappointed, as the Roman foundations of delict proved too ingrained to overcome. But it is these aspects of delict that could potentially provide a civilian foundation for Grotius' approach to wrongdoing.

CHAPTER 3

The Roman Law of Delicts

Delict and Crime

Obligation, the concept that binds together a sizable portion of Roman law, is not easy to define. Gaius defined obligations using their origins in contract and delict.[1] More promising, though not without controversy, is the definition provided by the Digest: '*obligationum substantia non in eo consistit ut aliquod corpus nostrum aut servitutem nostrum faciet sed ut alium nobis obstringat ad dandum aliquid vel faciendum vel praestandum*.'[2] A person bound by an obligation can be compelled 'to give', 'to do' or 'to perform'. All three verbs connote action; there is no way in which an obligation can be used to force a person to suffer something being done to them. Thus for as long as Roman society viewed matters such as homicide to be punishable rather than compensable, they were barred from the realms of delict.

Forms of wrongdoing that were redressed other than through doing, performing or giving fell under the criminal law of Rome. This operated principally through isolated jurisdictions and a dedicated system of courts (*quaestiones perpetuae*) and so became isolated from the mainstream of the civil law.[3] This would not have affected their importance within the Roman legal system, but it did serve to greatly obscure the significance of non-delictual wrongdoing to later generations, whose knowledge of Roman law comes principally from the *Corpus Iuris Civilis*.[4] Given the inevitable focus of the later civil law tradition, this section's content is skewed towards delictual wrongdoing. Nevertheless, it must be remembered that delict represents only one slice of the total Roman law on wrongdoing.

There were four main delicts: liability under the *lex Aquilia* for wrongfully caused loss (also known as *damnum iniuria*), *iniuria*, *furtum* and *rapina*.[5]

1 G.3.88–89.

2 D.44.7.3.pr: 'The essence of obligations does not consist in that it makes some property or a servitude ours, but that it binds another person to give, do, or perform something for us'.

3 Olivia F. Robinson, *The Criminal Law of Ancient Rome* (London: Duckworth, 1995), 2–6.

4 One book of the Digest is given over to criminal law: book 48. It is comprised of texts taken from commentaries on particular *leges*, and insights into criminal law snatched from other contexts. It thus provides an incomplete and warped view of Roman criminal law.

5 See generally William W. Buckland, *A Text-book of Roman Law: From Augustus to Justinian*, 3rd ed. Peter Stein (Cambridge: Cambridge University Press, 1963) 576–608 and Zimmermann, *The Law of Obligations*, 902–1206.

 | DOI 10.1163/9789004344372_004

These four delicts were singled out for special consideration by Gaius in his student textbook, and were again presented as the 'main' delicts by Justinian.[6] The centrality of these four wrongs to the law of delict is not borne out by the Digest, which treats all but the *lex Aquilia* as individual members of a list of over a dozen delicts.[7] Nevertheless, given the importance of the institutional framework to the later history of delict, the taxonomy adopted by Gaius and cemented by Justinian represents a sensible starting point for our exploration of the classical law of delict.

The Delicts as Conduct-Centric Wrongs

Each of the four institutional delicts was built around prohibited conduct. This can be seen most clearly in *furtum*, which responded to *contrectatio*. This is a term that defies translation.[8] There is a strong sense of tangibility to the word, and it is generally assumed that *furtum* originally required physical interference with another's property.[9] By classical law this requirement had slackened, though the degree to which *contrectatio* could exist without physicality is disputed.[10] A particular problem arose in the context of living property, which could be compelled from the possession of its owner without any direct physical contact, such as where a person drives away donkeys or chases

6 G.3.182–225; J.4.1–4.

7 The precise number of delicts depends on whether one treats the various specific instances of theft as one delict or many. Regardless, there are many that simply do not accord with the institutional delicts: harbouring criminals (D.47.16), breaking out of prison (D.47.18), extortion (D.47.13) and altering boundaries (D.47.21).

8 E.g. David J. Ibbetson, 'The danger of definition: *contrectatio* and appropriation' in *The Roman Law Tradition*, eds David J. Ibbetson and Andrew D.E. Lewis (Cambridge: Cambridge University Press, 1994).

9 The modern form of this position is traceable to Daube, '*Furtum probium* and *furtum improbium*' (1936–1938) 6 Cambridge Law Journal 217, in which he refutes the suggestion that the *res furtiva* of the Twelve Tables could be distinguished from the *res subrepta* of the *lex Atinia* on the grounds that the XII Tables brand of *furtum* was about fraudulence, not theft. This long-neglected stance stems from Paul Huvelin, *Etudes sur le furtum dans le très ancien droit romain* (Lyon: A. Rey, 1915).

10 E.g. William W. Buckland, '*Contrectatio*' (1941) 57 Law Quarterly Review 467; Alan Watson, '*Contrectatio* as an essential of *furtum*' (1961) 77 Law Quarterly Review 526; Joseph A. C. Thomas, '*Contrectatio*, complicity and *furtum*' (1962) 13 IURA 70; Alan Watson, '*Contrectatio* again' in *Studies in Roman Private Law*, ed. Alan Watson (London: Hambledon Press, 1991).

peacocks.[11] In light of such concerns, it is preferable to think of *contrectatio* as any interference with property. It is equally possible that the requirements differed according to the affected property: living property could be encouraged to run away without making physical contact, while the only way to deprive an owner of his inanimate property is to physically abscond with it. In the former case we might use the word 'interference', while in the latter 'handling' will suffice.

More complicated is *rapina*. This delict targeted a wide range of conduct, a fact sometimes obscured by its persistent treatment as little more than an aggravated form of *furtum*. This view stems from Ulpian's statement that *rapina* was a delict introduced to deal with force.[12] But his quotation from the praetor's edict reveals a wrong that is a bit more complicated: '*si cui dolo malo hominibus coactis damni quid factum esse dicetur sive cuius bona rapta esse dicentur, in eum, qui id fecisse dicetur, iudicium dabo*'.[13] One of the two wrongs described, forcefully depriving another of his property, clearly accords with the typical account of *rapina* as an aggravated form of *furtum*. But what of the other wrong: causing loss as an armed gang?

Ulpian treats the gathering of armed men as one of the ways in which force might be displayed.[14] Moreover, the requirement is trivialised by the interpreting 'men' as 'man'—simply having one armed person with you is sufficient for the action.[15] The need for violence is similarly rendered hollow, with mere beguilement sufficing.[16] The proper action where loss is caused by a gang is clearly supposed to be the *lex Aquilia*.[17] But from the topics he discusses, albeit somewhat sparingly, one can see that prior discussions hinted at *rapina* being a different sort of wrong targeted at ringleaders whose underlings caused loss. One such clue is to be found in D.47.8.2.12, in which Ulpian deals with the problem of identifying the specific wrongdoer. If you can identify the pool of possible suspects by pointing to a gang, but cannot name which one in particular caused you harm, the action will nevertheless lie. Ulpian does not say

11 D.47.2.52.20; D.47.2.37. This is the line advanced in Buckland, '*Contrectatio*' (1941) 57 Law Quarterly Review 467.

12 D.47.8.2.1.

13 D.47.8.2.pr: 'If any loss be said to have been inflicted with deliberate wrongfulness by armed men on someone or if his goods be said to have been forcibly taken, I will grant an action against the person alleged to have done this'.

14 D.47.8.2.2, 4.

15 D.47.8.2.6

16 D.47.8.2.8.

17 D.47.8.2.10.

against whom, but an earlier text places responsibility on whoever gathered the group, though actions against individual members are also permissible.[18]

The association with gang violence could also be supported by D.47.8's oft-neglected second half, dealing with loss caused '*de turba*'. Such loss merited an *actio in factum* giving damages of double the value of the property harmed, awarded under its own edict.[19] A tumult (or *turba*) was a significant disturbance, which Labeo distinguished from mere brawls.[20] Though no precise definition is given, Labeo implies that a tumult must involve a crowd.[21] This form of wrongdoing was clearly taken less seriously by the jurists, as can be seen in the very action awarded, a mere *actio in factum*. But if the two edicts that fall under the heading *rapina* are conjoined, as the classical jurists so clearly thought they were, it could point towards a common mischief. And, in both cases, the focus of the jurists is centred firmly on the type of conduct that constitutes the delict.

Iniuria is a similarly difficult delict to pin down. Its plural nature is revealed by the name of the action through which it was enforced, the *actio iniuriarum*. A great many types of wrong came to be dealt with through the delict. These were initially introduced piecemeal by the praetor, but were given a conceptual core by Labeo. The disparate strands of *iniuria* were brought together through the notion of *contumelia*.[22] Whether the specific wrong was a physical assault or public defamation, the actionable criterion was the disrespect manifested in the act towards the victim.[23] A heightened form of liability for *atrox iniuria* could be imposed where the disrespect manifested was particularly potent by virtue of the act itself, the person targeted or the location of the offence.[24] Though an injury's severity might be sufficient for rendering it *atrox*, the examples given suggest that it is the public exposure of the insult or the public stature of the victim that is at the core of aggravated liability. Thus slapping someone in the theatre is *atrox* despite there being no real harm because of the potential audience to the disrespect.[25]

The final delict, established under the *lex Aquilia* but often referred to as *damnum iniuria*, covered two sets of wrongs. Chapter one concerned the killing

18 D.47.8.2.12.

19 D.47.8.4.11.

20 D.47.8.4.3.

21 D.47.8.4.3.

22 D.47.10 1.pr.

23 David J. Ibbetson, '*Iniuria*, Roman and English', in *Iniuria and the Common Law*, eds Eric Descheemaeker and Helen Scott (Oxford: Hart, 2014).

24 D.47.10.7.8.

25 D.47.10.9.1.

of slaves and *pecudes*.[26] The verb used for killing, *occidere*, requires more explanation. It has a narrow meaning for a killing verb—it is not simply to bring an end to life, but doing so in a violent manner. This violence was described as *occidere*'s distinguishing feature by the grammarian Sextus Pompeius Festus in the late second century, and there is little to suggest that this was a new connotation.[27] The violence of the verb was reflected in its legal interpretation through a criterion of bodily directness: some modicum of force was needed for direct liability on chapter one of the *lex Aquilia*.[28] A series of examples involving poisoning illustrate the boundary between *occidere* and *necare*, the verb used to connote killing generically.[29] In the first, a midwife administers a drug that results in death. This is actionable on the *lex*.[30] In the second, the poisoner persuades their victim to allow the administration. The facts are constructed in such a way as to minimise the level of force involved: the patient consents, and the only force used is that required to introduce the poison, apparently by way of an enema. This still results in liability on the *lex Aquilia*.[31] In the third, the midwife gives the poison to the patient and has them administer it themselves. The absence of even a modicum of force pushes this case across the boundary, and a direct action on the *lex* would not be available.[32]

This slavish adherence to literalism was only possible because of the availability of a parallel form of liability: *actiones in factum* and *actiones utiles*. These praetorian remedies, collectively known as the decretal actions, were used to expand the scope of liability under the *lex Aquilia*. Within chapter one, they were available wherever a killing occurred that was not *occidere*.[33] Thus the third poisoning case involving self-administration by the victim would result

26 D.9.2.2.pr.

27 Festus, *De verborum significatu quae supersunt*, ed. Emil Thewrewk (Budapest, 1889), 195: '*occisum a necato distinguitur. Nam occisum a caedendo dictum, necatum sine ictu*' ('Slaying is to be distinguished from killing. For slaying suggests striking, while killing can occur without a blow'). Though the paucity of Latin texts contemporary with the *lex Aquilia* means any etymological argument ought to be viewed with caution.

28 A criterion reflected in the abstract test proposed by Gaius, who required that the harm be caused '*corpore corpori*' (G.3.219).

29 The term *causa mortis praebere* frequently appears in place of *necare*.

30 D.9.2.9.pr.

31 D.9.2.9.1.

32 D.9.2.9.pr.

33 Dieter Nörr, '*Causam mortis praebere*' in *The Legal Mind: Essays for Tony Honoré*, eds Neil MacCormick and Peter Birks (Oxford: Clarendon, 1986), an argument greatly expanded (but fundamentally unchanged) in Dieter Nörr, *Causa Mortis: Auf den Spuren einer Redewendung* (Munich: Beck, 1986).

in an *actio in factum*.[34] It is not clear how closely the decretal actions paralleled direct actions on the *lex Aquilia*. Direct actions were subject to an unusual procedural quirk known as *lis crescens* or litiscrescence, the doubling of liability for unsuccessful denials of responsibility. A clearly penal rule, it would be bizarre if it were not used to punish needlessly cruel means of causing death that fell short of *occidere* such as starvation.[35] The evidence is ultimately ambiguous. Texts elsewhere in the Digest have been used to support the idea that the generic term 'liability on the *lex Aquilia*' was used to refer to both direct and decretal actions, suggesting it was a boundary without substantive or procedural implications.[36] Nevertheless, decretal actions are sometimes said to be '*ad exemplum legis Aquiliae*', implying that without such a tag they would not be based on the *lex*.[37] The very existence of this verbal formulation suggests that by default there were procedural differences between direct and decretal actions. Such a distinction does not alter the basic scope of chapter one: anyone who blameworthily caused the death of a slave or *pecus* would be liable, one way or the other.

Chapter three of the *lex Aquilia*, as recorded in the edict and reported by Ulpian, read:

> <ceterarum rerum> <praeter hominem et pecudem occisos> si quis alteri damnum faxit, quod usserit fregerit ruperit iniuria, quanti ea res erit in diebus triginta proximis, tantum aes domino dare damnas esto.[38]

The phrasing of chapter three is slightly troubling, and the source of this discomfort can be traced to the first two clauses, demarcated by angular brackets. It would be unfortunate if one had to doubt the very wording of the edict, and so before considering the doctrinal detail of chapter three some effort must be made to isolate and expunge our worries.

---

34 D.9.2.9.pr.

35 D.9.2.9.2.

36 Alan Watson, 'D.7.1.13.2: The *lex Aquilia* and decretal actions' in *Studies in Roman Private Law*, ed. Alan Watson (London: Hambledon Press, 1991), 263.

37 John L. Barton, 'The *lex Aquilia* and decretal actions' in *Daube Noster: Essays in Legal History for David Daube*, ed. Alan Watson (Edinburgh: Scottish Academic Press, 1974).

38 D.9.2.27.5: 'In respect of other matters, except killed people and grazing animals, if anyone causes loss to another, by burning, breaking or smashing wrongfully, whatever that matter will be worth in the nearest thirty days, let him be condemned to pay so much bronze to the owner'. While 'slave' is a perfectly natural translation of *hominem* used by Ulpian through D.9.2, rendering it as 'person' emphasises the sloppiness of the clause in relation to chapter one.

'*Ceterarum rerum*' is not easy to translate. *Res* is one of the broadest nouns to be found in Latin, and among its many possible meanings are 'thing' and 'matter'. Thus two entirely plausible translations would be 'in respect of other things' and 'in respect of other matters'. Both would appear to be linking chapter three to the provisions that preceded it. This is extremely problematic for any scholar wishing to speculate on chapter three's original content.[39] The content of chapter two is referred to by Gaius alone, curiously concerning the liability of adstipulators following the fraudulent release of an obligation by the primary stipulator.[40] This is difficult to reconcile with chapters one and three, and it is curious that only one jurist considered chapter two worthy of discussion, especially in a student textbook. It seems likely that Gaius' comments are little more than an attempt at filling in the gaps in the law for his students, a problem exacerbated by his quasi-historical tendencies. Consequently it would be unwise to attach much weight to his account of chapter two of the *lex Aquilia*. Fortunately, the classical scope of chapter three is fairly clear from the Digest, and so it matters little for present purposes which translation of *rerum* is the more accurate, or even if the clause is entirely interpolated.

'*Praeter hominem et pecudem occisos*' is a far easier problem to solve.[41] It is almost unthinkable that the clause is original. It would be a supremely lazy draftsman who, having spelled out that chapter one applied to '*servum servamve alienum alienam*' opted in chapter three to use the imprecise '*hominem*'. Moreover the plural *occisos* paired with two singular nouns ought to raise an eyebrow. It seems extremely likely that the clause is an attempt at explaining its predecessor, likely written in the margins of a jurist's notes on the *lex* at some point in the long history of Roman law before slipping into the primary text. It can safely be ignored.

Chapter three of the *lex Aquilia* imposes liability for patrimonial loss (*damnum*) caused in a specific way. The original wording of the *lex* used three verbs to illustrate the nature of the damage covered: *urere, frangere* and *rumpere*. All three are indicative of a high threshold of property damage, though that alone is not sufficient to suggest that the *lex* was ever constrained only to the 'killing'

39 This has caused controversy in the Anglophone literature, with scholars divided over whether the best course of action is to account for the clause or expunge it. Compare David Daube, 'On the third chapter of the Lex Aquilia' (1936) 52 Law Quarterly Review 253 with Herbert F. Jolowicz, 'The original scope of the *lex Aquilia* and the question of damages' (1922) 38 Law Quarterly Review 220.

40 G.3.215.

41 See generally Tony Honoré, 'Linguistic and social context of the *lex Aquilia*' (1972) Irish Jurist 138.

of inanimate property.[42] By the earliest generations of jurists, *rumpere* was being interpreted as *corrumpere*, which is typically translated as 'spoiling'.[43] It is this word that is the focus of the Digest's analysis of chapter three. This, combined with Ulpian's view that *corrumpere* was sufficiently broad to encompass *urere* and *frangere* could lead to the view that *corrumpere* was the sole focus of the classical interpretation of chapter three. This view would be mistaken. A comparison of Ulpian's views in the Digest and the *Collatio* reveal that the compilers greatly reduced his treatment of *urere*. It is unclear whether he was similarly elaborate in dealing with *frangere*.[44] The tract of Ulpian on *urere* preserved in the Digest runs from D.9.2.27.6 to D.9.2.27.12. These seven texts are a truncated version of *Collatio* 12.7.1-10. The omitted passages make it clear that *urere* was a distinct form of wrongdoing in the early third century, not yet completely enveloped by the broader *corrumpere*. Arson, unlike generic spoiling, could attract capital punishment.[45] Moreover fire as the engine of harm attracted a unique set of considerations, such as how it ought to be contained and how liability reacts to a fire's escape.[46] These details are greatly simplified in the *Corpus Iuris Civilis*' account of loss caused by fire.

Nevertheless, the focus of D.9.2 is on *corrumpere*, and it is this verb that came to represent chapter three's scope in the later civil law. The verb had a wide semantic field, and it is difficult to find any one abstraction that would accurately convey its range of meanings. Celsus tried, arguing that it required a *mutatio* or change in substance.[47] This would be sufficient to cover changes of identity (e.g. turning wine into vinegar) and harm to property's physical structure (e.g. staining a shirt).[48] But it is no help with D.9.2.27.25, in which a person who picks grapes from the vine is liable on the *lex* only if the grapes were unripe. This cannot be seen as a *mutatio*—the grape is in precisely the same state in the picker's hand as it was on the vine. The source of loss lies in that fact that it has been rendered useless to its *dominus*. Once picked, the as yet unripe grape is deprived of its potential utility in the future, its purpose forever frustrated. Thus *corrumpere* came to deal with rendering property useless or less useful, a sense of the word that reappears in the context of *servi corruptio*.

42 For the methods of legislative drafting in a pre-juristic world, see David Daube, 'The influence of interpretation on writing' (1970) 20 Buffalo Law Review 41.

43 D.9.2.27.13.

44 Cf D.9.2.27.6–12 with *Collatio* 12.7.1–10.

45 *Collatio*, 12.7.2.

46 *Collatio*, 12.7.3 (mirrored D.9.2.27.8), 12.7.4–6 (without parallel in D.9.2).

47 D.9.2.27.14.

48 D.9.2.27.15, 18.

In formulating these rules Ulpian appears to have approached the verb as an anomalist, seeking only to map out its full semantic field without any attempt at unification through abstract rules and tests.[49] That frustration of purpose does not fit well with *mutatio* was of no concern.

By classical law chapter three required that the defendant cause patrimonial loss through *corrumpere*. The breadth of this verb meant that liability on chapter three was expansive, leaving little room for the decretal actions. Their primary area of application was where patrimonial loss was caused without *corrumpere*, an idea akin to pure economic loss. D.9.2.27.21 is evidence of clear reluctance to use the decretal actions in this way. A person knocks coins from my hand and they fall into a river or down a sewer grate. The coins are unimpaired: it is unlikely that the water will cause even the slightest physical deterioration to them. The harm I have suffered is entirely located in being deprived of their use. Thus Sabinus argues that the *lex* can only be used as a last resort: if any other action can be invoked, the *lex* ought not to be relied upon. The text is couched in extremely uncertain terms, with the jurists failing to agree even on whether a direct or decretal action would be appropriate. Elsewhere in the Digest the recovery of purely patrimonial loss through the decretal actions was seen as less problematic.[50]

The scope of chapter three was pushed in a second novel direction by the use of decretal actions. Ulpian writes that a free person who is injured can have a decretal action against the wrongdoer.[51] He is denied a direct action because nobody can said to be the owner of his own limbs. This looks to be inconsistent. The remedy to be awarded in a decretal action would be calculated according to the free person's *damnum*, or patrimonial loss caused by a reduction of their interest in the affected property. How can the injury be both unrecoverable because it is unmeasurable and the basis for the calculation of damages? The only possibility that avoids this inconsistency is that the decretal action is being used to recover only the loss flowing from the injury, such as medical expenses and lost wages. This turns a case that looks to be about personal injury into an instance of pure economic loss, as the patrimonial loss incurred is consequent on an unrecognised form of harm.

The conduct prohibited by chapter three of the *lex Aquilia* was generalised to such a degree it became trivial to show in practice. Nevertheless, the consternation displayed by some jurists in the face of attempts at circumventing

49 On anomalism as a juristic method, see Peter Stein, *Regulae Iuris: From Juristic Rules to Legal Maxims* (Edinburgh: Edinburgh University Press, 1966), 61–67.

50 D.19.5.23, D.19.5.14.2, D.41.1.55.

51 D.9.2.13.pr.

the need for *corrumpere* shows that it was still seen as a real requirement for liability.[52] As such the conduct-centric nature of the delicts was maintained. *Occisio, corruptio, contrectatio* and *contumelia* all remained definitive of their respective delicts, and with varying degrees of discrimination demarcated between worthy and unworthy wrongs. In light of this heavily conduct-centric mode of analysis, anyone looking to construct a rights-centric model of delict on Roman foundations faces an uphill struggle.

Piecemeal Doctrine and Historical Patchwork

It goes without saying that Roman law generally was a living system, developed over many centuries into the form enshrined in the *Corpus Iuris Civilis*. This is no less true of delict, which only began to take its institutional shape in the last days of the Republic. Existing before the Twelve Tables, *furtum* was the oldest of the delicts and broadly kept its original form, although its remedy underwent significant changes. The *lex Aquilia* and *iniuria* were both introduced to replace fixed penalties under the Twelve Tables, likely in the late third century BC.[53] The youngest of the institutional delicts, *rapina*, was introduced by edict in the first century BC, probably 76BC.[54]

Given the sheer expanse of time involved, it would be foolhardy to expect the pieces of delict to slot together perfectly. It was for the jurists to interpret

52 E.g. Sabinus' reluctance to allow an action in D.9.2.27.21.

53 This topic has spawned endless controversy, with no end in sight. The literature is sizable, and space prohibits detailed consideration. Briefly, modern scholarship looks to the purpose of the *lex* in order to date it. Ulpian (D.9.2.1.pr) claims that the *lex* derogated from earlier penalties, which we know to be fixed from the Twelve Tables (e.g. the penalty for *membrum ruptum*, Riccobono's reconstruction Table 8 Law 2; Crawford's reconstruction Table 8 Law 14). The shift from fixed penalties to the assessed damages found in the *lex* are likely a product of financial instability. This can be linked to the known inflation of the late third century caused by the Second Punic War (Tony Honoré, 'Linguistic and social context of the *lex Aquilia*' (1972) 7 Irish Jurist 138) or hypothesised deflation in the early third century or earlier (David J. Ibbetson, 'The dating of the *Lex Aquilia*' in *Judge and Jurist: Essays in Memory of Lord Rodger of Earlsferry*, eds Andrew Burrows, David Johnston and Reinhard Zimmermann (Oxford: Oxford University Press, 2013)). *Iniuria*, performing a similar function, ought to roughly coincide with this social impetus for assessed damages. This would align with the edict *de iniuriis aestimandis*—Ibbetson, 'The dating of the *lex Aquilia*', 176 n59, citing Otto Lenel, *Das Edictum Perpetuum*, 3rd ed. (Aalen: Scientia Antiquariat, 1927), 397–399.

54 Joseph A.C. Thomas, *Textbook on Roman Law* (Amsterdam: North-Holland Publishing Company, 1976), 377.

the delicts in such a way as to reduce whatever friction might exist between them, but this had its limits. The jurists could not alter the basic remedial structure imposed by each delict. Thus there was little that could be done to make sense of the bizarre contrast between *furtum* and *rapina*. By classical law the penalty for *furtum manifestum* had become pecuniary under the praetor's watch, valued at four times the claimant's interest in the stolen property.[55] The penalty for *furtum nec manifestum* remained double as under the Twelve Tables, but took the claimant's interest as its basis instead of the value of the property. *Rapina* resembled a somewhat neutered version of the *actio furti*. If brought within a year of the wrong, a successful action would result in four times the value of the property.[56] Unlike *furtum*, at no point in its history did *rapina* use the claimant's interest in the property as its basis. After a year, the damages in a successful action were simply for the value of the property. In most situations, it is clear that an *actio furti* would be preferable to an *actio vi bonorum raptorum*. Furthermore, the *actio vi bonorum raptorum* served to bar the claimant from bringing an *actio furti*, *vindicatio* or *condictio*.[57]

Similarly, the classical forms of chapter three of the *lex Aquilia* and *furtum* were difficult to distinguish. Both were concerned with interference with property of a very similar nature, but had different fault standards that nevertheless overlapped in cases of dolose interference. How were they to be distinguished? It is because of this similarity that Paul introduced an additional requirement for *furtum*: an *animus lucri faciendi*.[58] Chapter three was about causing loss and *furtum* was about making gains, though given the almost inevitable coincidence of these two factors in most cases this cannot have been a terribly helpful distinction. The language of 'causing loss' also infected *rapina*, as is clear from the very edict establishing that wrong.[59] The institutional delicts alone

55 G.3.189.

56 D.47.8.2.13.

57 D.47.8.1. This was because the fourfold damages awarded under the *actio vi bonorum raptorum* were seen as a threefold penalty (imperfectly performing the function of an *actio furti*) and a single measure of compensation (accurately acting as a *vindicatio*). Though the threefold penalty would clearly die with the wrongdoer, the questions remains whether the single measure of compensation was passively transmissible.

58 D.47.2.1.3.

59 D.47.8.2.pr: '*si cui dolo malo hominibus coactis damni quid factum esse dicetur sive cuius bona rapta esse dicentur, in eum, qui id fecisse dicetur, iudicium dabo*' ('If any loss be said to have been inflicted with deliberate wrongfulness by armed men on someone or if his goods be said to have been forcibly taken, I will grant an action against the person alleged to have done this').

were an awkward group. Matters are only made worse when one looks beyond these four to the mass of other wrongs that made up the Roman law of delict.[60]

Of the praetorian innovations one merits further consideration. The praetorian delicts of *metus* (fear or duress) and *dolus* (fraud) sit on the contract-delict boundary, and were primarily invoked as factors to justify the avoidance of contractual obligations. The mechanism by which this was achieved was the underexplored remedy of *restitutio in integrum*, which was something of a praetorian panacea. It was a legitimate response to a range of factors that cast doubt on the legitimacy of an arrangement, including *metus* and *dolus* but also deception (*calliditas*), infancy, error, change of condition and other similar circumstances.[61] These factors acted as *causae*—reasons for the praetor to intervene and grant discretionary relief to the parties.[62] Though the remedy was available to all, Callistratus claimed that cases ought to be heard according to the value of the sum at stake.[63] The actual operation of the remedy, at least in classical law, is a mystery. What does it mean to say that the matter must be 'restored in full'? Did the remedy bind both parties to unravel a previous transaction, or did it benefit only the party who had been wronged? To what extent did the transaction have to be undone—in the case of a sale, would simply returning the property for the price be enough, or would the buyer have to account for any profits made while in possession of the sold property? And, perhaps most interestingly, did these questions receive different answers according to the *causa* behind the remedy?

The circumstances of *restitutio in integrum* are discussed at length in Justinian's *Codex*. Despite the number of passages on the remedy, there is little insight to be gained into its actual nature beyond one scenario. The vast majority of the texts consider when and against whom minors can obtain *restitutio*.[64] The texts are for the most part routine: if the claimant is below twenty-five years old, a remedy lies unless there is supervening unconscionability (such as where the claimant is suing their parents or patron).[65] Nevertheless, some

60 E.g. the differentiation of *corruptio* of a slave under chapter three of the *lex Aquilia* and *servi corruptio* as a distinct delict; causing loss through contractual intimidation under chapter three and an *actio quod metus causa*, and many more besides.

61 D.4.1.1–2.

62 D.4.1.3.

63 D.4.1.5, 4.

64 C.2.21–41. This should not be surprising. Of all the possible triggers for the remedy, mismanagement of property during the owner's minority is likely to be among the most common in practice.

65 C.2.41.2.

generalisations can be made. Firstly, it needs to be shown that the arrangement in question owes its existence to the suspect factor. Thus when a person is threatened to encourage him to repay an existing debt, he cannot avail himself of the remedy to recapt his repayment.[66] The earlier debt was an underlying reason for the debtor to part with his property, though the threat of violence likely accelerated the transfer.

Secondly, the remedy concerned both parties. Suppose a claimant's ancestor was threatened into selling a tract of land. The land has since been sold on to a third party. The sale is ineffective proprietarily, so the innocent third party would need to acquire ownership prescriptively. Before this process has been completed, the defendant could ask for the original transaction to be reversed, but only if he first repaid the price.[67] That it is the price (*pretium*) and not the value that is restored shows that the remedy was concerned with the transaction itself, and not its effects. The innocent third party would presumably have to rely on a direct personal action against the coercive seller.

The greatest barrier to *restitutio in integrum*'s evolution into the sort of general remedy envisaged by Grotius was its exceptional and residual nature. In classical law any proceedings for restoration first had to consider whether any other action was available.[68] Praetorian relief was a last resort. The inclusion of D.4.4.16.pr in the Digest suggests that this was still the position in Justinianic law, particularly in the absence of any contradictory evidence. *Restitutio in integrum* filled the gaps in the law of obligations, but was not a worthwhile cause of action in itself.

A Plurality of Fault Concepts

The piecemeal approach of Roman law to wrongdoing can be seen again in the mishmash of fault concepts found across the delicts. This is perhaps surprising. Each delict is defined primarily by the conduct it prohibits. This pushes fault into a subordinate role: it simply sets out the state of mind attendant on the conduct that constitutes the delict. Fault is not so intrinsic to the identity of each individual delict as the conduct element. As such, we might expect to see the first pushes towards generalisation in relation to fault—a single

66 C.2.19.2.

67 C.2.19.3. On the proprietary significance of this text, see Fritz Schulz, '*Die Lehre vom erzwungenen Rechtsgeschäft im antiken römischen Recht*' (1922) 43 Zeitschrift der Savigny-Stiftung 171.

68 D.4.4.16.pr.

standard such as 'intention' or 'blameworthiness' could easily have been applicable across the field. Instead we find a miscellany of fault standards that approach liability from a variety of directions.

Paul's definition of *furtum* gives two mental elements: *fraudulosa* and (*animus*) *lucri faciendi*.[69] The latter was omitted in Justinian's definition of *furtum*.[70] *Fraudulosa* required the thief to act with the knowledge that the property's owner would not consent to his interference with the property, and a genuine lack of consent on the part of the owner. If the owner was indifferent to who did what with his property, there could be no question of liability in *furtum*.[71] Similarly, if the alleged thief genuinely believed the owner would not object to his interference with the property, an *actio furti* against him would fail. The focus of inquiries into *fraudulosa* was originally the state of mind of the owner, but as it became increasingly common for non-owners to deal with property the emphasis shifted to the thief's positive intentions. This is reflected in a second term occasionally used in place of *fraudulosa*: *animus furandi*.[72] In this context *animus* appears to be to mean something akin to 'intention'. The meaning of the third element of classical *furtum*, the intention to make a gain (*animus lucri faciendi*), is clear from its name. As has already been suggested, its introduction was likely motivated by a need to distinguish between the classical forms of *furtum* and the *lex Aquilia*, both of which prohibited interference with property. The result was a two-pronged approach to wrongs to property: one delict covered wrongfully caused loss, while the other covered wrongful gains. The trivialisation of each delict's conduct element left the onus of definition to questions of fault.

On its face the delict of *iniuria* did not have a fault standard. To understand this unusual absence, we must return to the delict's conduct element. It matters a great deal whether *contumelia* is translated as 'disrespect' or 'insult'. Whether an act is insulting is determined by the sting felt by its recipient, whereas disrespect is evaluated according to the intentions of the purported wrongdoer. Imagine a student who, rushing to a class while reading over his notes, snubs a wave from his teacher across the street. The teacher might feel insulted by this spurning of his greeting. But the student was oblivious to the teacher's existence, let alone his friendly overtures.

69 D.47.2.1.3.

70 J.4.1.1. It is possible to attribute the omission to the somewhat slavish adherence of Justinian's *Institutes* to Gaius' *Institutes*, which also omits any mention of *animus lucri faciendi*.

71 G.3.198.

72 E.g. D.47.2.33, D.47.2.53.20.

It is very difficult to think of the student as acting disrespectfully in this scenario.

If *contumelia* is translated as disrespect instead of insult the Digest's treatment of *iniuria*'s fault standard begins to make sense. It is clear that the wrongdoer had to be capable of forming wrongful intentions, as the insane and children could not be liable for disrespectful or violent acts.[73] We find *animus* lurking beneath the surface of the delict as a criterion of rationality governing capacity. Because *contumelia* fulfils the role of both *actus reus* and *mens rea* there is no need for a separate fault concept to be articulated. It is only if *contumelia* is translated as 'insult' that the absence of a fault standard becomes troubling.

Though the delict of *iniuria* might not have had a freestanding fault standard, the noun served as the original fault standard for liability under both chapters of the *lex Aquilia*. In the words of Ulpian, *iniuria* has two senses: the former sense of *iniuria* is its special meaning while the latter is its general meaning.[74] Most agree that the *iniuria* in *damnum iniuria* ought to be given its general meaning, though the position is not universal.[75] Similarly, most agree on the meaning of *iniuria*'s general sense. It refers to an objective standard of liability, asking whether the wrongdoer had a right to act as he did. If he had no such right, he is liable. There is no evaluation of the wrongdoer's state of mind. Rather, only his conduct and its objective justifiability matter. The Digest texts on the general sense of *iniuria* suggest that the only rights that can exculpate a wrongdoer are positive rights conferred by law. Thus there is no liability for killing a thief caught in the act, an adulterer or an attacker.[76]

By classical law *iniuria* was being read to include *dolus* and *culpa*, two of the fault standards behind the Roman law of contracts.[77] This is typically seen as a shift towards subjective liability, insofar as *culpa* involved some evaluation of the defendant's state of mind. The language of subjectivity does not preclude

---

73 D.47.10.3.1.

74 D.47.10.1.pr.

75 Maria F. Cursi, *Iniuria cum damno* (Milan: Giuffrè, 2002); Maria F. Cursi, 'What did *occidere iniuria* in the *lex Aquilia* actually mean?' (2011) 7 Roman Legal Tradition 16. It is worth noting that even Ulpian thought he was dealing with the general sense of *iniuria*: D.9.2.5.1.

76 Killing thieves: D.9.2.4.1, justified by the Twelve Tables; killing adulterers: D.9.2.30.pr, justified by the *lex Iulia de Adulteriis*. The justifiability of killing in self-defence is justified by natural reason, though it is said to be implied into every *lex*: D.9.2.4.pr. This imputation suggests that the *iura* in *iniuria* were categorically positive.

77 D.9.2.5.1, D.9.2.30.3.

measuring the defendant's motivations against some external standard. This is precisely what is found in a number of texts on *culpa* that take as their standard a failure of diligence. This can be seen in a fairly scattershot form across D.9.2 in texts dealing with professionals and tradesmen such as doctors and muleteers.[78] This approach to fault receives its most general formulation in a text of Paul:

> Si putator ex arbore ramum cum deiceret vel machinarius hominem praetereuntem occidit, ita tenetur, si is in publicum decidat nec ille proclamavit, ut casus eius evitari possit. Sed Mucius etiam dixit, si in privato idem accidisset, posse de culpa agi: culpam autem esse, quod cum a diligente provideri poterit, non esset provisum aut tum denuntiatum esset, cum periculum evitari non possit. Secundum quam rationem non multum refert, per publicum an per privatum iter fieret, cum plerumque per privata loca volgo iter fiat. Quod si nullum iter erit, dolum dumtaxat praestare debet, ne immittat in eum, quem viderit transeuntem: nam culpa ab eo exigenda non est, cum divinare non potuerit, an per eum locum aliquis transiturus sit.[79]

The rule is simple: *culpa* consists in failing to foresee that which the diligent man would have foreseen. However, this text is one of just a handful that approach *culpa* in this way. By far the more common form of analysis simply asks whether conduct was blameworthy or not.[80] In these texts there is no abstraction to be applied. It is not even clear whether they are asking whether the defendant's state of mind was blameworthy, or whether the activity in which he was engaged was blameworthy. It is as if the jurists are simply asking 'who is to blame?' A clear example is D.9.2.9.4, in which the outcome hinges entirely on

78 Doctors: D.9.2.7.8, D.9.2.52.pr; muleteers: D.9.2.8.1.

79 D.9.2.31: 'If a pruner or a person working on a scaffold throws down a branch and kills a slave, he is liable if it falls on a public place and he did not so that the accident could be avoided. But Mucius also said that an action could be brought for his fault if the same thing happened on private land: for there is fault where what could have been foreseen by a diligent man was not foreseen, or where the warning was given at a time that the danger could not be avoided. According to this reasoning it does not matter a great deal whether he was making his way across public or private land, since people often make their way across private places. But if there is no way, he should only be liable for deliberate wrongdoing, that he should not aim at a person whom he saw walking along; for he is not to be regarded as being at fault when he could not divine whether someone would be walking through that place'.

80 E.g. D.9.2.9.4, D.9.2.10, D.9.2.11.pr, D.9.2.29.2–4, D.9.2.52.1, D.9.2.57.

the location in which javelins were being thrown. If the defendant was throwing javelins in a public space, he is to blame. If the hapless slave wandered into a military training ground, the reverse is true. This is appended with the caveat that positive malfeasance trumps this causative analysis: *dolus* results in liability in any case. In these texts *culpa* resembles a causative tool more than a fault concept.

These two approaches to *culpa* appear to co-exist within the Digest, though it is not clear how. Those texts that treat *culpa* as diligence all deal with professional malfeasance, an area where there would likely be concurrent contractual liability. Moreover, a handful of texts explicitly link *culpa* under the *lex Aquilia* to *culpa* in *locatio conductio*.[81] It might be that where delictual and contractual liability overlap the contractual approach to *culpa* is sufficient. In straightforwardly delictual cases, the causative analysis was more helpful than inquiries founded on diligence.[82]

In total there were four approaches to fault in relation to the *lex Aquilia*. The original standard of *iniuria* asked whether the person had a positive right justifying his conduct, without any attempt at evaluating his state of mind. This was replaced by *culpa*, a standard that was simultaneously a holistic analysis of blameworthiness and an abstract standard of diligence. Behind all of these was the residual idea that dolus would typically be sufficient for liability. The jurists picked among these approaches as required by the case at hand, and were perfectly willing to jump between approaches if needed.[83] Even within this one delict there was not a uniform approach to fault, let alone across the law of delict as a whole.

Beyond the *lex Aquilia*, it was even possible to be held accountable for harm in the absence of fault. Leaving aside the quasi-delicts, there were two doctrines that could impose liability in the absence of direct fault on the part of the defendant: noxal liability and the *actio de pauperie*. Both dealt with the anomalous scenario in which animate property caused damage. Responsibility for that damage would be attributed to the property's owner. This responsibility would be for the full extent of the harm, though it could be shirked by surrendering the malfeasant slave, animal or son (the principle from which

81 D.9.2.5.3 (Ulpian), D.9.2.7.8 (Ulpian citing Proculus), D.9.2.27.9 (Ulpian citing Neratius), D.9.2.27.34 (Ulpian citing Mela).

82 For example, a standard of diligence would be of no use in the scenarios discussed in D.9.2.11.2 and 3.

83 E.g. D.9.2.52.1: Alfenus flits between *iniuria* and causative-*culpa*; and D.9.2.31: Paul analyses both through diligence-*culpa* and *dolus*. See generally Sandro Schipani, *Responsabilitá 'ex lege Aquilia'* (Turin: G. Giappichelli, 1969).

this type of liability takes its name: '*noxa caput sequitur*').[84] This mechanism was ancient, finding its origins in the XII Tables as a rule pertaining to *furtum*.[85] Linked to the *actio de pauperie* was an aedilician edict imposing responsibility on those who kept dangerous animals in close proximity to public spaces. Should such an animal escape and cause damage, its former owner would be liable for twice the value of the damage. Should an unfortunate freeman be killed by a dangerous animal, a fixed penalty of two hundred *solidi* was imposed.[86] Whatever residual role fault might have played in the creation of these heads of liability (presumably the original justification for the aedilicean action was that it is culpable to keep dangerous animals near public highways), they were irrelevant to the operation of each doctrine.

The Narrowness of the Interests Protected by Delict

The law of delict provided a comprehensive regime for the protection of property rights. Even in their original forms, the *lex Aquilia* and *furtum* acting together protected owners from the most damaging forms of interference with property, namely asportation and destruction. But both expanded to offer a fuller range of protection. It has already been seen how *furtum* came to treat *contrectatio* not as appropriation but interference. This allowed for non-physical interference with animate property, but also impacted the types of rights that could be affected by the delict. Thus it was possible for a person to be liable in *furtum* for stealing his own property, as the delict could be invoked to protect the interests of creditors such as the pledgee.[87] Similarly one could be branded a thief for, having borrowed a horse, riding it further than allowed by the underlying contract.[88] The reasoning behind these texts is clear: the first recognises that the interests of individuals besides the owner need to be protected, even as against the owner. The second treats any interaction with another's property beyond that specifically authorised by contract as sufficient for theft. Nevertheless, these scenarios are a far cry from the original notion of *furtum* found in the Twelve Tables. In any case, the remedy awarded in *furtum* could be up to four times the interest of the claimant in the affected property, representing a highly punitive measure of damages. *Rapina* imposed a more

84 D.47.2.18.
85 D.9.4.2.1.
86 D.21.1.40.1.
87 G.3.200.
88 G.3.196.

moderate penalty, of no more than triple the property's value. Both remedies were shaped primarily by the circumstances of the specific wrong, and the timing of the action.

Similar expansions are evident in the *lex Aquilia*. The interpretation of *rumpere* as *corrumpere* greatly expanded the scope of chapter three, effectively creating a delict that could address any and all property damage (and perhaps even pure economic loss). Further developments were made in relation to the remedy. From its enactment damages under chapter three were calculated according to the owner's *damnum*, or patrimonial loss.[89] But chapter one looked instead to the value of the killed slave or animal, calculating damages according to the highest value in the previous year. Awarding the highest value of the property in the past year ensures that damages reflect the seasonal peak in prices, thereby avoiding under-compensation. This rationale would become less compelling as Rome's economy moved away from its agrarian roots, but would not have vanished completely.

By classical law the measure of damages was not simply the value of the property, but the interest of the *dominus* in its existence.[90] This criterion involved modifying the basic objective value of the slave or animal with a pair of doctrines known as *damnum emergens* and *lucrum cessans*: consequential loss and failure to make a gain.[91] These modifications of the basic measure of damages interacted poorly with the one year rule, leading to the potential for colossal over-compensation. This is made readily apparent by a series of texts in D.9.2.23. The most accessible of these is D.9.2.23.3, which deals with the case of an artistically talented slave. Suppose this particular slave is internationally recognised for his talents, and the sales of his paintings generate most of his owner's income. An unfortunate accident leaves the slave dismembered, and he can paint no more. A few months later he is blameworthily killed by a party unrelated to the dismembering. Damages are to be calculated to reflect the highest value the slave had to its owner in the previous year. This would naturally be a point before his dismemberment, and so the killer would be liable for a sum that would dwarf the actual value of the slave moments before

89 Daube, 'On the use of the term *damnum*' in *Studi in Onore di Siro Solazzi* (Naples: E Jovene, 1948) 93–156 argues convincingly that *damnum* refers to the owner's loss and not the damage to the affected property. It is worth noting, however, the pair of texts in relation to *damnum infectum* that seem to suggest otherwise: D.39.2.39.2 and D.43.23.1.14. Both appear to use *damnum* to refer to property damage, though Daube attributed this to a scribal elision in an identifiable formula used to describe '*damnum in re*'.

90 Daube, 'On the use of the term *damnum*', 93–156.

91 D.9.2.22.1, 9.2.23.3.

his death. It is irrelevant that the master might have already recovered damages for the dismemberment, or that the killer had nothing to do with the slave's initial reduction in value. Similar examples are dealt with where the reduction in value is linked to an inheritance, or even to knowledge on the part of the slave.[92] This new measure of damages could be justified by the *lex*'s penal dimension, but it is unconvincing: the penalisation through punitive damages would be arbitrarily linked to the particular facts of a case, with no necessary correlation to the blameworthiness of the actor or the loss of the *dominus*. The development of chapter one's remedy, doubtless intended to bring it parallel with chapter three, injected a chaotic arbitrariness into its operation. Nevertheless, the expansion of chapter one's remedy served to protect every interest an owner might have in his property, bringing it into line with chapter three.

It is only *iniuria* that purports to deal with an interest other than property. Identifying the precise parameters of the interest harmed by *iniuria* is not easy. The variety of terms used in the Digest suggests it was not a precise concept. The most common term is *existimatio*, but *pudor*, *fama* and *honor* are also used on occasion. Perhaps the most informative route to the meat of the concept is through the related idea of *adversus bonos mores*, a requirement for *convicium* laid down in the edict establishing the offence and later edicts creating sub-delicts.[93] The idea of *boni mores* is more commonly found in the Roman law of contracts as a limit on the freedom of the parties to create legally enforceable agreements. A wide range of texts give individual examples of agreements *contra bonos mores*, but attempts at definition are rare.[94] Building on D.28.7.15 and Papinian's threefold suggestions of *pietas*, *existimatio* and *verecundia*, Zimmermann offers the following characterisation of the concept:

> The sense of duty and the natural affection towards gods, parents or near relatives, the respect or esteem enjoyed by a person in society and the innate sense of shame: these are the values which had from ancient times held together the community at large, and which in their entirety constituted the unquestioned and self-evident core of *bonos mores*.[95]

92 D.9.2.23.1, 4. On the former, see Alan Rodger, 'Labeo and the fraudulent slave' in *The Roman Law Tradition*, eds David J. Ibbetson and Andrew D.E. Lewis (Cambridge: Cambridge University Press, 1994). On the latter, see Alan Rodger, 'Damages for the loss of an inheritance' in *Daube Noster: Essays in Legal History for David Daube*, ed. Alan Watson (Edinburgh: Scottish Academic Press, 1974).

93 Lenel, *Edictum Perpetuum*, 400–401.

94 For an overview, see Zimmermann, *The Law of Obligations*, 709–11.

95 Ibid., 711.

The remedy itself was straightforwardly pecuniary. The plaintiff would name a sum in the formula, and this was the maximum sum the court could award.[96] The remedy for aggravated *iniuria* was fixed by the praetor, and in practice the courts did not interfere with this. *Iniuria* sat on the boundary of delict and crime, with the Digest attesting to an increasing number of cases being dealt with criminally in the Empire.[97] Affronts to *existimatio* apparently came to be seen as too serious for mere compensation, and *extraordinarium iudicium* became the normal form of redress for *iniuria*.[98] Nevertheless, the delict is unique for its focus on an interest other than property rights.

Gaps in the Roman Law of Delicts

From the discussion thus far it is clear that Roman law offered fairly comprehensive protection for property rights and, to a lesser degree, personality interests. However, there are several glaring holes in the scope of the Roman law of delict. There are two which may prove insurmountable barriers to a generalised model of delict in the civil law tradition, namely the delictual protection of the lives and limbs of freemen. That is not to say that there were not legal consequences for such forms of wrongdoing. It is almost inconceivable that a legal system could reach even the crudest levels of development without some form of sanction for homicide. But at an early stage both forms of wrongdoing were viewed as problems deserving of their own jurisdictions and their own systems of punishments. This severance of jurisdiction from the mainstream of the civil law proved almost irreversible. Its main consequence was a compensatory hole in the law of delict, which stands as one of the major barriers to the generalisation of delict in Roman law. Nevertheless, over the millennium of Roman legal history it is possible to identify attempts at providing compensation for harm to life and limb, and some of these attempts would provide the bedrock for the medieval and early modern pushes towards generalisation in delict.

A law attributed to Numa Pompilius stated that '*si qui hominem liberum dolo sciens morti duit, paricidas esto*'.[99] Further details are to be found in the XII Tables. Homicide was not the most serious offence in the XII Tables. It was

96 G.3.224.

97 D.47.10.45.

98 Ibid. According to status, *iniuria* could result in exile, forfeiture or corporal punishment.

99 Salvatore Riccobono, *Fontes iuris Romani antejustiniani* (Florence: Barbèra, 1941).

expressly subordinate to the theft of crops.[100] The Rome of the XII Tables was still primarily an agrarian economy, with the self-providing and self-sustaining family unit at its core. Depriving a family of their crops could mean the end of several lives, so it is understandable why the theft of crops was treated so seriously. The passage above confirms that homicide was indeed an offence, though its precise requirements are not articulated in the XII Tables.[101] There was a distinction drawn between lawful and unlawful homicides, as shown in the killing of thieves caught in the act: *si nox furtum faxsit, si im occisit, iure caesus esto.*[102] Lives could also legitimately be taken by society as a punishment. In addition to the theft of crops, various forms of capital punishment were imposed for giving false testimony, public verbal abuse, and causing a person to be rendered infamous.[103]

It wasn't until almost four centuries later that a further law on homicide is known to have been enacted. This considerable gulf has been explained as a shift in the context of homicide.[104] Intentional killings typically occur in relationships with strong emotions, with a majority of murders being committed by family members. So long as this was the case, homicide would fall under the jurisdiction of the affected *paterfamilias*. Where a homicide was not contained within a single family, recourse could be had to a local official. Robinson argues that the second century BC saw an increasing concern for the effects homicide could have on public order.[105] Alternatively, it could be the case that the rules in the XII Tables simply worked. Just as students of English criminal law are still taught Sir Edward Coke's definition of murder, there may not have been a need for an offence beyond that found in the XII Tables and *Leges Regiae*, which created an offence that was sensitive to the different intentions that can underlie the taking of a life, and was accepting of at least two justificatory defences.

100 Table 8 law 24b. Text as recreated in Riccobono, *Fontes iuris*, using Pliny the Elder, *Naturalis Historia*, book 18 paragraph 12.

101 Crawford (ed.), *Roman Statutes*, vol. 2, table 7 law 13: 'If anyone knowingly and maliciously kills a freeman, he shall be guilty of a capital crime. If he kills him by accident, without malice and unintentionally, let him substitute a ram to be sacrificed publicly by way of expiation for the homicide of the deceased, and for the purpose of appeasing the children of the latter.' This passage appears to be an incorporation of the law attributed to Numa Pompilius cited above into the XII Tables.

102 Table 8 law 12. Text as in Riccobono, *Fontes iuris*, relying on D.9.2.4.1 and Gellius, *Noctes Atticae*, book 20 section 7, among others.

103 Ibid., table 8 laws 1b and 23.

104 Robinson, *The Criminal Law of Ancient Rome*, 41–42.

105 Ibid., 42–43.

The *lex Cornelia de sicariis et veneficiis* of 81 BC provides significant support for Robinson's assertion that homicide became at least partially a matter of public order in the first century BC. The *lex* concerned not acts, but people: *sicarii* are people who habitually or professionally carried a *sica* (a type of dagger), the *-arius* ending implying a regularity to their conduct.[106] Cloud observes the peculiarity of the *lex* referring not to a crime, but to a class of criminal.[107] Moreover, *sicarii* was a label given to hatchet men who operated in cities alone.[108] The professional nature and urban environment of the *sicarius* make it fairly easy to link the *lex* to organised violence in Rome.[109] But this is not to say that the *lex* covered only professional killers: Seneca shows that (at least in the first century AD) the primary focus of the *lex* was killing in general.[110] The *lex Cornelia* drew additional focus and weight to certain types of killing, but it did not alter the basic shape of the crime. The same approach can be seen thirty years later, in the *lex Pompeia de parricidiis*.[111]

The framework created by the *leges regiae*, *lex Cornelia* and *lex Pompeia* endured throughout Roman history. Some further points of detail were established by Hadrian, such as punishing an attempt on a person's life as if it had been successful.[112] Otherwise the protection of life never left its discrete bubble, and was consistently dealt with by dedicated courts. The only lives that could ground a cause of action in the law of obligations were the lives of chattels: slaves and animals. The lives of *pecudes* were protected by chapter one of the *lex Aquilia*, with chapter three encompassing the lives of lesser creatures. The protection offered by the *lex* was not grounded in the value of the slave or animal's life *per se*, but in their value as *res* to their owner. The interest vindicated was not life but property. It is only on extremely rare occasions that we see any attempt at the valuation of free lives in a criminal context. A rescript of Hadrian confirmed an earlier rule partially manifested in the *lex Cornelia* that the punishment for homicide attached not to the outcome but to the intention.[113] Thus a failed assassin could be executed while an accidental killer

106 Duncan Cloud, '*Leges de sicariis*: the first chapter of Sulla's *lex de sicariis*' (2009) Zeitschrift der Savigny-Stiftung 114, 117.

107 Ibid., 117.

108 Ibid., 118.

109 Cloud uses Cicero's *Pro Roscio Amerino* to link the organised violence targeted by the *lex* specifically to assassins: Cloud, '*Leges de sicariis*', 121–128.

110 Ibid., 142; Seneca, *De Beneficiis*, 5.14.2.

111 D.48.9.1.

112 D.48.8.1.3.

113 *Collatio*, 59.

could go free. Accidental killings could result in lesser penalties. A text in the *collatio* alludes to mitigation being a fairly routine arrangement:

> Verba consultationis et rescripti ita se habent: 'Inter Claudium, optime imperator, et Evaristum cognui, quod Claudius Lupi filius in convivio, dum sago iactatur, culpa Mari Evaristi ita male acceptus fuerit, ut post diem quantum moreretur. Atque adparebat nullam inimicitiam cum Evaristo ei fuisse. Tamen cupiditatis culpa coercendum credidi, ut ceteri eiusdem aetatis iuvenes emendarentur. Ideoque Mario Evaristo urbe Italia provincia Baetica in quinquennium interdixi et decrevi, ut impendi causa duo milia patri eius persolveret Evaristus, quod manifesta eius fuerat paupertas.' Verba rescripti: 'Poenam Mari Evaristi recte, Taurine, moderatus es ad modum culpae: refert enim et in maioribus delictis, consulto aliquid admittatur an casu.' et sane in omnibus criminibus distinction haec poenam aut iustam provocare debet aut temperamentum admittere.[114]

The text appears to attach significance to the poverty of the victim's family, suggesting that claimants could not rely on being awarded a financial remedy. Moreover, such a remedy would only be available in cases of accidental death, as a commutation of the death penalty. These factors alongside the wide discretion granted to the investigating judge both in determining the type of relief offered as well as its value makes it difficult to think of there being a reliable remedy for the taking of a life from the perspective of the victim and their family. Justinian's compilers cut the same text short, omitting any mention of the fine.[115] This could reflect a change in policy by the time of Justinian, or that they thought it was a poor fit with the consensus of classical law.

114 *Collatio*, 62: 'The terms of the case remitted to the Emperor, and of the latter's Rescript, are as follows: "Your Imperial Majesty, I had before me the following case of Claudius and Evaristus. Claudius, the son of Lupus, while being tossed in a cloak at a banquet, was, though Marius Evaristus' fault, so roughly handled that, five days after, he died. It was clear that there was no ill-will between him and Evaristus. Nevertheless, I thought that recklessness should be checked, so that other young men of the same age might mend their ways. I therefore banished him for five years from Rome, Italy, and the province of Baetica, and ordered him to pay 200 sestertia as costs to the deceased youth's father, whose poverty was manifest." The terms of the Rescript: "You have acted rightly, Taurinus, in mitigating the penalty (and adjusting it) to the character of the offence; for even in the more serious classes of delicts, it is of moment whether a thing was done designedly or by accident, and in all crimes this difference will necessarily require the infliction of the full penalty or permit of a mitigation"'.

115 D.48.8.4.1.

Injuries to free persons attracted liability under the XII Tables. Though reconstructing the content of the legislation is an undertaking prone to ruffling academic feathers, universally recognised is the provision '*si membrum rup[s]it, ni cum eo pacit, talio esto*'.[116] Equally widely incorporated into recreations of the legislation is the quantification clause: '*manu fustive si os fregit libero, CCC, si servo, CL poenam subito*'.[117] This can be contrasted with the fixed penalty for *iniuria*, which likely incorporated less serious physical injuries: '*si iniuriam [alteri] faxsit, viginti quinque poenae sunto*'.[118] Taking these three penalties together gives a rough gradation of wrongs, allowing for an estimate of their comparative gravity to the early Roman mind. It is perhaps unexpected that the body of a free person is worth just twice as much as the body of the slave, though given the absence of any alternative remedies for property damage the award of 150 asses would have to cover all loss flowing from the slave's injury. Similarly striking is the relatively small penalty attached to *iniuria*, just one sixth the value of a slave's limb, particularly given the availability of capital punishment for spoken defamation that merely has the potential for causing dishonour.[119]

The level of harm punished under the XII Tables is ambiguous. The language of *membrum ruptum* is powerful, but there is a danger in taking it literally or definitively. Precision in legislative drafting in a hallmark of legal learning, and should not be read into early legal systems.[120] It is far more likely that the term *membrum ruptum* was symbolic of the type of harm intended to fall within the law's scope. Whether this means "personal injury" or "serious personal injury" is impossible to say, though the latter is suggested by the high penalty imposed as well as the smaller penalty for *iniuria*, assuming that covered lesser physical injuries.

The delictual aspects of the XII Tables were superseded by the delicts of *damnum iniuria* and *iniuria*. While damage to property, including *membrum ruptum* of a slave, fell under the *lex Aquilia*, injuries to the bodies of free persons became the original backbone of *iniuria*.[121] However, the focus of the delict changed drastically following the introduction by the praetor of new types of liability.

116 Riccobono, *Fontes iuris*, table 8 law 2.

117 Ibid., table 8 law 3.

118 Ibid., table 8 law 4.

119 Ibid., table 8 law 1b. Although this law deals with utterances of a decidedly more occult nature: '*cum perpaucas res capite sanxissent, in his hanc quoque sanciendam putaverunt si quis occentavisset sive carmen condidisset, quod infamiam faceret flafitiumve alteri*'.

120 Daube, 'The influence of interpretation on writing'.

121 Made abundantly clear by Gaius' definition of the delict in G.3.220.

These were given a common core by Labeo based on *contumelia*. This was to stifle the development of a delictual regime protecting the health of freepersons. Although such injuries were still capable of grounding liability in *iniuria*, the injury was ancillary to the delict's primary instigator: *contumelia*. Under the XII Tables the bodies of all free persons carried the same value. *Iniuria* attached greater significance to the difference in status between the parties. It is conceivable that *iniuria* as a violent offence had a continued existence in its own court (*quaestio perpetua*). Several of the *leges Cornelia* passed by Sulla established such courts, though the content of the *lex Cornelia de iniuriis* and its most detailed reference in the Digest makes no mention of a *quaestio perpetua*.[122]

Barriers to Generalisation

Anyone wishing to use Roman law as the foundation for a generalised theory of delict would have to overcome three major hurdles: the significantly variable approaches to remediation, the plurality of fault standards, and the significant gaps in the protection afforded by delict. Little more needs to be said about the last of these: the law of delict was simply an incomplete system of compensation. Legal mechanisms clearly existed to combat harms such as murder and assault, but their focus was not on compensation. Such areas of law were simply beyond the scope of delict.

All three problems are clearly consequences of Roman law being a system of actions. The law of delict was not an intellectual construct from its genesis, though the institutional scheme went a long way towards rationalising its disparate parts. It would be foolhardy to expect a series of wrongs enacted over centuries to represent a cohesive whole. The only way in which the scope of each delict could be changed without positive legislation or praetorian intervention was for the jurists to alter their interpretations. Unfortunately it is extremely difficult to subvert the actual remedies offered through clever juristic methods: if the *actio furti* decrees that a person found guilty of manifest theft must pay a fourfold penalty, there is no way to interpret that as a threefold or twofold penalty. All the jurist can do is, assuming the wording of the edict allows it, suggest a different base measure of damages to which the multiplier would be applied.

Moreover, in a system of actions, the web of available remedies is the root of the area of law. The *actio furti*, *actio iniuriarum* and their ilk were not the

122 D.47.10.5.1. The text does, however, state that the *lex* concerned violence.

ingredients that made up delict, but the actions from which the concept of delict was extracted. This is entirely opposite to the approach of a natural lawyer, who begins with an idea of what an area of law ought to do, then thinks about the legal structures and mechanisms needed to achieve those ends. For Roman jurists, the law of delict *was* the *actio legis Aquiliae*, the *actio furti*, the *actio iniuriarum*, the *actio vi bonorum raptorum* and the various praetorian delicts. It was far beyond the capabilities of the jurists to redefine the very remedies that made up the law. If such changes were to be achieved, they would have to be made by the praetor through alterations to the edict. Given the function of the praetorship as a means of advancing a nascent political career, only the most courageous politician would risk his future by upsetting a system of remedies that by all accounts was functional. And, of course, such changes were eventually rendered impossible by the enactment of the perpetual edict.

The classical interpretation of the *lex Aquilia* shows that it was possible to redefine specific elements of delicts, where the words were capable of being given a different meaning. *Corrumpere* is simply the addition of a prefix to the existing *rumpere*, though its effect was to greatly expand the scope of chapter three. More adventurous is the reinterpretation of *iniuria* as *culpa*. The two are, however, fairly closely related. Among the manifold meanings of *iniuria* is 'wrongfulness', though this meaning is uncommon in specialist legal texts. This clearly overlaps with blameworthiness, or *culpa*. However, this reinterpretation was uncommon. Looking at the fault standards of the law of delicts as a whole reveals a great plurality: *culpa*, *animus* (*lucrandi*, *iniurandi*), and *dolo malo*. Alongside these core '*mens rea*' concepts were additional conditions such as *contra bonos mores* and *fraudulosa*. There was no attempt at reconciling the fault standards of the various delicts, and perhaps for good reason: given the variety of penalties involved, it is surely right that *furtum* requires a greater degree of culpability than liability under the *lex Aquilia*. Nevertheless, this plurality of standards is just another barrier to the generalisation of delict.

CHAPTER 4

Delict in the Middle Ages

The medieval history of delict is chaotic. From relatively early in the revival of Roman law the subject fragmented across a number of academic disciplines beyond the mainstream of Roman law scholarship. Within each of these groups piecemeal developments can be seen, with no small degree of crosspollination between them. The result is a smorgasbord of ideas and approaches that defies generalisation or unification. The goal of this chapter is to trace how this fragmentation occurred, and to examine doctrinal developments within each context. At the heart of medieval legal scholarship is the *mos italicus*, the methods of typical Roman law scholars. Readers of such works are confronted with a near total disregard for delictual theory and doctrine, a phenomenon that requires explanation. Rather than the *mos italicus* those searching for delictual content must look to two other groups of scholars working on delictual matters, though they did not necessarily see themselves as writing on Roman law. The first is the writings of canonists, for whom the association of delict with sin had long been established. The second is a literature devoted to criminal law that emerged later in the Middle Ages, which provided a side-practice for some of the greatest jurists of the *mos italicus*. Developments from within these two academic spheres sometimes filtered through to the orthodox Romanist scholarship of the commentators, but in a manner without the slightest hint of consistency. Consequently, when examining the medieval history of delict it must be accepted that the best one can hope to identify is a series of atomised developments, with little in the way of generalisation that could prove to be a foundation for Grotius' thought.

A Chronological Overview of Delict in the Middle Ages

European legal histories typically restart in the middle of the eleventh century.[1] The developments of the five centuries between Justinian's codification project and its subsequent 'rediscovery' are murky. Lawyers have been content to

1 E.g. John P. Dawson, *The Oracles of the Law* (Westport, Conn.: Greenwood Press, 1978), 124. Over the course of the page the discussion turns from why Justinian might have chosen to include a certain text to developments in the twelfth century.

 | DOI 10.1163/9789004344372_005

leave the work of deciphering the legal developments of this half-millennium to specialist historians, who find in the numerous enactments and 'codes' of the period a pathway to understanding political concepts that have long been the bread and butter of medieval history.[2] The law of the period, voluminous though it can be, offers little evidence of high-level thinking about legal concepts and constructs.[3] Where the centuries are covered by a textbook of European legal history, it is as little more than a list of developments accompanied by possible (and often sweeping) historical factors that likely shaped the direction of the law and legal authority.[4]

The background to the eleventh-century re-emergence of the *Corpus Iuris Civilis* as a focal point for academic endeavour has spawned a great deal of conjecture.[5] The reasons are unimportant to this work: all that matters is that in the mid-eleventh century a new class of jurists began working on Justinian's compilation. This uptake of Romanist academia is often called the rediscovery of the *Corpus Iuris Civilis*, implying that the work had been lost for some time. But it is probable that the manuscript was consistently available well before the renewal of interest that marked the rebirth of the civil law in Europe.[6] The significant change of the eleventh century was the manner in which the texts were used, from a rhetorical learning aid to a source of inspiration in the widespread legal reforms of the late eleventh century.[7]

The mid-eleventh century marks the start of Bolognese jurisprudence, through which the techniques that came to be known as the *mos italicus* were developed. There were two principal approaches to the *Corpus Iuris Civilis* under the *mos italicus*, each of which gave their name to a class of scholar who worked on Roman law in the Middle Ages: the glossators and the commentators.

2 An arrangement with which historians seem quite content, given the sizable literature that is developing on early medieval law. See the extensive bibliography in the footnotes Michael Humphreys, *Law, Power and Imperial Ideology in the Iconoclast Era* (Oxford: Oxford University Press, 2014), 1–11.

3 Peter Stein, *Roman Law in European History* (Cambridge: Cambridge University Press, 1999), 38–43.

4 E.g. Manlio Bellomo, *The Common Legal Past of Europe 1000–1800*, tr. Lydia G. Cochrane (Washington DC: Catholic University of America Press, 1995), 34–54.

5 For an overview, see Charles Radding and Antonio Ciaralli, *The Corpus Iuris Civilis in the Middle Ages: Manuscripts and Transmission from the Sixth Century to the Juristic Revival* (Leiden: Brill, 2007), 35–65.

6 Radding and Ciaralli, *The Corpus Iuris Civilis in the Middle Ages*, 67.

7 Peter Landau, 'The Development of Law' in *The New Cambridge Medieval History Volume 4: c.1024-c.1198*, eds David Luscombe and Jonathan Riley-Smith (Cambridge: Cambridge University Press, 2004), 113–114, 118.

As their names suggested, the glossators were content to gloss the margins of the *Corpus Iuris Civilis* whereas the commentators crafted freestanding commentaries, albeit often on parts of the *Corpus* rather than particular bodies of law. Whether one treats these as two separate academic movements or stages within one tradition is another popular topic for writers in the field. While there is value in differentiating between the two stages, it can create a false sense of opposition between their methods. There is a great deal of consistency between the approaches of the glossators and commentators to the *Corpus Iuris Civilis*. But their fundamental objects in interacting with Roman law were sufficiently different to merit their division into two classes, and both will be considered in this chapter.

The earliest days of the *mos italicus* were fruitful for the study of the *lex Aquilia*. The revival of Roman law scholarship was at first marked by a tendency towards conservativeness, but the *lex Aquilia* was an exception to this.[8] Chapter one grew to cover homicide.[9] This was founded on a need to distinguish the *lex Aquilia* from the *lex Cornelia*. It was decided that the *lex Cornelia* responded to *dolus* and resulted in punishment, while the *lex Aquilia* responded to *culpa* and gave compensation.[10] By the middle of the thirteenth century the tide had turned, and the *lex Aquilia* was beginning to be overlooked. Two clear examples of this are Accursius' (c.1182–1263) *Glossa Ordinaria* and Odofredus' (d.1265) *Lectura in Digesto Veteri*.[11] Both discuss the *lex Aquilia*—after all, the methods of the glossators required exegesis on every passage—but both are devoid of further developments or commentary.

This change in attitude coincides with the emerging canon law treatment of wrongdoing. The relationship between wrongdoing in law and in theology is clear for all to see, and by the time of Gratian's *Decretum* individual wrongs were being analysed as the secular manifestations of certain sins.[12] By

8 Rotondi, '*Dalla lex Aquilia all'art. 1151 Cod. Civ*', 504.

9 Robert Feenstra, 'Die Glossatoren und die actio legis Aquiliae utilis bei Tötung eines freien Menschen' in *Das römische Recht im Mittelalter*, ed. Eltjo J.H. Schrage (Darmstadt: Wissenschaftliche Buchgesellschaft, 1987), 205, 211, relying on Accursius, Bulgarus, Rogerius and Azo, among others.

10 E.g. Placentinus, *In Summam Institutionum*, 142 (ad J.4.3).

11 Odofredus, *Lectura Super Digesti Veteri*, ad D.9.2; Accursius, *Corpus Iuris Civilis Iustinianei cum Commentariis: Primus Digestum Vetus*, ad D.9.2.

12 Though all crimes were seen as sinful, not all sins were crimes. A clear articulation of the classifications in play can be found in Abelard (ed. Luscombe), *Peter Abelard's Ethics* (Oxford, 1971), 71. Here Abelard claims that criminal sins are those that carry the stain of 'great fault' and subtract from his reputation.

the early thirteenth century such wrongdoing had become a standard part of the canonist's exposition of the law, and was being analysed in a clearly legalistic way.[13] But Gratian's *Decretum*, like any other canonist treatise, lacked formal legal force, even if through time it acquired *de facto* authority through its constant application. It was no different in this respect to the writings of a glossator: influential by virtue of its usefulness, but without direct heft. The turning point was the collection of legally authoritative Decretals by Gregory IX in 1234. These contained dedicated sections on many forms of wrongdoing: homicide, adultery, theft, arson, usury and a multitude of other assorted wrongs. But fatally to the civilian study of the *lex Aquilia*, it went so far as to articulate a general principle of delictual liability for the mere blameworthy causation of loss:

> Si culpa tua datum est damnum, vel iniuria irrogata, seu aliis irrogantibus opem forte tulisti, aut haec imperitia tua, sive negligentia evenerunt: iure super his satisfacere tu oportet, nec ignorantia te excusat, si scire debuisti ex facto tuo iniuriam verisimiliter posse contingere, vel iacturam.[14]

This passage is somewhat unceremoniously presented at the end of a chapter entitled *'de iniuriis et damno dato'*, as something which *'habet plura dicta'*.[15] It serves to unite the eight preceding examples of specific ways in which loss might be caused. It has been suggested that both this principle and the details of its application borrow heavily from the *lex Aquilia*.[16] This is a claim that matters: if the canonists were channelling Roman law, there was room for the glossators (and later, the commentators) to contribute to the development of delictual doctrine. Unfortunately, matters are not so straightforward. The *Decretals* themselves present X.5.36 as a commentary on individual norms in Exodus. It is possible that they nevertheless represent a hidden strand of Romanist influence, masked behind Exodus to provide a theological veneer. But this is a claim that can only be tested by examining the eight scenarios that

13 Stephan Kuttner, *Kanonistische schuldlehre von Gratian bis auf die Dekretalen Gregors IX* (Vatican: Biblioteca Apostolica Vaticana, 1935).

14 X.5.36.9: 'If by your fault loss is caused, or a wrong is inflicted, or inflicted on others with your help, or by your inexperience or carelessness, by right you are bound to make satisfaction. And ignorance will not excuse you, if you ought to know that by your act a wrong was likely to occur or loss to be caused'.

15 X.5.36; X.5.36.9.

16 David J. Ibbetson, 'How the Romans did for us: ancient roots of the tort of negligence' (2003) University of New South Wales Law Journal 475, 484.

precede the general principle, and analysing whether they are compatible with an analysis under the *lex Aquilia*.

The first text describes a fight between adults that causes an injury severe enough to leave one party bedridden.[17] The person who struck the fateful blow is responsible for his wages and medical expenses, with an explicit reference to Exodus.[18] This scenario could be linked to the main Digest text dealing with injuries to freemen, but the detailed description of the remedy is without parallel in Roman law.[19] The text is compatible with Roman law, but there is no reason to doubt its connection with the cited passage in Exodus. The second text considers liability where a person digs a pit into which a cow or ass falls. The choice of animals, which would both certainly be *pecudes*, as well as the specific scenario might both indicate a Roman law basis, as the Digest discusses a very similar scenario.[20] However, the text is ripped *verbatim* from Exodus.[21] The pit digger must pay the price of a head of livestock to replace the injured animal; if the animal goes on to die, the wrongdoer is entitled to the carcass. This is not a remedial structure that meshes with the *lex Aquilia*. The third text deals with a bull who has a habit of goring other living things, yet its owner does not keep it confined. If it then gores another's bull, the careless owner is forced to hand over the rampaging bull and receive the carcass, '*bovem pro bove*'.[22] This text is also copied verbatim from Exodus, in which a series of verses deal with gore-happy bulls, and again proffers a remedy that is hard to reconcile with the *lex Aquilia*.[23]

The fourth text is about the harm caused when one person allows their animals to graze in another's fields. Here the remedy is straightforwardly '*pro damno aestimationem*'.[24] There is a clear Roman law parallel to be drawn with the *actio de pauperie*. But the remedial structures are once again different. The *actio de pauperie* gave the owner of the damaged land both damages and the nefarious creature.[25] Here only damages are awarded. However, at this point the text deviates from Exodus. The remedy clause in the Decretals is simply '*pro damno aestimationem restituat*'.[26] The original is more complicated:

17 X.5.36.1.
18 X.5.36.1; Exodus 21:18.
19 D.9.2.13.pr.
20 D.9.2.28.pr.
21 Exodus, 21:33–34.
22 X.5.36.3.
23 Exodus, 21:35–36.
24 X.5.36.6.
25 D.9.1.1.pr.
26 X.5.36.4.

'*quicquid optimum habuerit in agro suo vel in vinea pro damni aestimatione restituet*'.[27] It would appear that the Decretals is opting for a monetary remedy, whereas in Exodus the same harm would be met with a demand for restoration sourced from the produce of the wrongdoer's land. It is possible that the *restituat* of the Decretals is suggestive of a remedy in kind instead of damages, but that would not explain the omission of '*quicquid optimum habuerit in agro suo vel in vinea*'.[28] The fifth text is another faithful quote from Exodus.[29] Where a fire breaks out and spreads into another's fields, destroying his crops, the person who started the fire must '*reddet damnum*'. This is precisely the same language used in Exodus, though its use of *damnum* is also compatible with the *lex Aquilia*.

The sixth text is the first to attribute its contents to a source other than Exodus, relying instead on an unattributed Roman penitential. If someone voluntarily sets fire to their own home, '*omnia restituat et tres annos poeniteat*'.[30] The reference to penance is inconsequential, and the damages clause is ambiguous. The reference to *restitutio* is not typically Roman, and when combined with the omission of a reference to *damnum* suggests a foundation in canon law. The seventh text, this time drawn from Pope Honorius III, has no possible foundation in Roman law, discussing instead a problem that had arisen in Florence.[31] The eighth text, credited to Pope Gregory IX himself, simply provides an explanation for why *damnum* must be addressed at all. Across these eight passages it is hard to see any definitively Roman roots. When an ancient source is relied upon, it is Exodus. This is not a superficial veneer given to Roman principles for the sake of theological authority. The rules expounded parallel closely, or in some cases exactly, the content of Exodus, and often approach damages in a way that is irreconcilable with Roman law. It is only the general clause in X.5.36.9 that raises the possibility of a Roman law connection. But that connection is not made explicit. No reference is made to the *Corpus Iuris*

27 Exodus, 22:5: 'He shall be bound to restore whatever is best in his own field or vineyard for the loss'.

28 Moreover, X.5.36.6 uses *restituat* in relation to a burnt down house. Unless the remedy being advocated is the literal rebuilding of all the properties destroyed in a fire, it seems safe to assume the word can be understood as entailing pecuniary damages.

29 X.5.36.5; Exodus 22:6. Only one small point of detail is omitted: '*si egressus ignis **invenerit spinas** et comprehenderit acervos frugum* …' ('if a fire breaks out and spreads to thorn bushes and corn heaps') becomes '*si egressus ignis comprehenderit acervos frugum*…'. The thorn bushes are unlikely to hold legal significance.

30 X.5.36.6.

31 X.5.36.7.

Civilis. Instead, the general idea that loss caused blameworthily ought to be restored is said to be '*habet plura dicta*'—essentially common knowledge.[32] Whatever the origins of this intriguing sentiment, its implications for the medieval law of delict were clear. By the early thirteenth century canon law had a robust and comprehensive system for dealing with wrongdoing. It was equally well placed to deal with nominate wrongs like murder and theft, as well as the simple causation of loss. So far as the civil lawyers were concerned, unlike the commercial demands that necessitated the revival of the Roman law of contract, there was no underlying impetus to propel the reconstruction of the law of delict.[33] Their work had already been done.

This explains why glossators writing in the thirteenth century, such as Accursius and Odofredus, did not show the same zeal for delict as their predecessors. The *Decretals* were not an ordinary commentary: they were law. Canon law had staked a claim to wrongdoing, and this was not a claim with which the academics of Bologna and elsewhere were likely to argue. It was in the nature of a gloss that some comment had to be made when examining delictual passages, but the comments did not need to be more than superficial. This lack of interest was carried forward into the commentators. No clearer insight can be given into the commentators' attitude towards delict than the manner in which it was taught. For this, we must turn our focus away from the great commentaries on the *Corpus Iuris Civilis* towards pedagogical lectures. Bartolus' curriculum survives in full, and is a testament to the irrelevance of delict to the medieval civilian imagination. The full course of lectures fills thousands of pages, working methodically through the Digest. From this bulk, just two pages are given to the *lex Aquilia*.[34] These represent a paraphrase of the already skeletal discussion of D.9.2 offered in his commentary on the Digest. His lectures on Books 47 and 48 combined, covering a total of 47 titles, fill a little over a hundred pages.[35] This is roughly the same amount of space given to D.45.1 on verbal obligations alone.

The sorry state of delict under the commentators was compounded by the fragmentary nature of its treatment in the *Corpus Iuris Civilis*. The Digest's treatment of delict is scattered. The vast majority of delictual topics are confined to the end of the *digestum novum*. Book 47 deals with *furtum* and *iniuria*

32 X.5.36.9.

33 An early example of the civilians' willingness to view delict as a matter for moralists can be found in Placentinus, *In Summam Institutionum*: '... *quia punitur a Deo omnis culpa*', 142 (ad J.4.3).

34 Bartolus, *Lectura Super Prima et Secunda Parte Digesti Veteris*, ad D.9.2.

35 Bartolus, *Lectura Super Prima et Secunda Parte Digesti Novi*, ad D.45.1.

alongside a miscellany of other wrongs as varied as cattle rustling and plundering public baths.[36] Alongside this is Book 48, dealing with what would now be termed Roman criminal law, both substantive and procedural. These two books are almost entirely concerned with wrongdoing. Meanwhile, Book 9 of the *digestum vetus* deals with four specific wrongs, including liability under the *lex Aquilia*. Sandwiched between books on servitudes and the partitioning of land, it would be easy to think that these wrongs were being conceptualised as part of the law of property, though noxal liability is difficult to fit into this picture. Book 11 contains a similarly anomalous list of wrongs that sits awkwardly between the Digest's sections on property and contract. At a structural level there is little unity to be found, even when one is looking for it. This separation of delict across the Digest would prove to be a hurdle for the medieval exploration of the subject. The *digestum vetus* and *digestum novum* were glossed separately, and so any links between the two would have been evidenced only by the Institutes.[37] This taxonomical separation of the individual heads of delictual liability, combined with the absence of any need to develop the subject, meant that delict remained a fragmentary subject under the *mos italicus*.

Fault and Diligence

Perhaps the most convoluted delictual development in the Middle Ages was the growth of a plurality of fault concepts. One must tread carefully, for the same few words are used to describe a wide array of positions. Moreover, one must look beyond the civilian mainstream to get a fuller picture of from whence later ideas of culpability might have emerged. Beginning in the twelfth century, it is easy to discern two distinct approaches to culpability. The first focuses on actions and results, and is clearly grounded in the approach of much of D.9.2 to questions of responsibility under the *lex Aquilia*. The second focuses on the inner machinations of the wrongdoer, and has roots in both the *lex Aquilia* and contractual *culpa*. The difference between the two is significant: it is the gap between asking whether it is blameworthy *per se* to throw javelins in a public location, and asking whether it was blameworthy for this particular defendant to do so. But from the twelfth century onwards jurists from a range of intellectual traditions drew unsystematically from both approaches, creating a raft of models of culpability. As such, it is unfortunate that the view that emerged as dominant represents little advance over the

36 D.47.14 and D.47.17 respectively.

37 Landau, 'The development of law', 120.

formulation of fault in Roman law: orthodoxy and adherence to their source material won the day.[38]

Much of the glossatorial treatment of *culpa* resembles the first approach to culpability, focusing not on actors but blameworthy acts. They were familiar with an array of terminology from their exploration of the Digest, but its full import did not strike them as obvious.[39] Though the language of *culpa lata, levis* and *levissima* was employed, they failed to effectively differentiate between degrees of culpability. It was sufficient to maintain only the boundary between *culpa* and *dolus* that separated the *lex Aquilia* from the *lex Cornelia*.[40] More problematic was the famous statement by Ulpian that 'even the slightest blame comes into account' when establishing liability under the *lex Aquilia*.[41] If the *lex Aquilia* imposes liability equally for *culpa levissima* and *dolus*, it begins to look like the two are being equated. Thus even this basic use of the various fault standards was not always maintained.[42] The preferred solution was to avoid engaging with the Roman hierarchy of fault standards so as to avoid the morass entirely.

Culpability was clearly linked to a failure to take due care in the writings of early canonists. Kuttner linked this view to Hugoccio, widely considered one of the most influential canonists of the twelfth century, who equated *negligentia* with wrongdoing.[43] Hallebeek identified a similar link between wrongdoing and *imprudentia*, a term apparently deployed to evidence *culpa* without supplanting it.[44] A recurring example in canonist texts is the responsibility of a bricklayer for allowing a brick to fall from a height, striking and killing

38 Ibbetson, 'How the Romans', 507.

39 E.g. the confusion in Azo, *Summa Codicis*, book 3 title 35 when delineating between *culpa* and *dolus*.

40 E.g. Placentinus, *In Summam Institutionum*, 142 (ad J.4.3). Of course, the *lex Cornelia* and *lex Aquilia* would never have coincided in Roman law as they concerned two completely different wrongs: homicide and property damage.

41 D.9.2.44.pr.

42 A gloss in the *Summa Vindobonensis* equates *dolus* and *culpa levisimma*: *Summa Vindobonensis*, IV.3; Emanuel G.D. Van Dongen, *Contributory Negligence: A Historical and Comparative Study* (Leiden: Brill, 2014), 109. This work, thought to have been compiled by a single student of Bulgarus, appears to be a compilation of very early glosses on the Institutes: Hermann Kantorowicz & William W. Buckland, *Studies in the Glossators of the Roman Law* (Cambridge: Cambridge University Press, 1938), 66–67.

43 Kuttner, *Kanonistische schuldlehre*, 227.

44 Jan Hallebeek, 'Negligence in Roman law' in *Negligence: The Comparative Legal History of the Law of Torts*, ed. Eltjo J.H. Schrage (Berlin: Duncker & Humblot, 2001), 85, citing in n.42 an anonymous gloss ad D.50.13.6 ('*per imprudentiam*') discussing manifold instances of *imprudentia*.

a pedestrian below.[45] This analysis is clearly grounded in the anomalous *lex Aquilia* text '*si putator*'.[46] In these scenarios *culpa* and *negligentia* are equated. This can also be seen readily in the *Decretals*, in which *culpa*, *imperitia* and *negligentia* are used interchangeably.[47]

These two approaches to fault shared a chaotic symbiosis, and it is impossible to ascribe one approach as representative of a given legal tradition once one leaves the twelfth century. Individuals drew upon ideas from both traditions, all while explaining the single word '*culpa*'. Even among the early glossators, there is clear evidence that some of the leading authors were viewing *culpa* in terms of duty. For example, Placentinus (d.1192) drew an early link between the role of punishment and the wrongdoer's failure to exercise his God-given capacity for reason.[48] But despite this haphazard development it is possible to identify an overall movement towards subjective models of fault, examining not the blameworthiness of the act but the defendant's state of mind. A recent study has cogently linked this to a broader 'turn to individualisation', itself the product of an increasingly Augustinian intelligentsia.[49] In direct contradiction to Aristotelianism, Augustine's writings provided a basis for a theory of culpability that responded to individual choices rather than entire lifetimes of habituation. This provided a sufficient basis for judging individuals within a criminal context, which was readily exploited by the Decretists in giving substance to their emerging criminal jurisdiction, which rested on the delineation of internal and external aspects of wrongdoing.[50]

An attempt at dislocating Augustine's approach from a theological context can be seen in Albertus Gandinus' *Tractatus Maleficiorum*, which has been presented as a turning point in the history of fault.[51] This manual, though primarily

45 Harry Dondorp, 'Crime and Punishment' in *Negligence: The Comparative Legal History of the Law of Torts*, ed. Eltjo J.H. Schrage (Berlin: Duncker & Humblot, 2001), 101 n.2.

46 D.9.2.31.

47 X, 5.36.9; Ibbetson, 'How the Romans', 498 n.131.

48 Placentinus, *In Summam Institutionum*, 144 (ad J.4.3): '*homo semper est rationalis, licet non semper ratione utat*'. Similar ideas can be seen in Dynus, *De Regulis Iuris*, c.10 ('*ratihabitionem*'), cited by Hermann Kantorowicz, 'Baldus de Ubaldis and the Subjective Theory of Guilt' (1934) 1 Social Research 358, 359 n5.

49 Virpi Mäkinen and Heikki Pihlajamäki, 'The individualization of crime in medieval canon law' (2004) 65 Journal of the History of Ideas 525, 526–530; see also Dietmar Willoweit (ed.), *Die Entstehung des öffentlichen Strafrechts* (Cologne: Böhlau Verlag, 1999).

50 Mäkinen and Pihlajamäki, 'The individualization of crime', 533 citing Rufinus of Bologna, *Summa decretorum*, ed. Heinrich Singer (Paderborn: F. Schöningh, 1902).

51 E.g. Hermann Kantorowicz, *Albertus Gandinus und das Strafrecht der Scholastik*, 2 volumes (Berlin: J. Guttentag, 1907–1926).

concerned with points of procedure, deals with a number of general questions concerning the nature of liability. He presents liability as existing only through the proper combination of conduct, fault and result.[52] His discussion of fault is focused primarily on proving intention, but is presented at a general level. The same questions apply regardless of the wrong being judged, and will always require culpability beyond mere chance.[53] This approach stands somewhere between the two stances traceable to Roman law. It looks to the defendant's state of mind, exculpating the insane or incapacitated, but does not use the language of duty.

More promising is the *Lectura Codicis* of Baldus de Ubaldis (1327–1400).[54] Wrongs (*delicta*) are said to have three components: manifestation, name and quality. The first '*stat in consummatione delicti*', essentially requiring that penalisation be based on the occurrence of prohibited results or conduct. The second aspect is included simply to note that not all forms of wrongdoing are given names. A direct parallel is drawn with the innominate contracts—there is scope for redressable wrongdoing in the interstices of the nominate delicts. It is the third element that is of interest to the development of fault. By 'quality' Baldus appears to mean the severity of the wrongdoing—every factor that aggravates liability is said to be a quality of the wrong. These can be divided into two sets of considerations: the internal machinations of the wrongdoer, and the circumstances within which he acted. The internal considerations can be evidenced either through positive volition, blameworthiness, or a failure to live up to some legally imposed standard.[55] The example given is homicide: though the taking of life may well be a crime even when unaccompanied by direct intention, volition makes the crime even more serious. This analysis detaches fault considerations from the act and relocates them in the defendant. No more should one ask only whether throwing a javelin in a public space is *culpa*, but also whether the defendant was *culpa* to do so. Moreover, Baldus

52 In so doing he appears to have relied upon the 13th century jurist Odofredus—Mäkinen and Pihlajamäki, 'The Individualization of Crime', 535.

53 Gandinus, *Tractatus Maleficiorum*, 210.

54 The descent of manuscript versions of this work is complicated: Kantorowicz, 'Baldus', 360–3. A reconstructed Latin version of the key passage, C.9.2.5, can be found ibid., 364–370.

55 Kantorowicz, 'Baldus', 365–66, recreating C.9.2.5: '*qualitas vero delicti est duplex. Una est qualitas inherens ipsi delinquent, alia est inherens circumstantiis vel concomitantiis ipsius delicti. Et iterum qualitas inherens deliquenti potest esse duplex. Una est que provenit ex anomi, ut dolus, vel ex circumscriptione, ut culpa; alia est qualitas que non provenit ipso iure, sed ex eo, quia ipsa persona est qualifcata a iure*'.

follows the lead of the criminal treatise authors in dealing with such questions at a general level, rather than containing his discussion to individual delicts.

Writing between Gandinus and Baldus was the latter's teacher, Bartolus (1313–1357), the most influential of the *mos italicus* jurists. He examined the term '*culpa*' in two distinct contexts. The first is a minimalist examination of the delictual sense of the term in his commentary on the *lex Aquilia*. The only text discussed is D.9.2.11pr, which is viewed as a matter of causation.[56] Far more substantial is his exploration of contractual *culpa* in relation to the contract of deposit in D.16.3.32. Here *culpa* is given a definition: 'a deviation from that which is good, which could be foreseen by a diligent person'.[57] That Bartolus did not extend this definition to the delictual sense of *culpa*, which retained the insubstantial form given to it by earlier civilians, was no more than the retention of the Roman distinction between '*culpa*' in the *lex Aquilia* and the more nuanced contractual *culpa levis in abstracto/concreto*. The maxim '*nemo bonus iurista nisi bartolista*' proved unfortunately influential in the development of fault concepts within the civil law tradition. The Roman bifurcation of *culpa* across contract and delict persisted, causing considerable terminological ambiguity.[58] The specific approach adopted by an individual jurist or judge appears to have been a matter of personal preference.[59]

Doctrinal Developments in the *Lex Aquilia*

It was in the nature of many of the commentators, as with the glossators, to write on every aspect of Roman law, even those that had ceased to be relevant to their concerns. This is less evident in commentaries dedicated to specific topics, but so long as their works focused on specific passages of the *Corpus Iuris Civilis* discussion of the totality was unavoidable. Thus despite their pervasive lack of interest in delictual matters, under the *mos italicus* a number of

56 Ibbetson, 'How the Romans', 506 n.185.

57 Bartolus, *Commentaria*, ad D.16.3.32 at n.7: '*culpa est deviatio ab eo, quod bonum est, quod per diligentiam potuit praevideri*'; translation taken from Ibbetson, 'How the Romans', 506 n.185.

58 Something that even at the turn of the seventeenth century caused despair: Lessius, *De Iustitia et Iure*, 2.7.6.

59 It is perhaps possible to identify regional practices across extended periods of time. E.g. Venetian practice in the mid-fourteenth century favoured an Augustinian approach: Guido Ruggiero, 'Excusable murder: insanity and reason in early renaissance Venice' (1982) 16 Journal of Social History 16.

doctrinal developments were made in relation to the *lex Aquilia*. These developments reflect the attitude of the authors of the *mos italicus* towards delict, smacking more of indifference than thought. The result was ironically to greatly expand the *lex Aquilia* beyond its ancient strictures, allowing it to encompass several new types of harm.

Damages for injuries to free men

Injuries to free persons up to and including homicide appear to have been readily accepted as falling under the *lex* from an early date. This accretion to the *lex Aquilia*'s scope was made almost without comment or discussion. In the earliest days of the glossators this development was resisted on the grounds given by Ulpian in D.9.2.13.pr: a free person's body and life are beyond valuation. This was put forward in an influential form by Bulgarus of the Four Doctors.[60] But the opposite view, typically ascribed to Azo (1150–1230), clearly found favour.[61] The *glossa ordinaria* offers a very straightforward analysis of D.9.2.13: 'a free man is forcefully killed. Does a direct action on the *lex Aquilia* lie? The answer is no, but an *actio utilis* does lie'.[62] The text being glossed is on a mere injury, and is apparently taken at face value before being extended to cover even homicide.[63] The absence of any commensurable property, though flagged as an interesting topic, was not by this point a concern. The same disregard can be seen in Bartolus' commentary on the *Digestum Vetus*, which omits any mention of D.9.2.13.

As has already been seen, at a very early point in the revival of Romanist scholarship the *lex Aquilia* and *lex Cornelia* became conjoined.[64] Both were viewed as dealing with homicide, and so the pertinent question came to be how each was invoked. The rule that quickly emerged was that the *lex Cornelia* responded to *dolus*, while the *lex Aquilia* was triggered by the lesser *culpa*. This aligned neatly with the differing purposes of the actions, with the *lex Cornelia* being used to punish while the *lex Aquilia* sought to remediate *damnum*.[65] The

60 Feenstra, 'Grotius' doctrine of liability for negligence', 211.

61 Azo, *Summa Codicis*, book 3 title 35 (*lex Aquilia*) and book 9 title 16 (*lex Cornelia*).

62 Accursius, *Corpus Iuris Civilis Iustinianei cum Commentariis: Primus Digestum Vetus*, ad D.9.2.13: '*sic ponitur: homini libero manus incisa est. An ei directa Aquil. competat? Et respond. quod non: sed utilis sic*'.

63 For a full overview of the glossatorial treatment of damages for homicide, see Feenstra, 'Die Glossatoren und die actio legis Aquiliae utilis bei Tötung eines freien', 211.

64 E.g. Placentinus, *In Summam Institutionum*, 142 (ad J.4.3).

65 Ibid., 142 (ad J.4.3). While the canonists viewed such remediation as itself punitive, this does not appear to have informed the reasoning of the glossators.

damages would be determined according to the lost income of the deceased, showing that the Roman rule that the body itself was beyond valuation was still lurking beneath the surface.[66]

The recovery of pure economic loss has unmistakeable roots in the Digest. Perhaps the clearest example is to be found in D.9.2.27.21:

> Si quis de manu mihi nummos excusserit, Sabinus existimat damni iniuriae esse actionem, si ita perierint, ne ad aliquem pervenirent, puta si in flumen vel in mare vel in cloacam ceciderunt: quod si ad aliquem pervenerunt, ope consilio furtum factum agendum, quod et antiquis placuit. Idem etiam in factum dari posse actionem ait.[67]

The principle seems clear: where no other action can lie, an action on the *lex* will be granted. Whether the action is direct or decretal is irrelevant at this point—all that matters is that the *lex* could be used to remedy pure economic loss. However, a German audience might doubt the extent to which this text can be described as dealing with *pure* economic loss. For example, Zimmermann argues that the text stands for the broader proposition that 'the defendant's conduct has to have related to a specific corporeal asset in the plaintiff's property'.[68] The basis of this boundary might be questioned. The text is clearly dealing with a scenario in which the only loss suffered is economic in nature. The coins are unscathed and still perfectly usable—in no sense can they be said to have been spoiled. To limit pure economic losses to those felt without any connection to a corporeal asset seems to restrict the concept needlessly. Nevertheless, on the German conception there is no evidence of the *lex Aquilia* being used to redress pure economic loss in the *Corpus Iuris Civilis*.

Regardless of how one views D.9.2.27.21, it was not that text that grounded the medieval expansion into the recovery of pure economic loss. Instead the glossators latched onto a text from Justinian's Institutes:

> ... sed si non corpore damnum fuerit datum neque corpus laesum fuerit, sed alio modo damnum alicui contigit, cum non sufficit neque directa

66 Jansen, 'Duties and rights in negligence', 451.

67 D.9.2.27.21: 'If someone knocks coins from my hand, Sabinus believes there is an action for wrongful loss provided that are lost and do not come to another person, as where they fall into a river or the sea or a drain; but if they come to another person there will be an action for aiding and abetting theft, and the ancient jurists also believed this. He says that an *actio in factum* can also be given.'

68 Zimmermann, *The Law of Obligations*, 1022.

> neque utilis Aquilia, placuit eum qui obnoxius fuerit in factum actione teneri: veluti si quis, misericordia ductus, alienum servum compeditum solverit, ut fugeret.[69]

Commentaries on this passage invariably treat it as providing for the recovery of any *damnum* whatsoever.[70] A particularly useful example is given by Durandus (c.1230–1296): a person drops litter in front of another person's door. The property owner is fined by the local authority under a civic *lex*. He can then use the *lex Aquilia* to recover the cost of meeting that fine from the person who dropped the litter.[71] This is a scenario without any precedent in the *Corpus Iuris Civilis*, showing the abstraction of a principle from the Justinianic sources and its application to a new problem. There is no way to construe the loss caused as other than purely economic in nature. A similar idea lies behind Baldus' discussion of the liability of a secretary who discloses confidential information.[72] This is another clear accretion to the delict's scope.

Penalisation and Remediation

The medieval jurists were writing in an environment that had an established tradition of viewing laws on wrongdoing as the secular reflection of sin. Thus when turning to the medieval treatment of delict it should be no surprise that the original tension between the compensatory and penal dimensions was typically resolved in favour of categorising the action as penal. However, the way in which damages were interpreted served to undermine this penal label.[73] Sometimes the dissonance between the association of wrongdoing with sin and the increasingly compensatory focus of the *lex Aquilia* is

69 J.4.3.16: '…If damage be done, not by the body or to a body, but in some other form, neither the direct nor the modified Aquilian action will lie, though it is held that the wrongdoer is liable to an action on the case; as, for instance, where a man is moved by pity to loose another's slave from his fetters, and so enables him to escape'.

70 E.g. Placentinus, *In Summam Institutionum*, 143 (ad J.4.3): '*tertio capite … cavetur de omni caetero damno dato*'.

71 Durandus, *Speculum Iudiciale*, 4.4.2; Zimmermann, *The Law of Obligations*, 1023; Gordley, *Foundations of Private Law*, 266.

72 Baldus, *Commentaria*, ad D.9.2.41; Gordley, *Foundations of Private Law*, 266. This served to extend the Roman rule on the destruction of wills. It is the information in the will that is truly valuable, thereby determining the size of the award of damages. So what if the information can be separated from a physical document?

73 Rotondi, '*Dalla lex Aquilia all'art. 1151 Cod. Civ*', 507: '*che l' a. l. Aq. sia penale, i glossatori non lo possono negare; ma, di fronte alla funzione da essa esercitata, cercano per quanto è possibile di interpretare restrittivamente questo carattere*'.

apparent. Placentinus, for example, shows his working: an action *ex maleficio* must always be penal, but an action on the *lex Aquilia* is mixed.[74] As a failure to use reason is not always *maleficium*, it follows that this liability is not always penal—it depends on the case at hand. In his commentary on Justinian's *Institutes*, Baldus straightforwardly asserted that the action on the *lex* is penal, though the only consequence of this he labours is the passive intransmissibility of the action.[75] That Bartolus also viewed the *lex Aquilia* as a penal form of liability can be seen most clearly in his treatment of *lis crescens*. He justified the continued existence of this procedural quirk as an additional penalty, essentially for adding to the claimant's work.[76] Upon the defendant's denial of liability the claimant has a fresh burden of proving his claim, and if the defendant is found guilty that burden could (and should) have been shirked from the outset. But while casting the *lex* as a penal source of liability, Bartolus also sought to narrow the troubling scope for over-compensation under chapter one. This can be seen in his treatment of ambiguous causation.[77] Dealing with a series of formulations in which wounds are struck sometimes simultaneously, sometimes consecutively, and over varying periods of times, in each Bartolus found a way to ensure the damages awarded were roughly proportionate to the harm inflicted, primarily by limiting the number of causative agents who could be held accountable. In so doing he removed one of the most punitive aspects of the delict's original operation.

This conflict between the compensatory and penal dimensions of delict had a further manifestation within the terminology of medieval private law: the use of the term *restitutio* by canonists. The verb *restituere* was sometimes used to describe a particular punishment (*poena*).[78] Some care is required with this terminology and the significance attached to it. The language of restoration bears a special significance to Grotius' formulation of delict, and any encounter with it in earlier legal traditions needs to be dealt with cautiously. The *restitutio* of the canonists has been presented as being directly compensatory.[79] Dondorp has argued that this is misguided, and that it was

74 Placentinus, *In Summam Institutionum*, 144 (ad J.4.3).

75 Baldus, *Lectura Super Institutionibus*, 44 (ad J.4.3).

76 Bartolus, *Consilia, Quaestiones et Tractatus*, (Venice, 1585), q.8.n.17; see also Durandus, *Speculum Iudiciale*, 213.

77 Bartolus, *Commentaria*, ad D.9.2.11.

78 Dondorp, 'Crime and punishment', 103.

79 Scott, 'Passive transmissibility of delictual actions in old canon law' (1978) Acta Juridica 17: 'Canon law ... rejects the possibility of any amount being awarded in excess of actual damages sustained'.

not uncommon for fines to be awarded as 'restitution'.[80] In so doing, he argues that the canonists were inspired by the punitive approach to *iniuria* of Roman law. Though the word implies a directly compensatory measure of damages, *restitutio* was nevertheless a *poena* to the canonists, and so could exceed mere reipersecution.[81] This reading of *restitutio* was further supported by the Digest texts on the *lex Aquilia*, which spoke of restoration and punishment in the same breath.[82]

How is it that Scott and Dondorp could take such diametrically opposed stances on the meaning of *restitutio*? To answer this, one needs to begin in the twelfth century. In its original canon law usage, the term was used to describe an aspect of penance in the *forum internum*.[83] This is the sense in which Gratian used the term, not as an action but a moral principle: absolution required restoration.[84] It was not until the Decretals of Gregory IX that one can see the juridification of *restitutio* into a cause of action.[85] The *restitutio* of the decretalists, now known as *restitutio in integrum*, mirrored the remedy of Roman law described in D.4.1 and responded to any breach of natural justice in human relations.[86] This general principle worked its way into the *glossa ordinaria*.[87] Thus in the thirteenth century there were two parallel notions of *restitutio*. The noun used on its own could still refer to an aspect of penance that might require a monetary offering be made in excess of the strict loss caused to redress particularly heinous wrongdoing. But this should not detract from the literal restoration imposed under the canonical *restitutio in integrum*, which was typically defined in terms of restoring '*in pristinum statum*'.[88] This latter remedy, though directly compensatory, remained confined to the works of the canonists. Though it was known to secular jurists, its exceptional nature in Roman

80 Clear and seemingly conclusive evidence is offered in X.5.36.6, in which the verb *restituere* is used in relation to a fine of fourfold damages: Dondorp, 'Crime and punishment', 103–4.

81 It is clear that canonists regarded damages under an *actio legis Aquiliae* as penal regardless of the harm inflicted: e.g. Dondorp, 'Crime and Punishment', 107 n.23 citing Bernardus Papiensis.

82 D.9.2.30.3.

83 Richard H. Helmholz, *The Spirit of Classical Canon Law* (Athens: University of Georgia Press, 1996), 93.

84 Andrea Bettetini, *La 'restitutio in integrum' processuale nel diritto canonico* (Padua: CEDAM, 1994).

85 X.1.41.1.

86 Helmholz, *The Spirit of Classical Canon Law*, 95.

87 Ibid., 97.

88 Ibid., 89.

law did not escape their notice.[89] Consequently it has little significance to the medieval law of delict beyond the realms of canon law.

Iniuria

The delict of *iniuria* was the form of wrongdoing most specific to Roman society. The interest harmed, variously *existimatio*, *fama* and *pudor*, was a very Roman notion. While it is very common for a legal system to develop laws against rumourmongering or other hurtful speech, the form that these norms ought to take is not immediately obvious. Different aspects of the speech can be focused upon. Is it spreading untruths that deserves redress? Or harm to a person's reputation, whether caused by truth or lies? And what is it that the law protects: social standing, affection, reputation, commercial viability, or some other factor? In the treatises of the medieval criminal lawyers it was common for some form of injurious words to be dealt with, but not necessarily the *iniuria* of Roman law. A leading example is Gandinus' *Tractatus Maleficiorum*, which examines only one verbal wrong: *falsari*.[90] Others still saw *iniuria* as something broader than its Roman counterpart. Gambiglioni, while commenting on the meaning of *verba iniuriosa*, wrote that many wrongs can be committed verbally, chief among them *contumelia* and adultery.[91] This effectively bumps the Roman *iniuria* down to a subspecies of a broader category, so as to unite otherwise disparate types of wrongdoing.

When it was studied, the medieval substance of *iniuria* remained broadly consistent with Roman law.[92] By late classical law the criminal dimensions of the delict were being emphasised over any compensatory role it might once have played.[93] Its penal aspect was similarly the focus of medieval scholarship. And although *iniuria* became a matter of considerable interest to criminal lawyers, little was done to take it beyond its original strictures. In the late

89 Accursius, *Corpus Iuris Civilis Iustinianei cum Commentariis: Primus Digestum Vetus*, ad D.4.1.7.1.

90 Gandinus, *Tractatus Maleficiorum*, c.35.

91 Gambiglioni, *Tractatus de Maleficiis*, 115. He also deals with threats and blasphemy, among others, under this heading.

92 E.g. Placentinus, *In Summam Institutionum*, 144–145 (ad J.4.4); the *glossa ordinaria* on D.47.10 is primarily a list of other actions that might lie in the scenarios discussed, or variations thereof. The core concepts are left undefined.

93 D.47.10.45, a text credited to Hermogenian, a jurist of the late third and early fourth centuries.

fourteenth century Bonifacio Vitalini's (c.1320-c.1388) *Super Maleficiis* had pushed the need for *animus iniurandi* to the fore, making explicit the seemingly implicit requirement of Roman law.[94] Later works simply built on this basis, offering ever more precise formulations of the requisite standard of intention. This approach to *iniuria* peaked in Angelo Gambiglioni's *Tractatus de Maleficiis* in 1472, which provided a framework of presumptions which determined when intention could be inferred and when it had to be positively shown.[95] Crucially, it remained immune to any push towards generalisation, remaining in a distinct delictual bubble.

Although the *iniuria* of civil and criminal law remained close to its Roman roots, a parallel remedy developed in the writings of the canonists that took defamatory comments in a different direction. The substance of the wrong remained the same as in the civil law, but the remedy was something new. Rather than a pecuniary remedy, it sought to undo the harm caused through apologising, or publicly retracting the injurious statement.[96] Drawing on theological doctrine, a failure to recant acted as a barrier to salvation. This remained a canon law remedy throughout the Middle Ages, finding application in secular courts only in the sixteenth century through the *actio iniuriarum ad palinodiam*.[97]

The interest harmed by *iniuria* was inconsistently defined across the wrong's civil and criminal conceptions. Gambiglioni did not define *contumelia* nor the thing it targets, bar the occasional tangential reference to *honor*.[98] There is a strong sense that one is expected to recognise it on sight. Vitalini was similarly vague. Though he faithfully describes the full variety of conduct that could ground an *actio iniuriarum* in Roman law, it is the conduct itself that justifies an action. Beating somebody is injurious not because it is disrespectful, but because it is violent.[99] Injurious words are actionable simply because they are *mala verba*. The focus is, as in Roman law, firmly on the conduct rather than

94 Antonio Marongiu, *Enciclopedia del Diritto*, 46 volumes (Milan: Giuffrè, 1958–1993), vol. 12, 477.

95 Ibid., 477; Gambiglioni, *Tractatus de Maleficiis*, 116ff. Examples include whether factors such as anger and provocation excuse a contumelious outburst. This development is consonant with the developing role of presumptions in canon law.

96 Gordley, *The Jurists*, 58.

97 Zimmermann, *Law of Obligations*, 1072. The origins of this action are unclear, with no apparent precursor in the medieval civil law tradition. The use of *palinodia* is particularly curious: a Greek term that within the *Corpus Iuris Civilis* is not connected to *iniuria* even once. This hints at a possible humanist origin; a new name for the *malum carmen* perhaps. But this is little more than speculation.

98 Gambiglioni, *Tractatus de Maleficiis*, 116.

99 Vitalini, *Super Maleficiis*, ad tit. *de iniuriis* n.4–8.

the harm. In both of these works, the meat of *iniuria* is explored through a prolonged series of examples. The same methods are seen in civilian treatises. While Azo associated *famosi libelli* with *fama* but was silent on the harm caused by *iniuria*, Placentinus tentatively linked *iniuria* to *honor*.[100] He did, however, choose to substantiate the delict through examples of injurious conduct.[101] The *glossa ordinaria* retains the same focus and, over a century later, this approach was still favoured by Bartolus.[102]

This conceptual looseness is not indicative of the broader approach to personality interests in the medieval civil law. In other areas of law such concepts were rigidly defined. *Fama*, for instance, became an important aspect of legal personality, determining one's capacity to act in court and hold certain public offices, an antonym to the Roman *infamia*.[103] *Fama* was an idea with a definite function within legal procedure, and so needed to be understood in the same light wherever the civil law found application. *Fama* as understood by lawyers was closely related to a person's reputation in the real world, but it was necessarily distinct from such concerns. A person's legal capacity cannot fluctuate with public sentiment. Thus as *fama* became more of a concern to lawyers, it bore less and less resemblance to an actual personality interest. It is for this reason that Kuehn speaks of '*fama* in the streets' and '*fama* in law'.[104] The interest harmed by *iniuria* must be closer to '*fama* in the streets', but this notion was a product of mutable public opinion.

This fairly uneventful history likely reflects the sparing use made of *iniuria*. Many localities had statutory regimes governing insults, and eminent jurists would advise upon these. Dean reports a *consilium* of Bartolus on the definition of an insult.[105] A statute in Chiusi imposed a fixed penalty for every insulting word, and it was for Bartolus to determine whether a particularly vituperative tirade ought to lead to damages calculated literally according to the

100 Azo, *Summa Codicis*, book 9 title 35; book 9 title 36.

101 Placentinus, *In Summam Institutionem*, 144–145 (ad J.4.4).

102 Accursius, *Corpus Iuris Civilis Iustinianei cum Commentariis: Digestum Novum*, ad D.47.10; Bartolus, *Commentaria*, ad D.47.10.

103 Francesco Migliorino, *Fama e infamia* (Catania: Editrice Giannotta, 1985).

104 Thomas Kuehn, '*Fama* as a legal status in renaissance Florence' in *Fama: The Politics of Talk and Reputation in Medieval Europe*, eds Thelma S. Fenster and Daniel L. Smail (Ithaca, NY: Cornell University Press, 2003); the foundations for a similar distinction were laid in Roman law (e.g. D.50.17.104) and built upon early glossators: Bulgarus, *Ad Digestorum Titulum de Diversis Regulis Iuris Antiqui Commentarius*, para.104.

105 Trevor Dean, *Crime and Justice in Late Medieval Italy* (Cambridge: Cambridge University Press, 2007), 116 n.13.

word, or whether words might be combined into insulting clauses. In so doing, the sixty word attack was reduced to just eight insults.[106] Similar regimes are to be found across Italy in the Middle Ages, and even further afield.[107] In their local statutory form insults were typically remedied through a fixed penalty. In light of such adequacy, there was little impetus for the development of the Roman conception of *iniuria*.

Conclusion

The haphazard development of delict in the Middle Ages does not give the impression of design. The early formulation of a general principle of delictual liability for the infliction of loss in canon law through the Decretals served to ossify what had previously been a fertile branch of Roman law. Consequently the subject was barely taught in the classrooms and studied in the libraries of the Roman law faculties of medieval Europe. Such doctrinal developments as did exist were the product of the early burst of energy that delict (or, more specifically, the *lex Aquilia*) experienced before the thirteenth century, and were perpetuated in the writings of the commentators almost as if they were traditional. These did, however, serve to advance the degree of generalisation visible within delict. The expansion of the *lex Aquilia* to cover personal injuries up to and including homicide took delict beyond its ancient core of proprietary wrongdoing. The later development of wrongdoing and associated doctrines such as fault was achieved not under the *mos italicus*, but through the development of canon and criminal laws. These ideas fed back into the writings of the commentators to a degree—it would be hard for Baldus to ignore his own writings on criminal responsibility when putting on his Roman law hat. But such developments lacked the slightest hint of systematisation. Individual heads of liability remained inconsistent in their approach to basic questions such as fault and remediation, with iniuria in particular far removed from the *lex Aquilia*. Under the *mos italicus*, delict remained a fragmentary and under-explored discipline.

106 Ibid., 117.

107 E.g. the regular usage made of *amende honorable* by the Parlement of Paris in the fourteenth century: Bernadette Auzary-Schmaltz, 'Liability in tort in France before the Code civil' in *Negligence: The Comparative Legal History of the Law of Torts*, ed. Eltjo J.H. Schrage (Berlin: Duncker & Humblot, 2001), 322.

CHAPTER 5

Delict in the Sixteenth Century

Delict and the Mainstream of 'Legal' Humanism

Legal humanism, also known as the *mos gallicus* for the largely French bias of its constituent scholars, holds a special place in many legal histories. From Petrarch's first call for a return to the law of antiquity, scholars sought to disentangle the essence of Roman jurisprudence from the medieval bindings that they thought threatened to snuff out its intellectual value.[1] This leads to the claim that, in the words of a recent scholar, 'the humanist program led to the sixteenth-century revolution in the methodology of law and history'.[2] The purpose of this chapter is to determine whether this methodological revolution filtered down to the development of delictual doctrine.

Within the authors typically taken as representing the *mos gallicus* there are at least two distinct groups. The first consists of those humanists who used legal sources to further their understanding of the ancient world. Their interest was not in law for its own sake, but the insight into social norms and values that the subject can provide.[3] Budeaus (1467–1540) is perhaps the best example of this approach, whose lengthiest tract on the *lex Aquilia* focuses on D.9.2.7.4 and the meaning of the word '*pancratium*'.[4] Though unquestionably

1 Petrarch, *Letters from Petrarch*, 166–170, ed. Morris Bishop (Indiana: Indiana University Press, 1966), cited in Donald Kelley, 'The Rise of Legal History in the Renaissance' (1970) 9 History and Theory 174, 176 n4. The famous description of the *mos italicus* as 'barbarism [that] has smothered the pure law like a giant creeper' stems from Zasius: Georg Dahm, 'On the Reception of Roman and Italian law in Germany' in *Pre-Reformation Germany*, ed. Gerald Strauss (London: Macmillan, 1972), 300, citing *Zasii Epistolae*, ed. Joseph A. Riegger (Ulmae, 1774), part 2 number 8.

2 Gordley, *The Jurists*, 111. See also Julian H. Franklin, *Jean Bodin and the Sixteenth-Century Revolution in the Methodology of Law and History* (New York: Columbia University Press, 1963).

3 This is not to downplay the significance of the source criticism instilled in scholarship by this class of essentially philological humanism. It simply reflects that the basic fact that just because someone is using legal sources does not mean they are interested in legal doctrine.

4 Budeaus, *Opera Omnia*, III, 163.

 DOI 10.1163/9789004344372_006

one of the most mysterious words in D.9.2, there is little about it that suggests legal import. Rather, Budeaus seizes upon it as a further insight into the quotidian of classical Rome. In the words of Stein, he was 'little interested in legal questions', and far preferred 'the new knowledge of antiquity resulting from humanist researches'.[5]

The members of the second group were genuine in their interest in law. They adapted the methods of the humanists to unravelling the Byzantine construction and medieval interpretation of the *Corpus Iuris Civilis*, thereby restoring the letter of the law to its original form. It is with these authors that this chapter is concerned, and in their writings alongside the more orthodox commentaries of the sixteenth century that it will search for doctrinal developments within delict. But the humanist methods to some degree presuppose the existence of a medieval gloss, the unstitching of which provided them with a focus. As has already been seen, the *mos italicus* left delict in an emaciated form, leaving little for the humanists to unravel. As such, there was not much for the *mos gallicus* to contribute to the law of delict through its ordinary methods. This chapter will focus first on how the biggest names in humanism dealt with delict in the Roman sense, rather than the broader idea of wrongdoing. Having shown that delict fared as well at the hands of humanism as it did under the *mos italicus*, it will focus on a number of individual treatments of delict. This division serves to emphasise that though delict was not entirely ignored in the years leading up to Grotius, it was severely malnourished.[6]

Humanism and the lex Aquilia

The medieval neglect of delict survived into humanism, and can be seen in the writings of many of its central figures. This can easily be illustrated through the writings of Alciatus (1492–1550), one of the most prolific legal humanists. The following table is a reconstruction of his commentary on the Digest, with the topics arranged to mirror their location in the Digest:

5 Peter Stein, 'Legal humanism and legal science' (1986) 54 Tijdschrift voor Rechtsgeschiedenis 297, 299.

6 A clue in support of this conclusion can be found in the tendency in seminal works on the history of delict to skip from the commentators to the *usus modernus pandectarum*. See, for example, Rotondi, '*Dalla* lex Aquilia *all'art. 1151 Cod. Civ*', 501–526 which devotes less space to each successive century in the Middle Ages; Zimmermann, *The Law of Obligations*, 1017, which leaps from Justinian to the *usus modernus*.

Subject	Location
Iustita et iure	D.1.1
Officio eius, cui mandata est iurisdictio	D.1.21
Officio assessorum	D.1.22
Iurisdictione omnium iudicum	D.2.1
Quod quisque iuris in alium statuerit	D.2.2
Si quis ius dicenti non obtemperaverit	D.2.3
Rebus creditis, si certum petatur, et de certi condictione	D.12.1
Depositi, vel contra	D.16.3
Soluto matrimonio, quemadmodum dos petatur	D.24.2
Liberis et posthumis haeredibus instituendis	D.28.2
Haeredibus instituendis	D.28.5
Vulgari et pupillari substitutione	D.28.6
Adquirenda vel omittenda hereditate	D.29.2
Legatis et fideicommissis	D.30.1, 31.1, 32.1
Ad legem Falcidiam	D.35.2
Ad senatusconsultum Trebellianum	D.36.1
Bonorum possessione contra tabulas	D.37.4
Bonorum possessionibus	D.37.11
Novi operis nuntiatione	D.39.1
Donationibus	D.39.5
Adquirenda vel amittenda possessione	D.41.2
Usucapionibus et usurpationibus	D.41.3
Quae in fraudem creditorum facta sunt	D.42.9
Verborum obligationibus	D.45.1
Appellationibus et relationibus	D.49.1

Immediately apparent is the scant consideration of obligations as a whole. The picture given by the titles alone is, however, misleading. Alciatus' commentary on D.45.1 consumes almost a quarter of his entire *Opera Omnia*, and half of his treatment of the Digest. Clearly he was interested in aspects of the law of obligations, and his interest could be genuinely legal. It simply did not extend to delict. Only one title of the five books with content relevant to wrongdoing, namely books 9, 11, 47, 48 and 49 of the Digest, is examined. Instead, it is readily apparent that Alciatus is interested in the Roman laws that govern life when it is going well. Significant tracts are dedicated to the *lex Falcidia*, which bars the complete disinheritance of one's heirs, and the *senatusconsultum Trebellianum* on the management of fruits under a *fideicommissum*. As well as inheritance, there are sections on marriage, property and commercial dealings. This is coupled with the expected passage on the underlying jurisprudence of Roman law, a typically humanist amalgam of commentary and history.[7]

Alciatus did not see fit to comment on delict in relation to the Digest. His collected works also include a commentary on the *Decretals* of Gregory IX. The very last passage of this is entitled '*de poenitentiis et remissionibus*'.[8] This is as close as Alciatus comes to touching on wrongdoing—a little over a page on penance. The institutional delicts are almost entirely absent from his written corpus. The only exception to this is *furtum*, which is dealt with extremely briefly. Unsurprisingly, this is solely a means of getting at the oddities of Roman society to which *furtum* can attest. Thus Alciatus' sole discussion of *furtum* as a discrete topic deals with the bizarre *furtem per lancem et licium* to which Gaius alludes.[9] Similar patterns can be seen at the end of the sixteenth century. Albani (1509–1591), in his *Lucubrationes in Bartolum*, uses chapter one of the *lex Aquilia* to explore the Roman understanding of the passage of time. Starting with the number of days in a year, a matter surely relevant to a proper reading of the *lex*, he continues to consider how many years had elapsed between the dawn of creation and the birth of Christ.[10] While it might be thought perfectly natural for the nocturnal musings of a cardinal to turn to such spiritual matters, his somnolent thoughts on the *vindicatio* make for distinctly more legalistic reading.[11]

This lack of interest in delict is not entirely representative of the humanist tradition. However, it is not uncommon for those humanists who wrote on delict to neglect it in favour of more interesting topics, typically the law of contract or inheritance. Though Zasius' (1461–1536) *Paratitla* deals with book 9 of the Digest, it is not sufficiently important to merit inclusion in the summary of key points provided at the start of that work. Again, the *lex Aquilia* is not being seen as a topic that will generate interest, but something that ought to be included for the sake of completeness. As a consequence, the *lex Aquilia* is dealt with in just five columns. The starting point is trite: the *lex Aquilia* is about *damnum* caused through *iniuria*.[12] The expansions of the commentators

7 Including, for example, a passage on how the English came to recognise Roman sovereignty: Alciatus, *Opera Omnia*, I, 9 (point 42). Similar passages deal with Sicily, Spain and France.

8 Alciatus, *Opera Omnia*, III, 793. He omits any reference to X.5.36.

9 Ibid., IV, 353; G.3.192–193.

10 Albani, *Lucubrationes in Bartolum*, 221–222.

11 Ibid., 209ff.

12 Zasius, *Operum Omium*, I, 86, point 1.

are incorporated, such as the now familiar claim that wounds to a free man are to be remedied through an indirect action.[13] Zasius even refers to the medieval rule that dolose homicides are to be treated criminally, while culpose homicides merit an action on the *lex Aquilia*.[14] *Iniuria* is to be read as *dolus* and *culpa*, the latter of which is defined as a failure of diligence.[15] This promising definition, arrived at through D.9.2.31, is substantiated through a list of familiar scenarios: self-defence, necessity, killing a thief caught in the night, and so on.[16] These cases are not concerned with diligence, but the absence of right and blameworthiness of conduct, a more authentically Roman approach to fault than that adopted by most medieval jurists. It is clear that the duality of *culpa* was still an issue. Having set out the basic features of the *lex Aquilia*, Zasius moves on to more difficult topics. But even here his discussion is safely confined to the issues raised by the Digest with the occasional humanist interjection.[17] In short, as the name of the work suggests, Zasius' *Paratitla* offers an accurate and probing summary of D.9.2, but it does not depart from earlier Romanist scholarship. We find in his work neither new ideas, nor an attempt at wiping away the medieval gloss on the *lex Aquilia*. Instead the established orthodoxy is continued.

The writings of Baron (1495–1550) discuss the *lex Aquilia* in two locations: a commentary on the Institutes, and a selection of interesting Digest titles. The latter show a preoccupation with contract similar to that found in Alciatus. It discusses a sole text on the *lex Aquilia*: D.9.2.54.[18] This text concerns the effects of *mora* on delictual liability where the animate property to be delivered is killed. Little is made of the delictual issue at the heart of the text. Rather, it is being read for its contractual content. His discussion of the text glosses over any difficult points of terminology by referring to Bartolus, perhaps surprising for a humanist. It goes without saying that this discussion purporting to pertain to the *lex Aquilia* is among the shortest entries in his commentary. However, unlike Alciatus, this interest in contractual problems did not entirely preclude Baron from considering the detail of delictual doctrine. His commentary on J.4.3 deals with a number of difficult points. The most novel is his discussion of the meaning of *culpa*. He notes the troublesome duality discussed in the previous chapter, writing that *culpa* ought to consist in doing, but for many it means

13 Ibid., I, 86, point 3.
14 Ibid., I, 88, point 22.
15 Ibid., I, 87, point 5.
16 Ibid., I, 87, point 6.
17 E.g. Ibid., I, 88, point 26 on the *pancratium*.
18 Baron, *Commentariorum ad Varios Digestorum Iuris Civilis Titulos*, III, 97–98.

negligentia.[19] He tries to incorporate both views: *culpa* is the fault standard for loss caused by actions, and *negligentia* for loss caused by omissions. In so doing he brings together texts discussing situational *culpa* (e.g. the case of the thief killed in the night) and texts on failures of diligence.[20] The remainder of the passage is curiously silent on the expansions of the commentators. He allows an action for blameworthily inflicted personal injuries, but there is direct Justinianic authority for this. His discussion of the objects of chapter one focuses entirely on the meaning of *pecudes*, noting that camels and elephants came to be included. He says nothing of whether the *lex* could be used to redress any type of homicide in Roman law.[21]

Cujas' (1522–1590) commentary on the *lex Aquilia* is of a comparable level of detail to Baron, but displays a greater tendency to think about the law rather than simply provide an explanation of the Latin. The starting point is familiar: the *lex Aquilia* rests on the twin pillars of *iniuria* and *damnum*.[22] His commentary on the *Institutes* is preoccupied with linguistic points significant to the reconstruction of Justinian's text, but his works as a whole are far from devoid of legal detail.[23] In a passage on the law of sale, he defines *damnum* as necessarily consisting in valuation (*aestimatio*).[24] Consequently, in a significant departure from the orthodoxy of the day, he would not allow an *actio legis Aquiliae* for the homicide of a free person *per se*, but only where there was remediable loss.[25] This rule applies equally to wounds, effectively ignoring the *mos italicus* reading of D.9.2.13.pr. This is indicative of the nature of the effect humanism had on delict. It informed small points of detail, sometimes to great effect, but couldn't change the overall shape or characteristics of liability for wrongdoing.

Humanism and iniuria

The leading humanists did not find *iniuria* as compelling a topic as might be expected. The humanist project was driven by a desire to rediscover and revive

19 Baron, *Institutionum seu Elementorum Iustiniani*, 357: '*Ait iniuria. Interpretatur cum Ulpian verbum iniuria, ut sit non iure factum, sed contra ius, et culpa actum, quae in faciendo est fere, not etiam in negligendo ... scio negligentiam pro omni culpa, quae extra dolum sit, usupari* [sic]'.

20 Ibid., 358.

21 He does, however, consider the position in French law: ibid., 359.

22 Cujas, *Opera*, VIII, 1041E.

23 The first three points flagged for discussion in his commentary on J.4.3 are the construction of the clause, and the meaning of the words '*pecudes*' and '*latrones*': Cujas, *Opera*, VIII, 1043C-1044A.

24 Cujas, *Opera*, X, 715E.

25 Ibid., III, 578C.

antiquity. In using legal sources, for many the goal was not to understand the mechanics of the law but how the Romans structured their society, and to uncover behind the institutions the values and principles of Ancient Rome. *Iniuria* ought to have been a perfect fit for this ambition, evincing characteristically Roman values such as honour, reputation and shame. Moreover, it is difficult to find an alternative means of exploring these concepts through legal sources. Nevertheless, the works of the leading legal humanists contain only occasional references to the word *iniuria*, and when it does arise attention is torn between the general and specific usages of the term. Budaeus' *Annotationes* contains only the most fleeting reference to *existimatio*.[26] Even this snippet more closely resembles a tract on etymology than on law, referencing not jurists but the likes of Cicero and Quintilian. *Iniuria* is not to be found in either of its forms. The works of Alciatus make for slightly more fruitful reading. References to fault (*culpa*) lead not to texts on delict but on contract, but at least they lead to law.[27] The term *convicium* was deemed interesting enough to a humanist audience to earn a place in his *De Verborum Significatione*.[28] He claims that *convicium*, unlike *convocium*, need not be vocalised. This is a conscious break with Labeo, but appears to conflate *contumelia* with *convicium* with no mention of the other forms *contumelia* could take. As one might expect of a humanist, the brief text on *convicium* discusses the propriety of spelling it with a 't' instead of a 'c' (opting for the latter) instead of probing any legal depths.[29] Zasius is more legalistic yet again, but nevertheless *iniuria* is omitted.[30] A reference to '*laus boni viri*' leads only to a particularly fawning passage on the virtues of a number of jurists.[31]

By contrast, there is no shortage of references to *iniuria* in the index of Jacques Cujas' *Opera Omnia*. However, the vast majority of what he has to say relates to the general meaning of *iniuria*. Indeed, taken as a whole his references to *iniuria* can be seen as little more than a tally of the use of the word in the entire *Corpus Iuris Civilis*. Thus for the meaning of *iniuria* the reader is directed to passages on the *actio empti*, the respect owed to matrons, and actions between fathers and sons.[32] Cujas' comments on Digest 47.10 are telling. *Iniuria* is explicitly lesser than the other three institutional delicts, seemingly because

26 Budaeus, *Annotationes*, 531–2.

27 Alciatus, *In Digestorum*, 68.

28 Alciatus, *De Verborum Significatione*, 209.

29 Ibid., 210.

30 Zasius, *Singulares Intellectus*, 9 (*culpa*), 50 (*furtum*).

31 Ibid., 104.

32 Cujas, *Opera*, XII, 605, referencing VII, 1185, I, 111, and VII, 1073.

it is not available to heirs.[33] Its definition is simply given as '*agit causam doloris*', itself borrowed from Valentinianus and chosen by Cujas on account of its elegance.[34] The only other treatment of substance to be found across the twelve volumes of his *Opera Omnia* is a very superficial explanation of the outline of the delict.[35] In particular, the physical *iniuria* of the Twelve Tables seems to be at the fore of Cujas' mind, categorising the forms of *iniuria* as *aut in corpus aut extra corpus*.[36] *Iniuria extra corpus* consists of *convitiis et famosis libellis*.

No effort is made at defining or describing these terms. Instead he offers a truncated version of the substance of D.47.10.[37] Where points of details are explored, it is for their humanist and not legal interest. Thus a passage on the meaning of *atrox iniuria* contains the references to Ulpian that would be needed to ground the concept in Roman legal thought, but is supported further by references to Livy, Caesar and Cicero.[38] In spite of the fertile ground *iniuria* should have proven for humanist endeavours, in most of the leading legal humanist texts of the sixteenth century it is woefully underdeveloped.

Delict and the Mainstream of 'Legal' Humanism

Two fundamental aspects of the mainstream of legal humanism ran counter to the steps required for the generalisation of delict: their interests and their goal. The conclusion that the humanists were uninterested in delict seems inescapable. Indeed, many of the leading figures of the *mos gallicus* held little interest in law at all, instead using legal sources for antiquarian scholarship. And for those humanists who were genuinely interested in the letter of the law, contract and its monumental medieval scaffolding held far greater sway. The humanist goal was the rediscovery of the true law of Ancient Rome, the older the better. For delict, this meant the restoration of a messy framework of overlapping remedies protecting property and little else from various types of interference. And as all the institutional delicts were known to have pre-classical existences, their classical forms were of even less interest. The *lex Aquilia* and *iniuria* remained isolated from one another, and little was done to harmonise the common elements of the institutional delicts. Each retained their focus on prohibited conduct, and each operated under different requirements.

33 Ibid., III, 293.
34 Ibid., III, 293.
35 Ibid., V, 2188.
36 Ibid., V, 2188.
37 Ibid., V, 2188–2198.
38 Cujas, *Opera*, V, 2191.

Individual Strands within Sixteenth-Century Delictual Scholarship

We now have an overview of the shape of delict as dealt with by the major scholars in the both the *mos gallicus* and *mos italicus* up to the mid-sixteenth century. From this point on, it becomes harder to maintain a valuable distinction between the two traditions, as the humanist context became increasingly normal in the academic world. Instead we must turn to individual jurists to understand developments. Before turning to the writings of Donellus (1527–1591), which served to revive interest in delictual matters to a significant degree, there is value in first considering a number of smaller problems that arose in specific works on delict. These will serve to underscore the state of scholarship on this long-neglected branch of private law.

What is Delict?

In some late sixteenth-century works there is a sense of rediscovery to their exploration of delict. In his tract on the practice of criminal law, Giulio Claro (1525–1575) uses three words interchangeably to describe wrongdoing: *crimen, delictum* and *maleficium.*[39] The work adopts an interesting structure. A long list of individual wrongs is bookended by an initial discussion of general principles and a final treatment of procedure. The list of wrongs is clearly of a strongly criminal character, and it includes those Roman delicts which had long been assimilated into the criminal law of the canonists, such as *furtum*. However, alongside homicide, treason and blasphemy Claro includes *iniuria.*[40] This, along with his formulation of general principles governing responsibility for wrongdoing, deserve further exploration.

Claro divides wrongdoing along three boundaries. Firstly, wrongs are divided into two categories: private and public.[41] Some wrongs are by their nature public because they attack not an individual but the community. The obvious example

39 This can be seen within the first page of Claro's volume on wrongdoing: Claro, *Opera*, V, 1. The word crimen is used in the title of the volume ('*liber quintus ... in quo omnium criminum materia ...*'); the title of the first section, on general principles governing liability for wrongdoing, uses *delictum* ('*in quo generalia quaedam, ad delictorum materiam*)'; and the very first sentence of this section reads '*superiore libro dictum est de contractibus, sequitur nun cut de maleficiis videam.*'

40 The full list might give a sense of how truly criminal this work is: *adulterium, assassinium, blasphemia, falsum, fornicatio, furtum, haeresis, homicidium, incestus, iniuria, laesae maiestatis, ludus, parricidium, periurium, raptus, sacrilegium, simonia, sodomia, stuprum, usura.*

41 Claro, *Opera*, V, 1 at point 1.

is treason, but the list also includes adultery, homicide, violence and bearing false witness. Secondly, wrongs can be further subdivided into ecclesiastical, secular and common offences. This division is sensibly drawn according to jurisdiction. Those wrongs that are dealt with solely in ecclesiastical courts are *mere ecclesiastica*, while wrongs that are handled entirely by secular courts are *mere secularia*.[42] Only a handful of offences have implications in both jurisdictions.[43] Finally, wrongs may be identified as nominate or innominate wrongs.[44] This is simply making the point that imaginative wrongdoing that cannot be neatly categorised does not excuse liability. Of these three divisions, the second is noteworthy. The distinction to which it alludes is by no means new—homicides and similar wrongs had long been dealt with in secular courts instead of ecclesiastical courts. But Claro uses this jurisdictional boundary to draw an intellectual divide: the wrong is by its nature secular, and it is not for canonists to offer legal advice on secular wrongs. This is reflected in the sources found in his examination of individual wrongs. Secular wrongs rely on civil law sources, while ecclesiastical wrongs are dealt with using the writings of canonists.

The absence of property damage or any mention of the *lex Aquilia* alludes to a further distinction that Claro does not explicitly make. Wrongdoing can be civil or criminal. This can be seen in his treatment of *iniuria*, where he states that the same insult can give rise to both criminal and civil liability.[45] Claro is only interested in the criminal consequences, and does not deal at all with civil responsibility. Nevertheless, it is curious that the language of *delictum* has been appropriated by a humanist to refer to wrongs other than the delicts of Roman law. It shows that even in the late sixteenth century there was no consensus on how the law ought to approach wrongdoing, even at a taxonomical level.

The same indeterminacy can be seen in the writings of Vigelius (1529–1600). He wrote two tracts on delict. The first, entitled '*de quatuor maleficiorum generibus*', deals with the four institutional delicts along fairly orthodox lines.[46] The second, '*de reliquis maleficiis et quasi maleficiis*' deals with noxal liability, pauperies, *servi corruptio* and the other miscellaneous wrongs examined in chapter three of this work.[47] At the outset of the first of these tracts, Vigelius provides a general account of the institutional delicts. They are, together,

42 Ibid., v, 2 at point 7. Examples of ecclesiastical wrongs would be heresy and simony, while secular wrongs are *furtum* and homicide.

43 Ibid., v, 3 at point 7. E.g. adultery.

44 Ibid., v, 3 at point 8.

45 Ibid., v, 63 at point 4.

46 Vigelius, *Digestorum Pars Sexta: De Obligationibus et Actionibus ex Delicto Descendentibus*, 7.

47 Ibid., 8.

known as the penal actions.[48] At first the terms *maleficium* and *delictum* are treated as equivalents, though both in chapter headings and in the body of his treatment he almost invariably prefers the language of *maleficium*.[49] This terminological indeterminacy is to be found in treatments of delict up to and including Donellus.[50] Delict was to many jurists a category of obligation with uncertain content.

Commentaries on the Lex Aquilia

The scope of the *lex Aquilia* oscillated in sixteenth-century discussions of the delict. Some claimed that the medieval gloss allowing for an action for an injury to a free person ought to be expunged.[51] Others implicitly disagreed by discussing scenarios in the Digest dealing with injuries to '*homines*' (meaning slaves) by explicitly reinterpreting the term as '*liber homo*'.[52] Between these two positions no consensus was reached. On the one hand was the maxim '*liberum corpus nullam recipit aestimationem*'. On the other, the ambiguous references to injuries to *homines* instead of *servi*. Furthermore, the *lex Aquilia*'s penal dimension was re-emphasised, perhaps an inevitable consequence of allowing *lis crescens*.[53] Beyond this, remarkably little attention was paid to the remedy that might be awarded. Baron was content to describe it as the owner's interest before moving swiftly on.[54] He was far more interested in the rules on transmissibility, themselves entwined in considerations born of the action's penal nature. Maran's (1546–1621) commentary on the Digest barely mentions the *lex Aquilia*, and focuses entirely on noxal liability.[55] Schneidewein (1519–1568) includes a brief comment on how damages are to be calculated, '*secundum aestimationem commune, et non singularem affectionem*'.[56] This is expanded using a threefold notion of *valor*, founded on *precium conventum, precium*

48 Ibid., 9.

49 Ibid., 9: '*Ex delicto seu maleficio...*'.

50 Donellus, *Commentariorum de Jure Civili*, 15.24.1, 3, 5.

51 Schneidewein, *In Quatuor Institutionum Imperialium Iustiniani Libros Commentarii*, 591.

52 Baron, *Institutionum seu Elementorum Iustiniani*, 359; Zasius, *Operum Omnium*, I, 86, point 3; Cujas, *Opera*, I, 280D (provided the killed person was of financial importance to the claimant).

53 Baron, *Institutionum seu Elementorum Iustiniani*, 359; Bode, *In Quatuor Institutionum Imperialum Libros Commentarii*, 251.

54 Baron, *Institutionum seu Elementorum Iustiniani*, 358.

55 Maran, *Paratitla Digestorum*, 142. Curiously, his discussion of D.9.4 on noxal liability is somehow even shorter.

56 Schneidewein, *In Quatuor Institutionum Imperialium Iustiniani Libros Commentarii*, 592: 'following common value rather than individual affections'.

commune and *precium singulare*.[57] But these insights are not delictually informative. Instead commentaries tended to focus on when an action is available at all, marking a return to the casuistic analysis of the Digest.[58]

For all the medieval theorising about the nature of responsibility, and the many different approaches to fault that can be found in the works of earlier jurists, the treatment of those questions by the humanists was uninspired.[59] D.9.2.31 was still the text through which such matters, at least so far as they concerned delict, were addressed.[60] But many were content to simply explain the concept through examples drawn from the *Corpus Iuris Civilis*. An example of this is a commentary on the Institutes by Schneidewein which includes a section on '*si putator*'.[61] The only definition offered is confined to situations involving doctors, for whom *culpa* is synonymous with *imperitia*.[62] Schneidewein reluctantly says that this might be extended to other professions: judges, teachers, advocates and '*quocunque artifice locum habent*'.[63] For some jurists, fault was not even a relevant consideration.[64] For others, it was a word that did not merit definition. When defining *iniuria* in his *Paratitla* entry on the *lex Aquilia*, Wesenbeck (1531–1586) simply states that it '*... generaliter quod non iure factum est: hoc est, si contra ius et per culpam quis occiderit. Igitur iniuriam hic accipiemus, damnum culpa datum, etiam ab eo qui nocere noluit*'.[65] The medieval rule

---

57 Ibid., 592.

58 Vigellius, *Digestorum Pars Sexta: De Obligationibus et Actionibus ex Delicto Descendentibus*, 46.10.3 (*causae ex quibus actio proposita competit?*) dominates his discussion; see also Baron, *Institutionum seu Elementorum Iustiniani*, 357–8, Schneidewein, *In Quatuor Institutionum Imperialium Iustiniani Libros Commentarii*, 591–2.

59 Indeed, the medieval theorisation was rarely acknowledged. A rare exception is Baron, *Institutionum seu Elementorum Iustiniani*, 357, which contains the somewhat dismissive line '*scio negligentiam pro omni culpa, quae extra dolum sit, usupari*'. The verb is presumably a misspelling of *usurpari*.

60 E.g. Baron, *Institutionum seu Elementorum Iustiniani*, 358; Schneidewein, *In Quatuor Institutionum Imperialium Iustiniani Libros Commentarii*, 595.

61 Schneidewein, *In Quatuor Institutionum Imperialium Iustiniani Libros Commentarii commentarii*, 595.

62 A rule with clear Justinianic authority: D.9.2.7.8.

63 Schneidewein, *In Quatuor Institutionum Imperialium Iustiniani Libros Commentarii*, 596.

64 Take the treatment found in the commentary on the lex Aquilia by Maran, *Paratitla Digestorum*, 142, which omits any reference to fault.

65 Wesenbeck, *Paratitla in Pandectas*, 190 (ad 9.2): 'Generally [*iniuria means*] that which is done without right, such as where without right and through blameworthiness someone is killed. And so we understand *iniuria* here to mean loss caused through blameworthiness, even where the killing wasn't intended'.

that *dolus* leads to liability on the *lex Cornelia* instead of the *lex Aquilia* persists, which ought to make the definition of *culpa* even more central. But this need is unmet. Reflecting the approach of Ulpian in the Digest, *culpa* is impliedly a term that the reader ought to be familiar with through intuition alone.[66]

Commentaries on iniuria

Commentaries on D.47.10

At times it can seem like *iniuria* was simply alien to sixteenth-century jurists. There is an ambivalence that can be seen in commentaries on individual titles of the Digest that purportedly contain delictual material. These headings are an effective insight into what sixteenth-century scholars saw as the focus of the Roman writings. Easily the most informative example of this is D.47.10, today viewed at least in part as a title on the delict of *iniuria*. But for Wesenbeck, who first published his commentary on the Digest in 1566, D.47.10 is given the heading '*Ad lex Corneliam de Falsis*'.[67] One might think it is not so great a misrepresentation. After all, D.47.10.5 and a miscellany of other texts across the title do focus specifically on the *lex Cornelia*. But the title contains a total of forty-five laws, and well in excess of a hundred fragments, the majority of which are on *iniuria*. Despite this, Wesenbeck's commentary makes no mention of the term at all.

Other sixteenth-century commentaries simply follow the medieval tradition and pare back their discussions of delict to the bare essentials. Maran dedicates less than a hundred words to his commentary on the *lex Aquilia*, giving a truly anaemic summary of its operation ('… *veniunt occasione rerum quae nobis servient, hoc est, servorum vel animalium*') and a few passing comments on whether the action can be used noxally.[68] But *iniuria* suffers a worse fate. His commentary on the Digest ends abruptly at book 42, meaning the vast majority of delictual material is simply omitted.[69]

Detailed considerations of *iniuria* were rare in the sixteenth century, but they did exist. The most detailed is in a commentary on the Digest written by Vigelius. This is a noteworthy work in several respects, one of which is the

66 The same approach can be seen in Vigelius' commentary on the *lex Aquilia* which discusses *si putator* (D.9.2.31) simply by saying that it is consistent with J.4.4: Vigelius, *Digestorum Pars Sexta: De Obligationibus et Actionibus ex Delicto Descendentibus*, 46.10.3.11.

67 Wesenbeck, *Paratitla in Pandectas*, ad D.47.10.

68 Maran, *Paratitla Digestorum*, 142: 'This is used for the killing of things that serve us, namely slaves or animals'.

69 Bizarrely, the longest examination of a delict belongs to liability for *pauperies* in D.9.1: Maran, *Paratitla Digestorum*, 141–2.

amount of space spent on the delict of *iniuria*. Its content is far from revolutionary, but as this is a rare examination of *iniuria* its contours are worth tracing briefly. He begins with a quote from Ulpian:

> Iniuria ex eo dicta est, quod non iure fiat. Omne enim quod non iure fit, iniuria fieri dicitur. Hoc generaliter. Specialiter autem iniuria dicitur contumelia. Interdum iniuriae appellatione damnum culpa datum significatur, ut in lege Aquiliae dicere solemus.[70]

Straightforward, but as will shortly be seen sixteenth-century jurists could not always be trusted to reproduce this definition accurately. Two distinctions are then drawn. The first is between the ways in which *iniuria* might be committed: *aut re aut verbis*.[71] The second is the range of interests it might harm: '*Labeo ait, omnem iniuria aut in corpus inferri, aut ad dignitatem, aut ad infamiam perinere*'.[72] Both of these are lifted directly from the Digest.[73] This is representative of much of the substance of his analysis, which is largely a restructuring of D.47.10 according to *causae* he has identified. The upshot of this is a fairly rigorous examination of the various instances in which civil liability on the *actio iniuriarum* would exist. The criminal action under the *lex Cornelia* is considered separately.

Commentaries on J.4.4

Unlike D.47.10, J.4.4 cannot be seen as dealing with any subject other than *iniuria*. Nevertheless, sixteenth century jurists rarely engaged with the Justinianic treatment of the subject. In his commentary on the Institutes, Porporato (1517–1581) heavily emphasised the criminal dimension of the delict, dealing with the civil rules only insofar as they explained on whose behalf a *paterfamilias* could bring an action.[74] Bodei (1519–1568) offers a more balanced account of the delict's civil and criminal dimensions, though his concluding remarks

---

70 Vigelius, *Digestorum Pars Sexta: De Obligationibus et Actionibus ex Delicto Descendentibus*, 132: '*Iniuria* means all that is done without right; everything that is done without right is said to occur wrongfully [*iniuria*]. This is the general meaning. Specifically, *iniuria* means contumely. Furthermore, sometimes the word *iniuria* refers to loss caused by blameworthiness [*culpa*], as we say in the *lex Aquilia*'.

71 Vigelius, *Digestorum Pars Sexta: De Obligationibus et Actionibus ex Delicto Descendentibus*, 132.

72 Ibid., 132: 'Labeo says that every *iniuria* is aimed at the body, at dignity or at causing infamy'.

73 *Aut re aut verbis*: D.47.10.1.1; interests: D.47.10.1.2.

74 Porporato, *In Quatuor Institutionum Iustiniani Libros Commentaria*, 196–7.

make it clear that the latter holds more interest.[75] His account of the civil dimension is little more than a restatement of Justinian's text. Perhaps the most telling example is Baron's commentary on the distinction found at the outset of J.4.4. Justinian's text reads:

> Generaliter iniuria dicitur omne quod non iure fit specialiter alias contumelia, quae a contumendo dicta est, quam Graeci ὕϐριν appellant; alias culpa, quam Graeci ἀδίχημα dicunt, sicut in lege Aquilia damnum accipitur; alias iniquitas et iniustitia, quam Graeci ἀδίχιαν vocant.[76]

In Baron, these three meanings are reduced to just two:

> Ait, Generaliter. Iniuriae verbum varie accipi oste[n]dit: generaliter pro eo quod non iure sit, ut si forte furiosus servum occiderit. Specialiter iniuria in lege Aquiliae accipitur pro culpa, cuius appellatione et dolus continetur, ut dixi.[77]

He goes on to discuss liability for *contumelia*, but this too focuses primarily on the *lex Cornelia*. Indeed, it is said that '*actio civilis iniuriarum ex lege Cornelia descendit*'.[78] His *commentarii particula reliqua* makes it clear that the French law developed its own rules independently of Roman law as the product of French *mores*, presumably explaining his lack of interest in the Roman doctrine.[79]

Donellus and the Generalisation of Delictual Scholarship

In histories of delict Donellus is often given a leading role. Sometimes he is cast as the individual who shaped the future direction of delictual scholarship

75 Bodei, *In Quatuor Institutionum Imperialum Libros Commentarii*, 254.

76 J.4.4.1: 'Generally *iniuria* means all that is done without right, but specifically means contumely directed at others, which the Greeks call *hubris*. In other contexts it means blameworthiness, which the Greeks call *adikema*, as is recognised in the *lex Aquilia*. And it sometimes means inequality, which the Greeks call *adikan*'.

77 Baron, *Institutionum seu Elementorum Iustiniani*, 361: 'It can be said, generally, that the word *iniuria* has a variety of meanings. Generally it refers to that done without right, as where a madman kills a slave. Specifically *iniuria* in the *lex Aquilia* means *culpa*, which it comprises alongside *dolus*, as has been said'.

78 Ibid., 363.

79 Ibid., 364.

singlehandedly,[80] though more often he is seen as simply laying the groundwork for Grotius to innovate.[81] Whatever the truth, he is clearly a scholar whose formulation of delict deserves detailed consideration. There are two aspects to his alleged influence: structure and generalisation. The first of these is in line with the methods typically seen as the humanist contribution to European legal history, a systematic rationalisation of the *Corpus Iuris Civilis* in a manner reminiscent of the Institutes.[82] In this respect Donellus might be significant, but he would be by no means unique. Far more interesting are the claims that Donellus had a role to play in the generalisation of delict, and it is on this claim that this section will focus.

The Procedural Bias of Earlier Movements towards the Generalisation of Delict

The first pushes towards the generalisation of delict came long before Donellus. The very idea of delict being a source of obligation is itself an attempt at generalisation, borne of the institutional framework adopted early in the classical period of Roman law. This generalisation is most readily seen through the classification of actions, with delictual actions typically being seen as *actiones poenales*. This label was an effective way of packaging together certain procedural norms applicable to all penal actions, such as passive intransmissibility and the use of a multiplier in the assessment of damages.[83] Penal actions were distinguished from reipersecutory actions, although there was a degree of overlap. A handful of actions were known as the *actiones mixtae*, as their remedy incorporated both compensatory and penal measures. These actions were principally delictual, including both the *actio legis aquiliae* and the *actio vi bonorum raptorum*. There were, however, non-delictual examples.[84]

80 E.g. Descheemaeker, *The Division of Wrongs*, 220.

81 E.g. Feenstra, 'Grotius' doctrine of liability for negligence' 143–4; Ibbetson, 'How the Romans' 284–5; Daniel Visser and Niall R. Whitty, 'The structure of the law of delict in historical perspective' in *A History of Private Law in Scotland*, eds Kenneth Reid and Reinhard Zimmermann (Oxford: Oxford University Press, 2001), II, 425; Peter Stein, 'Donellus and the origins of the modern civil law' in *Melanges Felix Wubbe: offers par ses collègues et ses amis à l'occasion de son soixante-dixième anniversaire*, ed. Hans A. Ankum (Freiberg: Editions universitaires, 1993).

82 E.g. John W.F. Allison, *A Continental Distinction in the Common Law: A Historical and Comparative Perspective on English Public Law*, rev. ed. (Oxford: Oxford University Press, 2000), 114–115.

83 Though there were exceptions: Buckland, *Text-book of Roman Law*, 691–2.

84 J.4.6.19.

The Roman category of delict was formed through flexible common rules. Typically delictual actions would be actively transmissible, but they need not be in order to be a delict. Typically damages would be awarded as a multiple of the claimant's interest or the value of the affected property, but if an alternative framework was adopted it did not make the wrong any less of a delict. Thus the *actio iniuriarum* was undeniably delictual, even though it did not conform with these basic tenets of delictual liability. This is because of the manner in which the category of delict was created—as a model superimposed onto an existing framework of remedies. The best it could ever hope to achieve was the identification of broad commonalities.

Similar in style but more rigorous in approach are the generalisations of the medieval criminal treatise authors. Again, these jurists were bound by the law already posited and the need to be practical.[85] But unlike the classical jurists of antiquity they were in a position to be creative, especially in areas underdeveloped in the *Digest*, principally procedure and punishment. An early example is the *Tractatus de Maleficiis* of Albertus Gandinus (1245–1310), which is primarily concerned with questions such as how a formal accusation ought to be made, and what presumptions ought to be relied upon in a trial. Precisely the same concerns are found in the manual of criminal law written by Prospero Farinacci (1554–1618), which is divided into five parts: inquisition, accusation, punishment, incarceration and torture.[86] These two authors bookend the period in which criminal treatises might have shaped delictual thought, but their approach towards the basic structure of the law is unchanged. Farinacci's division of procedure and consideration is undeniably more sophisticated than that found in Gandinus, as he benefitted from centuries of doctrinal refinement.

Before Donellus, it is difficult to find any attempt at the generalisation of delictual doctrine. The rigid structure of the law of actions remains in place, with only its procedure being unified. There are, however, signs that individuals were starting to draw the strands of delict together. An example that stands out is a commentary on the Digest by Vigelius, the sixth part of which is structured as follows:

85 A fact evident from the titles of many criminal treatises. Just one reminder is Farinacci, *Praxis et Theoricae Criminalis*.

86 The third of these is titled '*De delictis et poenis*'. But the matters considered are clearly procedural, such as when and how a wrongdoer's property can be confiscated, and the range of *poenae* that might be used: Farinacci, *Praxis et Theoricae Criminalis*, 1, titles 19 and 25.

Book 46: *De quatuor maleficiorum generibus, sum suis actionibus*	Book 47: *De reliquis maleficiis, et quasi-maleficiis, nec non praecedentium actionum adfinibus remediis*
1. *De poenalibus actionbus in genere*	1. *Si quadrupes pauperiem fecisse dicatur*
2. *De furtis*	2. *De noxalibus actionibus*
3. *De furti actione*	3. *Si familia furtum fecisse dicetur*
4. *Quibus competit furti actio?*	4. *Si is qui testamente liber esse iussus est, post mortem domini ante aditam hereditatem subripuisse quid dicetur*
5. *Adversus quos competit furti actio?*	5. *Rerum amotarum*
6. *Quid, quantumque veniat in furti actione?*	6. *De actione in factum adversus publicanos*
7. *Adfinia furti actionis remedia, et de vindicatione rei furtivae*	7. *De crimine peculatus, sacrilegii, et de residvis*
8. *De condictione furtiva*	8. *Expilatae haereditatis*
9. *Vi bonorum raptorum*	9. *De servi corrupti actione*
10. *De actione legis Aquiliae*	10. *De libero homine exhibendo interdictum*
11. *De exceptionibus praecedentium causarum generalibus*	11. *De abigeis actio*
12. *De reliquo Aquiliae actionis iure*	12. *Arborum furtim caesarum*
13. *De iniuriarum actione*	13. *De tigno iuncto*
14. *De exceptionibus praecedentium causarum generalibus*	14. *De damno in turba dato actio*
15. *Quibus actio iniuriarum competit?*	15. *De incendio, ruina, naufragio, rate, nave expugnata actio*
16. *Adversus quos, et per quos iniuriarum actio competit?*	16. *De his qui deicereint vel effuderint actio*
17. *Quid quantumque veniat in actione iniuriarum?*	17. *De posito et suspenso actio*
18. *De reliquo iniuriarum actionis iure*	18. *De crimine Stellionatus*
19. *De actione iniuriarum ex lege Cornelia*	19. *De variis extraordinariis delictis et criminibus*

We have already noted the breadth of his treatment of individual delicts, discussed above in relation to *iniuria*. But the structure imposed on this disparate group of wrongs is equally noteworthy. Vigelius is clearly drawing on the Institutional treatment of delict, as evident in his use of the *quatuor maleficia* on the one hand, and the remaining wrongs (as well as quasi-delict) on the other. But in this work he goes considerably beyond the Institutes, pulling together material from all over the Digest. He looks not only at the remedial structures available in response to wrongdoing (e.g. the use of the *condictio in furtum*), but where the Digest's treatment of a delict gives rise to multiple causes of action (e.g. '*de damno in turba dato actio*' under D.47.8). It is difficult to think of Vigelius' treatment of delict as itself a generalisation. Beyond a few fairly ephemeral comments on their shared qualities at the outset of book 46, attention is paid to each delict individually. But it is a significant step towards generalisation. With all the relevant material identified and pulled together it became easier for later jurists to continue his work.

Donellus' Approach to Delict

Donellus is a jurist who defies classification, despite often playing a very significant role in many histories of European private law.[87] He is often presented as the high point of legal humanism, placing him in the same tradition as the philologically motivated authors discussed at the start of this chapter. But this seems a poor fit for the substance of his works. Donellus, unlike many other humanists, bore a genuine interest in the letter of the law. References to classical authors other than the jurists of Ancient Rome are relatively rare, and when they do surface it is for their legal insights. Increasingly there has been an academic push towards viewing him as something *other*, a *sui generis* jurist. But his greatest contribution to the development of private law—its systematisation—is a direct product of a humanist desire to unravel the medieval and even Byzantine reordering of their Roman sources to discover the law's true form. As a jurist, his treatment of the letter of the law insofar as delict is concerned tends towards the unremarkable.

This duality of structural innovation paired with doctrinal orthodoxy defines Donellus' approach to liability for wrongdoing. It comprises two basic strands: lofty theorisation about the nature of delict, and a truly humanist exploration

87 Stein 'Systematisation of private law in the sixteenth and seventeenth centuries' in *Die Entwicklung der Methodenlehre in Rechtswissenschaft und Philosophie vom 16. bis zum 18. Jahrhundert*, ed. Jan Schröder (Stuttgart: F. Steiner, 1998); Robert Feenstra, '*Hugues Doneau et les juristes néerlandais du XVIIe siècle: L'influence de son système sur l'évolution du droit privé avant le pandectisme*' in *Jacques Godefroy (1587–1652) et l'Humanisme juridique à Genève*, eds Bruno Schmidlin and Alfred Dufour (Basel: Helbing & Lichtenhahn, 1991); Jean-Louis Thireau, '*Hughes Doneau et les fondements de la codification moderne*' (1997) 26 Droits: revue française de théorie, de philosophie et de culture juridiques 81.

of the doctrinal details. It is the former that is seen as his contribution to the development of delict within the natural law school, but the latter dominates his own treatment. There is a fundamental tension in his writings between a desire for generalisation and a humanist desire to understand the doctrinal mechanics of the ancient law of delict. In total Donellus spends nine chapters on liability for wrongdoing, with a smattering of further details to be gleaned from a commentary specifically on the Digest's treatment of the *lex Aquilia*.[88] The first of the nine chapters sets out his general theory, something markedly different from anything that came before it. In it he constructs a model of delict around the infringement of rights.[89] This is followed by a single chapter on *iniuria*, and seven on wrongs affecting property rights. The position of *iniuria* within delict is recognised as anomalous, providing within its content one of just two exceptions to his general theory of delict.[90] For all his theorisation about the structure of delict, the schism between *iniuria* and wrongs to property remained insurmountable.

His general theory of delict consists in a single action '*ex maleficio*'.[91] *Maleficium* is the source of obligations that had previously been identified with *delictum* and *peccatum*.[92] In truth these two ideas are just species of *maleficium*: '*maleficium est delictum omne et peccatum*', and so '*unde qui ex maleficio obligantur, idem dicuntur obligari ex delicto*'.[93] All three of these terms are grouped together and juxtaposed with *crimen*, which refers specifically to wrongs dealt with by public right (*jure publico*).[94] This enveloping of *delictum* within *maleficium* allows Donellus to take definitions of the former and extend them to the latter. Delicts are said to consist in either *faciendo* or *negligendo*, and so the same must be true of *maleficium*.[95] But *maleficium* is also given its own definitional core: the infliction of harm ('*nocetur detrahiturque quid alteri*').[96] Only two exceptions are recognised: *calumniatores* and those who convince a slave to steal from its master, both of which involve liability without harm.[97]

88 Donellus, *Opuscula Posthuma*, 427.

89 Jansen, 'Duties and rights in negligence', 454.

90 Donellus, *Commentariorum de Jure Civili*, 15.24.6.

91 Ibid., 15.24.5.

92 Ibid., 15.24.1–2.

93 Ibid., 15.24.2: '*maleficium* encompasses every delict and every sin' and so, 'whenever one is bound *ex maleficio*, they can also be said to be bound *ex delicto*'.

94 Ibid., 15.24.2.

95 Ibid., 15.24.4.

96 Ibid., 15.24.5.

97 Ibid., 15.24.6.

Every form of wrongdoing other than the two exceptions just enumerated share a core in the causation of harm to another. There are two ways in which such harm can be caused: literally through causing *damnum*, or through depriving another of their property.[98] *Damnum* can be caused through destruction (*allato interitu*) or through spoiling (*corruptio*).[99] This merges the two chapters of the *lex Aquilia* into a single wrong. Spoiling, so far as it applies to living property, can affect both the body and the mind.[100] Spoiling of the mind folds *servi corrupti* into the mix. Spoiling *a corpore* expressly brings together the *lex Aquilia* and the anomalous wrong of stealthy tree surgery dealt with in the Digest.[101] Deprivation also has two species, occurring either by stealth (*clam*) or force (*vi*). The former refers specifically to *furtum*, while the latter is further subdivided into taking forcefully property (*rapina*) and depriving another of possession by force (the interdict *unde vi*).[102] Thus through the simple notion of harming another's property interests Donellus unites disparate wrongs from across the Digest.

Damnum is the focus of Donellus' analysis. It is defined as '*a demendo, et quasi deminutione patrimonii*'.[103] Explicit reference is made to pure economic loss, '*cum res per se integram maneant*', as a recoverable species of *damnum*.[104] Moreover, the damages obtained under chapter one of the *lex Aquilia* are redefined in terms of *damnum*.[105] The action is straightforwardly for the recovery of the *damnum*, the value of which is to be determined by a judge.[106] This means things that cannot be given a value are excluded from this general action. Personal injuries are excluded '*quia liberum corpus non recipit aestimationem*'.[107] Nominally general, the action begins to fragment when considering the remediation of particular forms of wrongdoing. In relation to *servi corruptio*, Donellus says:

> Constituitur actio in duplum eius, quanti ea res erit. Quibus verbis non continetur tantum servi corrupti aestimatio, qui postquam corruptus est,

98 Ibid., 15.26.1.

99 Ibid., 15.26.2.

100 Ibid., 15.26.3.

101 Ibid., 15.27.9; D.47.7.

102 Ibid., 15.29.3; 15.32.1.

103 Ibid., 15.26.2.

104 Ibid., 15.26.2.

105 Ibid., 15.27.6: '*haec verba, quanti ea res erit, sic accepta sunt, non quanti erit ea res, quae occisa aut deterior facta est: sed quanti id damnum omne, quod ob rem corruptam contingit ...*'

106 Ibid., 15.26.5–6.

107 Ibid., 15.26.7.

> minoris esse coepit: sed omne damnum, quod propeter corruptelam servi domino contigit.[108]

This is an instance of friction between Donellus' humanist desire to remain true to the doctrines of Roman law, and to expound his newly systematised model of private law. The result is awkward: though the *actio servi corrupti* is brought under the general model of delict, and theorised as a variation on *corruptio* as a subspecies of *damnum*, it retains a unique remedy. By contrast, the focus of the general remedy for the recovery of *damnum* appears to be restorative, but the same is true of the classical interpretation of chapter three of the *lex Aquilia*. In classical law the picture was warped through penal mechanisms such as *lis crescens* and multiple recovery in cases involving multiple wrongdoers, both of which resulted in the claimant receiving damages out of proportion to the harm suffered. Interestingly, Donellus is silent on these considerations in relation to the generalised *actio ex maleficio*. It is clear that certain factors can aggrevate liability, turning it into a *crimen* deserving of a greater penalty.[109] An opuscule specifically on the *lex Aquilia* shows that he thought an *actio legis Aquiliae* was available against every person responsible for the harm, as in classical Roman law, but it is not at all clear whether this view can be carried over to the general action.[110] Perhaps the clearest insight is provided by his consideration of contributory negligence, a topic isolated from delict in his corpus. On this, van Dongen writes that 'Donellus came to the conclusion that negligence of one party implied that the resulting loss had to be imputed to himself and not to the other party'.[111] This would suggest that multiple recovery for harm caused by multiple wrongdoers was not a possibility, though the absence of such a rule from Donellus' discussion of *damnum* is curious.

Donellus' treatment of fault is largely orthodox. For the general *actio ex maleficio* to lie, the harm must have been caused *iniuria*, which is understood to mean *culpa*.[112] This is defined as '*non solum eum teneri hac lege ob damnum datum, qui dedit sciens dolo malo, sed et qui per imperitiam aut nihil minus cogitans*

108 Ibid., 15.26.5: 'This action is for double whatever the thing was worth. By these words we are not limited to an evaluation of just the value of the corruption of the slave, which after the corruption will be worth less, but rather all the loss to the master which stems from the corruption'.

109 Ibid., 15.26.9.

110 Donellus, *Opuscula Posthuma*, 427.

111 Van Dongen, *Contributory Negligence*, 198.

112 Donellus, *Commentariorum de Jure Civili*, 15.27.2.

quam damnum dare, si dedit culpa'.[113] The typical references to D.9.2.44.pr (*culpa levissima*) and D.9.2.31 (*'si putator'*) are provided as authority. In this context Donellus' humanist nature shows. He despairs of listing the various types of *culpa*, describing it as an endless toil (*infiniti laboris*).[114] Instead he adopts an authentically Roman analysis, going through individual scenarios drawn from the Digest that illustrate the boundary between blameworthy and blameless conduct.[115] There is nothing in his treatment of fault that is original.

Thus far Donellus has provided a harmonised account of delict. As such, his consideration of *iniuria* is particularly awkward. Rather than being assimilated into the core of delict, it stands alone—a disjointed addendum to the generalities explored above. This wrong is used to capture harm to any right other than property. Three are listed: *corpus incolumitas, libertas* and *existimatio*.[116] The diminution of any of these committed wrongfully (*iniuria*) is prima facie grounds for liability. It is noteworthy that an earlier list of fundamental rights included one further interest: *vita*.[117] Its omission at this juncture is understandable. The classical delict of *iniuria* could be readily invoked to address wrongs to the body, *existimatio* and in all likelihood *libertas*.[118] It had no role to play in homicide. However, wrongs to *vita* do not arise elsewhere within the law of *maleficia*, effectively excising it from the scope of delict. This leaves three rights to be remedied through the *actio iniuriarum*. Two of these are paid very little attention.

Violations of *corpus incolumitas* are linked with little fanfare or discussion to the *lex Cornelia*, but are nevertheless remedied through the *actio iniuriarum*.[119] The same action is said to lie for the diminution of a person's *libertas*, with no further explanation.[120] By far the most substantial treatment is given to wrongs to *existimatio*, which fills most of the chapter. This may have been because of the centuries of neglect the wrong had experienced. Uncovering its classical form was akin to new research on Roman law, something likely to cause excitement to a quasi-humanist scholar.

Iniuria is given a structure in much the same way as *damnum iniuria datum* that encompasses many narrow forms of wrongdoing within Roman law.

113 Ibid., 15.27.2.

114 Ibid., 15.27.3.

115 Ibid., 15.27.4.

116 Ibid., 15.25.2.

117 Ibid., 2.8.3.

118 This term, best translated into English as autonomy or the ability to make decisions freely for oneself, was dealt with primarily through the praetorian delicts of *dolus* and *metus*. It would nevertheless be contumelious to defraud or threaten someone in many cases.

119 Donellus, *Commentariorum de Jure Civili*, 15.25.3.

120 Ibid., 15.25.3.

Beginning with Ulpian's distinction between the general and specific meanings of *iniuria*, Donellus divides the special (delictual) *iniuria* into its private and public forms. Private *iniuria* maps onto the Roman delict, whereas public *iniuria* includes attacks on the state, such as insulting an official.[121] Private *iniuriae* consist of either words or deeds, and words can be written or spoken.[122] Affronts to the *existimatio* of another retain the Roman name *convicium*.[123] Beyond the requirement of an intention to defame, the actual contents of *convicium* appear to have caused Donellus some trouble. It doubtless included false accusations of certain offences (the examples given are homicide, theft, and poisoning) made in public. But among upstanding men (*honestos viros*) lesser offences could also constitute *convicium*, for they had no less deleterious an effect on the reputation of the defamed. Such accusations might cause the defamed to be seen as fraudulent or rude. This difficulty seems to stem from Donellus' imprecision in defining *existimatio*. The examples given suggest that he has relegated the status-centric model of Roman law to the domain of "public" *iniuria*. Instead it is the moral integrity of the defamed which determines the scope of actions that might be considered defamatory.

However, not all injurious words are spoken. Written or drawn instances of defamation are considered together as a distinct form of *iniuria*.[124] Any piece of writing or drawing that can cause the dishonour or infamy of another can be actionable. This is a more serious form of *iniuria* because it can reach a far larger audience than most spoken words. It is an even more serious offence where the tortfeasor publishes the defamation anonymously. Reputations can also be harmed by actions.[125] Here the intent to harm is paramount. The examples used by Donellus knowingly draw on Roman social mores, and are mostly regurgitations of Digest texts about mourning and untoward behaviour in the presence of virgins or married women. This is a clear reminder of Donellus' humanist roots, because of which the generalised notion of *iniuria* provided at the outset is broken down into an increasing number of discrete formulations, each with their own requirements for liability.

All three forms of *iniuria* share some common elements.[126] To be actionable, the relevant conduct or words must display *contumelia*, result in actual harm to the defamed, and the defamed must bring the action at once (or at least

121 Ibid., 15.25.1.

122 Ibid., 15.25.2, 3.

123 Ibid., 15.25.5.

124 Ibid., 15.25.6.

125 Ibid., 15.25.7.

126 Ibid., 15.25.8.

declare his intention to do so). If he chooses to ignore the *iniuria*, an *actio iniuriarum* cannot lie.[127] Having established liability, the action could be brought either by the defamed himself, or by a master, father, husband, father-in-law, heir or fiancé where the defamed herself could not sue, or where the defamed was *in potestates*.[128] The inclusion of heirs in this list is a departure from Roman law, with Donellus unambiguously stating the heir can bring an action only where the defamed is dead or where the *iniuria* took place at a funeral. Though the remedy is couched in language of restoration, it remains monetary in nature. The interest harmed, *existimatio*, is again left undefined. It seems to again be concerned with how *good* the defamed appears in the eyes of reputable men rather than with honour or social standing.

Taken as a whole, Donellus' account of liability for wrongdoing is structurally innovative but substantively conservative. The overall project is one of unification, although the scope of delict remains fundamentally fractured by the division of liability into the *actio ex maleficio* and the *actio iniuriarum*.[129] The *actio ex maleficio* aspires towards generalisation, offering a single fault standard (*culpa*) governing a single wrong (*damnum datum*). At a remedial level this wrong remained fragmentary, with the consequences of *servi corrupti* differing from the quotidian causation of loss, despite the former being rationalised as a species of the latter. The *actio iniuriarum*, on the other hand, remained hopelessly pluralistic. The piecemeal approach to *iniuria* found in Roman law is recreated by Donellus, with the fault standard oscillating between *dolus* and strict liability according to the manner in which the calumny was issued. While the *actio ex maleficio* strives for unity, the *actio iniuriarum* is content to contain the miscellaneous odds and ends of the Roman law of delict.

Donellus' influence can be seen fairly immediately, with small changes in the treatment of delict identifiable soon after the publication of Donellus' commentaries. There is a noticeable uptake in the study of *iniuria* in his wake, particularly in the first quarter of the seventeenth century. One example is the treatment of D.47.10 found in Hendrik Zoesius' (1571–1627) commentary on the Digest. The passage, entitled '*De iniuriis et famosis libellis*', bears many striking similarities to Donellus' treatment of the subject.[130] Similarly detailed but deeply confused is the analysis found in Faber's (1581–1622) commentary on

127 Ibid., 15.25.11.

128 Ibid., 15.25.14.

129 Though even in this respect Donellus is inconsistent. For example, in 15.25.1 *iniuria* is described as a *maleficium*. It is nevertheless incapable of being brought under the general model of *maleficium* advanced.

130 Zoesius, *Commentarius ad Digestorum*, ad D.47.10.

the Institutes.[131] Faber's account reads as little more than a man trying to make sense of the near absence of *iniuria* for the preceding few centuries, concentrating primarily on Azo's commentary. Thereafter *iniuria* received increasingly elaborate discussions.[132] However, one must be careful not to mistake correlation for causation. In many respects Zoesius' analysis goes beyond Donellus, and neither he nor Faber makes any reference to Donellus' commentaries. It is entirely possible the two 'rediscoveries' of *iniuria* are unrelated. If so, a further question arises: why did multiple people begin thinking about this long-neglected delict at the turn of the seventeenth century? Their own citations are no use in this regard, suggesting it was not an influence within the civil law tradition that was providing the impetus.

Conclusion

On the eve of the seventeenth century delict looked to have moved significantly beyond its medieval formulation, primary through the toils of Donellus, though its Roman heritage was still visible. However, looks can be deceiving. The end result of Donellus' labours was a formulation of delict different in form to any that came before it, but still burdened with the issues inherent in a slavish devotion to the content of Roman law. Reliant on the forms of action, delict remained fragmentary, although the actio iniuriarum was doing significantly more of the work than it had done for centuries by dealing with all recoverable wrongdoing that affected interests other than property. But there was no scope for an obligation to arise in the wake of homicide, following a conscious decision by Donellus to omit *vita* from the scope of *maleficium*. There remained a plurality of fault standards that might be applied to specific wrongs. The only advances Donellus brought to the table were at a theoretical level, though the conceptualisation of delict as the infringement of a natural right is of particular importance. These abstract refinements were not reflected at a doctrinal level. The action available would vary according to the right infringed, and across the range of actions on offer there was a variety of fault standards and remedies.

131 Faber, *In Quatuor Libros Institutionum Eruditissima Commentaria*, 112–113.

132 E.g. Manz (1606–1677), *Commenatarius Ratio-regularis in Quatuor Libros Institutionum Imperialium*, 45–61, itself longer than the sum treatments of delicts in many medieval and sixteenth-century commentaries.

PART III

Grotius' Thomist Sources

Grotius' Thomist Sources

This section comprises five chapters exploring the development of delictual doctrine within Thomism is the second half of the sixteenth century and early seventeenth century. It focuses on a particular string of Thomist authors who internally formed a tradition of their own, through each successive scholar's citation of his predecessors. Grotius himself falls into this pattern in relation to delict, focusing on the same five Thomists: Cajetan, Soto, Navarrus, Covarruvias and, above all others, Lessius. This narrow tradition of Thomists wrote in a variety of formats. Cajetan wrote a straightforward commentary on the secunda secundae of the Summa Theologiae, examining its content article-by-article. Soto wrote a freestanding treatise on the Thomist account of justice, though its content is very faithful to its source material. Navarrus wrote a commentary on the Ten Commandments known as the Enchiridion. And Covarruvias and Lessius wrote treatises on the Thomist theory of justice that departed significantly from Aquinas' structure.

The focus on these five authors will show that over the course of the second half of the sixteenth century the concerns of Thomism became steadily more pragmatic, and an increasing number of arguments from the civilian tradition were introduced to further this end. This can be seen mostly clearly where there were gaps in Thomism that would prevent its deployment as a model of delict. The most glaring gap of this sort was the absence of a sophisticated hierarchy of fault standards, and it is in this context that we find a significant reliance on Roman law ideas. Their goal the goal was to isolate and extract Roman ideas from their civilian context, and make them work within the Thomist theory of delict. The result by Lessius is a model of delict that is still recognisably influenced by Aquinas in many ways. It shares a vocabulary with the Summa Theologiae, and both its taxonomy and conceptual framework display strongly Thomist roots. But it is no longer bound to Aquinas' theological context, and can operate as a freestanding system of delict.

Chapter six will begin by considering the intellectual foundations of Thomism in Aristotelian thought. It will examine the treatment of wrongdoing in the Siete Partidas, in which the assimilation of Roman law, Aristotelian ethics and local law represents a prototype for the Thomist endeavours that might help explain why the Thomist movement under examination was so concentrated in Spain. Chapter seven will then set out the starting point for the Thomist model of delict by examining in detail the interactions between wrongdoing and justice in the Summa Theologiae. Chapters eight, nine and ten then explore the developments in each of the three main strands of the Thomist approach to delict: the remedy of restitutio, the individual forms of wrongdoing, and the concept of fault. In examining fault chapter ten will take a broader focus, exploring whether the dependence on civil and canon law seen in relation to fault is a theme that underpins more of the Thomist theory of delict as evidenced by the authors under consideration.

CHAPTER 6

The Foundations of Thomism

The very text of the *Summa Theologiae* bears witness to the powerful hold Aristotelian thought held over Aquinas. References to 'The Philosopher' abound, and often in a context wherein the invocation of Aristotle is deemed to be conclusive on a disputed point. Indeed, for centuries scholars have been comfortable labelling theories as 'Aristotelico-Thomistic'.[1] Despite this longstanding association, recent scholars have been more reluctant to read correspondence where Aristotle and Aquinas appear to refer to the same ideas, preferring instead to probe precisely how far Aquinas deviated from his inspiration.[2] This reluctance is readily understandable. The rediscovery of Aristotle's written corpus provided a direct challenge to many longstanding doctrines of the Church.[3] Aquinas' project was in no small part to reconcile Aristotelianism and Christianity, a task that inevitably entailed reinterpreting strands of Aristotelian thought to fit Christian doctrine. Thus when reading Aquinas it is important to bear in mind that no matter how Aristotelian his account of a problem might appear, he always wrote as a Christian Aristotelian. Nevertheless it is difficult to deny the profound influence the *Corpus Aristotelicum* had over Aquinas, both methodologically and substantively. And for this reason there is value in briefly considering the way in which Aristotle approached questions of law and wrongdoing.

Praise, Blame and Responsibility

The law's treatment of wrongdoing stands at the intersection of Aristotle's accounts of ethics and justice. To get a complete view of how such matters are resolved within Aristotelian thought, it is necessary to consider both strands. As will be seen in due course, a complete picture is in fact unattainable. Although

1 Joseph Owens, Aristotle and Aquinas' in *The Cambridge Companion to Aquinas*, eds Norman Kretzmann and Eleonore Stump (Cambridge: Cambridge University Press, 1993), 38.

2 Ibid., 2.

3 Consequently, it was not unknown for Aristotle's writings to be banned. See, for example, the Condemnation of 1210 issued by the synod of Sens proclaiming that no work by Aristotle on natural philosophy could be taught or read in Paris: Edward Grant (ed.), *A Source Book in Medieval Science* (Cambridge, Mass.: Harvard University Press, 1974), 42.

 | DOI 10.1163/9789004344372_007

both strands deal with matters of central concern to wrongdoing, Aristotle himself failed to draw the two together, leaving unanswered fundamental questions as to how the two interact. Within ethics, the relevant concept is responsibility, the key to determining under what circumstances a person can be praised or blamed for their actions. This is a topic of central importance to Aristotle's ethics, feeding directly into his conception of moral agency that acts as the gateway to both virtue and vice.[4] This is dealt with in two locations in the *Nicomachean Ethics*, although as might be expected the two accounts bear many similarities.

Aristotle's first account of responsibility begins with the basic proposition that praise and blame are only bestowed on actions that are 'voluntary'.[5] The word translated here as voluntary is *hekousion*, a word without a direct analogue in English. Although it certainly connotes actions performed without coercion, of one's own free will, there is an element of purpose to it that is not necessarily implicit in the idea of voluntariness.[6] As 'voluntariness' is the translation of choice in works both on ancient philosophy and legal philosophy, it will be maintained here.[7] Nevertheless, its ambiguity should be noted, especially when comparisons are drawn with the Latin variations on '*voluntas*' which, for simple reasons of etymology, are also translated as 'voluntariness'.

Actions are involuntary when compelled by an external force or performed through ignorance. External compulsion comes in many forms, and some are easier to justify as being irrelevant to ethical judgments than others. For example, it is straightforward to argue that a person whose ship is carried into dangerous waters by an overwhelmingly strong wind is not to blame for the damage done to the ship and its cargo. The reason given by Aristotle is simple: the actor contributed nothing to the harm.[8] He was simply carried into the path of harm by a force entirely external to him, and so there can be no question of blameworthiness. Matters are complicated when the actor is compelled to act by an external force, but the decision to act is his own. Within legal taxonomies the obvious example is duress, but Aristotle considers also actions motivated by noble purposes.[9] In both cases the simple fact that there is an underlying choice, even if that choice is constrained by the circumstances in which it is

4 See generally Susan S. Meyer, *Aristotle on Moral Responsibility: Cause and Character* (Oxford: Oxford University Press, 2011), 17–19.

5 Aristotle, *Nicomachean Ethics*, 3.1.

6 Ibbetson, 'How the Romans', n.91.

7 E.g. Ibbetson, 'How the Romans', 492; Gordley, 'Tort law in the Aristotelian tradition', 131, 138.

8 Aristotle, *Nicomachean Ethics*, 3.1.

9 Ibid., 3.1.

made, is sufficient to describe such actions as voluntary. This is a conclusion that troubled Aristotle, evidenced by his caveat that 'such actions, therefore, are voluntary, but in the abstract involuntary; for no one would choose any such act in itself'.[10]

Given the ambiguous treatment of compelled choices in the *Nicomachean Ethics*, it should not be surprising that his discussion of the same topic elsewhere is not consistent.[11] In the *Eudemian Ethics* he considers the case of a person who reveals a secret under torture.[12] The same indeterminacy found in the *Nicomachean Ethics* underscores his argument, but this time Aristotle comes down on the side of involuntariness. This change in opinion has recently been explained through the characterisation of the choice involved in coercion scenarios: is it legitimately a choice (and so internal to the actor, bringing him within the realms of voluntariness) or has the capacity for choice been negated by the circumstances in which the action was performed?[13] This inconsistency need not concern us. Although the *Eudemian Ethics* might have had an effect on Roman law due to its popularity in the ancient world, it is the *Nicomachean Ethics* that is cited consistently by Aquinas.[14] It is sufficient to note that compulsion of this sort appears to have marked the boundary between voluntariness and involuntariness within Aristotle's ethics, and that within the *Nicomachean Ethics* he characterised such actions, albeit reluctantly, as voluntary.

Aristotle's account of ignorance as the second form of involuntariness is straightforward:

> ... the term 'involuntary' tends to be used not if a man is ignorant of what is to his advantage—for it is not mistaken purpose that causes involuntary action (it leads rather to wickedness), nor ignorance of the universal (for that men are blamed), but ignorance of particulars, i.e. of the circumstances of the action and the objects with which it is concerned. For it is on these that both pity and pardon depend, since the person who is ignorant of any of these acts involuntarily.[15]

10 Ibid., 3.1.

11 Meyer, *Aristotle on Moral Responsibility*, 93–118.

12 Aristotle, *Eudemian Ethics*, 1225a.

13 Jozef Müller, 'Agency and responsibility in Aristotle's *Eudemian Ethics*' (2015) 60 *Phronesis* 206; Meyer, *Aristotle on Moral Responsibility*, 93–118.

14 Although the argument has been made that even in the classical world it was the *Nicomachean Ethics* that affected Roman law: Moshe Shalgi, 'Aristotle's concept of responsibility and its reflection in Roman jurisprudence' (1971) 6 Israel Law Review 39.

15 Aristotle, *Nicomachean Ethics*, 3.1.

Ignorance pertains to the circumstances of an action and its objects. One cannot be blamed for innocently revealing information believed to be public knowledge, but in fact a secret, for the actor is ignorant of the quality of his action that would make it wrongful. Actions performed through ignorance ought to result in the actor's repentance once his ignorance is corrected, but cannot be a sufficient basis for censure. At this point ignorance is approached at a strictly subjective level—no inquiry is made into whether the ignorance is justifiable, or whether there is any information that an actor *ought* to know.

It is on this point that Aristotle's second account of responsibility in the *Nicomachean Ethics* is thought to differ, insofar as it justifies judging ignorance according to an objective standard. This argument arises in relation to Aristotle's treatment of the culpability of mistakes:

> ... there are three kinds of injury in transactions between man and man; those done in ignorance are mistakes when the person acted on, the act, the instrument, or the end that will be attained is other than the agent supposed; the agent thought either that he was not hitting any one or that he was not hitting with this missile or not hitting this person or to this end, but a result followed other than that which he thought likely (e.g. he threw not with intent to wound but only to prick), or the person hit or the missile was other than he supposed. Now when (1) the injury takes place contrary to reasonable expectation, it is a misadventure. When (2) it is not contrary to reasonable expectation, but does not imply vice, it is a mistake (for a man makes a mistake when the fault originates in him, but is the victim of accident when the origin lies outside him). When (3) he acts with knowledge but not after deliberation, it is an act of injustice, e.g. he acts due to anger or to other passions necessary or natural to man; for when men do such harmful and mistaken acts they act unjustly, and the acts are acts of injustice, but this does not imply that the doers are unjust or wicked; for the injury is not due to vice. But when (4) a man acts from choice, he is an unjust man and a vicious man.[16]

It is the injection of terms like 'reasonable expectations' in scenario (1) that appear to invite questions of objectivity. The point of contention is whether 'reasonable' has the connotations of objectivity that it has borne in legal contexts for most of the last two millennia. Against the longstanding assumption that reasonableness implies some sort of evaluation of whether a belief was

16 Ibid., 5.8.

tenable according to an external standard, Daube argued that it was instead concerned with psychological fact.[17] His argument is founded in passages from elsewhere in Aristotle's *corpus*, drawn primarily from works on rhetoric instead of ethics to argue for a translation of 'against calculation' instead of 'reasonable expectations', thereby confining the evaluation to matters internal to the actor. The question becomes whether it was reasonable for the defendant, armed with whatever knowledge he actually possessed, to act as he did.

Daube's reinterpretation of mistake was roundly rejected by Schofield, who took issue with Daube's argument at a primarily methodological level. In seeking the handful of instances across Aristotle's vast corpus in which it seems untenable to associate mistake with objectivity, he overlooks the multiplicity of scenarios in which Aristotle can only be seen to be referring to objective reasonableness in relation to mistaken beliefs.[18] Daube's argument is the product of selective readings and 'extremely elastic statements of his own interpretation of the Greek'.[19] On the strength of Schofield's arguments, it appears safe to overlook the lone voice arguing for a subjective reading of Aristotelian mistakes. Aristotle's second account of responsibility gives every appearance of adding a criterion of reasonableness to questions of praise and blame, at least in so far as they stem from mistakes. But the sort of standard he had in mind is not clear, and the language of reasonableness might be leading.

Justice as a Virtue

The second relevant strand of Aristotelian thought is the virtue of justice. This is one of the four cardinal virtues in Aristotelian ethics, and so represents an indispensable strand of his ethics. *Eudaimonia*, the ultimate end of human endeavour, is to be achieved through virtuous action.[20] Almost all virtues are introspective, and culture the correct response to a given stimulus. When faced with a threat, the virtuous man will know whether it is best to respond courageously, fighting back, or cautiously, instead choosing flight. These internal responses to external factors are cultivated through *phronesis*, or practical reason. Justice stands alone among the virtues in its concern for 'transactions', or

17 David Daube, *Roman Law: Linguistic, Social and Philosophical Aspects* (Edinburgh: Edinburgh University Press, 1969), 133–137.

18 Malcolm Schofield, 'Aristotelian mistakes' (1973) 19 Proceedings of the Cambridge Philological Society 66, 67.

19 Ibid., 67.

20 Aristotle, *Nicomachean Ethics*, 1.4.

interactions between private parties. An aspect of *eudaimonia* is understanding how best to relate to your fellow man, and justice seeks to give shape to these relationships.

Justice is divided into two strains: distributive and corrective.[21] Distributive justice is an aspect of Aristotle's political theory, describing the ideal distribution of assets across society. Corrective justice links his ethics to his political theory, explaining under what circumstances actions that upset the balance of assets dictated by distributive justice need to be addressed. Such deviations from distributive justice can arise either voluntarily or involuntarily in reference to the disponee.[22] Aristotle barely pays attention to voluntary transactions—it is taken as obvious that a person can voluntarily part with their assets without ethical consequences. His focus is on involuntarily transactions. Under what circumstances does justice demand that a person who causes another to have less than he ought to, and does so against his will, be held responsible for the loss?

The archetypal situation of an inequality envisages a direct correspondence between the loss caused and the gain made through the injustice. An example of this is theft, wherein one man's gain matches perfectly another's loss. Justice demands that the thief be deprived of the gain he made and that the victim be restored to his fair share of wealth. This can be achieved simply by taking the stolen property from the thief and giving it to its rightful owner. The goal is, in Aristotle's own words, 'equalisation'.[23] How ought we to deal with injustices that do not result in material gain to the wrongdoer? Here too Aristotle uses the language of 'gain', although he concedes that it is not ideal.[24] This model of corrective justice as maintaining the equilibrium of assets applies just as readily to homicide and physical injuries as it does to theft through the use of penalties to take away the 'gain' from the wrongdoer.[25]

Behind these inquiries is the question of how responsibility interacts with justice. A person is responsible for their actions unless those actions were compelled by a force entirely external to the actor or were performed through reasonable ignorance. We are told that 'a man acts unjustly or justly whenever he does such acts voluntarily'.[26] Does this mean that the demands of corrective justice only apply where a person acts voluntarily? Answering this question is

21 Ibid., 5.2.
22 Ibid., 5.4.
23 Ibid., 5.4.
24 Ibid., 5.4: 'For the term "gain" is applied generally to such cases, even if it be not a term appropriate to certain cases, e.g. to the person who inflicts a wound and "loss" to the sufferer'.
25 Ibid., 5.4.
26 Ibid., 5.8.

complicated by a distinction between unjust acts and consequences that arises in a passage disconnected from Aristotle's main account of corrective justice.[27] It is perfectly possible for an unjust act to lead to just consequences, as where a creditor coerces a debtor into repaying his loan by threatening the wellbeing of his family. Similarly, it is possible to bring about unjust consequences without acting unjustly, principally where the act was involuntary. Under what circumstances is corrective justice invoked? Assuming corrective justice is ever employed, there can be three answers:

1) In response to unjust consequences caused involuntarily (and so not unjustly), as where a captain is driven onto rocks by a strong wind
2) In response to unjust actions alone, even where they do not cause an injustice, as where a debtor coerces by threats a creditor into repaying his loan.
3) In response only to unjust actions that cause unjust consequences.

Aristotle provides no guidance on whether any of these answers is incorrect. It would be perfectly compatible with the text of the *Nicomachean Ethics* to argue that all three necessitate corrective justice, which results in a strict liability reading of Aristotle. But this reading requires a complete divorcing of Aristotle's concepts of responsibility and justice. This is difficult to justify in the face of their association together at the beginning of V.8. What is the value in claiming that a person only acts unjustly if they act voluntarily, when it makes not a lick of difference to their liability under corrective justice? Can corrective justice operate in so mechanical a fashion, blind to questions of desert, within a theory of ethics? Distinctions founded on voluntariness were intended to have practical consequences in Athenian society within the context of laws against homicide.[28] Can it be that, against his legal context, Aristotle was pushing for a model of homicide founded strictly on the harm caused—that the mere causation of death, regardless of mental state, was deserving of punishment? While it is consistent with his text to read Aristotle as proposing a model of strict liability, it appears to rely on a lawyer's interpretation instead of a moralist's, and loses sight of why Aristotle wrote about justice in the first place: its function as a virtue within a broader moral context.

27 Ibid., 5.8.

28 Ibbetson, 'How the Romans', 493–4; W.T. Loomis, 'The nature of premeditation in Athenian homicide law' (1972) 92 Journal of Hellenic Studies 86. See generally Douglas M. MacDowell, *Athenian Homicide Law in the Age of the Orators* (Manchester: Manchester University Press, 1999).

Aristotelianism and Roman Law in Spain

Aristotle's writings represent the intellectual context for Aquinas' thought, constituting indirectly the foundations for the writings of the Thomists. The final task for this chapter is to seek to explain why Thomism came to be concentrated in the Iberian Peninsula. There are three strands to be considered: firstly, why did the changes occur so markedly in the early sixteenth century? Secondly, why were they concentrated to such a strong degree in the Iberian Peninsula? And thirdly, why did the Thomists focus so heavily on law? This is partly a matter of detailing the institutional history of Thomism, the migration of primarily Spanish scholars to primarily Spanish institutions that would accommodate their legal-theological endeavours. The impetus for the widespread resurgence in Thomism was the replacement of Lombard's *Sentences* with Aquinas' *Summa Theologiae* as the cornerstone of the university curricula. This was first adopted in Paris, but was systematically implemented in Spanish faculties starting with Salamanca in the 1520s.[29] It is no coincidence that this coincides with the return of Francisco de Vitoria to Spain from Paris, where he had been among the first students exposed to the Thomist curriculum, in order to take up the Chair of theology at the University of Salamanca in 1524. To this rationale is often added the need for theologians to show their practical side in the wake of an assault from humanism, though the accuracy of these claims is heavily disputed.

Institutional history can only do so much, and it leaves certain problems unanswered. Why were these changes so disproportionately manifested within Spain? This speaks to the academic climate of Spanish universities. Spain had long acted as the conduit by which Aristotelian ideas entered Europe. Sizable parts of Aristotle's corpus were translated out of Arabic and into Latin (and, later, Castilian) by the embryonic School of Toledo.[30] This same school was later patronised by Alfonso X, the monarch behind the *Siete Partidas*, which will be discussed shortly. While the study of Aristotle was banned in some European universities, it retained a constant foothold in Spain.[31] This foothold was

29 Lidia Lanza and Marco Toste, 'The *Sentences* in sixteenth-century Iberian scholasticism' in *Medieval Commentaries on the Sentences of Peter Lombard*, ed. Philipp W. Rosemann, 3 volumes (Leiden: Brill, 2001–2015), III, 416.

30 Grant, *The Foundations of Modern Science in the Middle Ages: Their Religious, Institutional and Intellectual Contexts* (Cambridge: Cambridge University Press, 1996), 23–24, 27; Anthony R.D. Pagden, 'The diffusion of Aristotle's moral philosophy in Spain, ca.1400–1600' (1975) 31 Traditio 287.

31 E.g. the Condemnation of 1210 banning Aristotle's natural philosophy from being taught, or even read, in the University of Paris: Grant (ed.), *A Source Book in Medieval Science*, 42.

only expanded when in the 1460s Aristotle's moral philosophy began to spread rapidly in the wake of printing, attaining 'a hitherto unprecedented intellectual importance'.[32] The Spanish universities were a natural home for an Aristotelian curriculum, and readily received Thomist scholars seeking to further explore Aristotelian ideas through the writings of Aquinas.

The Thomists didn't write on just any aspect of the *Summa Theologiae*. Their focus was overwhelmingly on the *secunda secundae* and, in particular, the virtue of justice. This virtue undoubtedly plays a central role in Thomist ethics, particularly as it is the sole virtue that governs human relationships. Even so, among some Thomists justice was studied to the exclusion of all others. This trend is particularly clear towards the end of the Thomist movement. The commentary on the *secunda secundae* by Cardinal Cajetan (1469–1534) explores every *quaestio* of that work in some detail. Although there is a lot of legally interesting material in his commentary on justice, there is no small degree of theological heft to his examination of other issues. This can be compared to the seminal treatise by Leonardus Lessius (1554–1623), entitled *De Iustitia et Iure Caeterisque Virtutibus Cardinalibus*. As the name suggests, it discusses all four of the cardinal virtues. But the attention paid to each is far from even. Prudence receives two chapters with four disputations each, fortitude two chapters with six disputations each, and temperance four chapters with between four and sixteen disputations. By contrast, justice is discussed across forty-seven chapters, some of which have up to thirty-eight disputations. Even within justice, their focus is narrowly on matters of legal import. As will be seen in due course, sins against justice with purely theological relevance were quickly marginalised.

How can this preoccupation with justice and, within justice, legal doctrine be explained? Again, it might be a product of the quite unique Spanish legal context, and in particular the *Siete Partidas*, that together explain why the juridification of Thomism was of such appeal to mostly Spanish theologians. The direction of Spain's legal history was determined by the strong interest taken by its royalty towards law. This is by no means an anomaly—legally interventionist monarchs can be found across Europe in every century. But in Spain it had a manifestation that is uncharacteristic of its period: a code (or perhaps, more accurately, a code-like authority).[33] This was known as the *Siete Partidas*,

32 Pagden, 'The diffusion of Aristotle's moral philosophy in Spain, 289.

33 It was not, however, the primary source of law. Royal legislation (compiled in periodic *recopilaciones*) were the highest source of law, followed by *fueros* (sets of local enactments). The *Siete Partidas* was subsidiary to both of these. See further Francisco Tomás y Valiente, *Manual de Historia del derecho Español* (Madrid: Tecnos, 1983), 232–280.

Alfonso X's great legislative enactment written in the mid-thirteenth century, though perhaps not enacted until a century later under the *Ordenamiento de Alcalá* of 1348, which also enacted a number of additional laws. The crown of Castile's strong authority (cemented by its union with the Habsburgs in 1516) coupled with the crown's assertion of supremacy in secular affairs, thereby forbidding deviation from the laws of the king, ensured this quasi-code survived beyond the Thomists.[34] But the *Siete Partidas* was more than just a body of laws: it was a code of ethics and rules by which citizens ought to live, expressly intended to ensure citizens lived according to their faith.[35]

The *Siete Partidas* has a considerable amount to say about wrongdoing, and in these discussions one can see an early and patchy attempt at uniting doctrinal Roman law with Aristotelian principles. Such attempts are far from universal, but can be seen piecemeal throughout the *Siete Partidas*. The claim by Alfonso X that he crafted the *Siete Partidas* himself, though almost certainly untrue, has obscured from history the true authorship of the code, along with the means by which it was constructed. It is thus impossible to trace individual contributors who were interested in Roman law and Aristotelianism. The best that can be done is an analysis of areas of law. To do this for the entire code, or even its treatment of wrongdoing as a whole, would be beyond the scope of this book. For present purposes, it will suffice to examine two aspects of wrongdoing, defamation and homicide, and see how and to what extent civilian and Aristotelian ideas were assimilated. This involves an examination of three tracts of the seventh part of the *Siete Partidas*, on wrongs to *fama*, wrongs to *honor*, and wrongs to life. Each of these wrongs shows a different approach to the sources of law. *Fama* is a melting pot of Roman law, Aristotelianism and local Castilian laws. *Honor* is overwhelmingly Roman. And homicide shows the adaptation of Roman rules drawn from a range of contexts to an Aristotelian way of thinking. Taken together they represent a piecemeal but firm foothold for the assimilation of Roman law and Aristotelianism in Spain, a task to be taken further centuries later by the Thomists.

Harm to *fama* is known as *infamado*, and harm to *honor* as *deshonras*. The basis of *infamado* is expressly Roman: it matters because it renders people *infamis*, and such a status has legally imposed consequences for that person's place in society.[36] The language of honour, a central concern throughout much

34 Carlos Petit, '*Derecho común y derecho castellano: notas de literatura juridica para su estudio* (*siglos XV-XVII*)' (1982) 50 Tijdschrift voor Rechtsgeschiedenis 157. Decock, *Theologians and Contract Law*, 34: '*non habenos major sobre nos en lo temporal*'.

35 Siete Partidas, 1.1.1.

36 Ibid., 7.6.7: 'infamy has such effect that such persons cannot again obtain any dignity or honor such as those for which men of good reputation are selected' (Scott).

of the *Siete Partidas*, is itself suggestive of an Aristotelian basis. A reduction in a person's *fama* occurs either through an act or by operation of law. So far as acts are concerned, questions of fault are immaterial. Thus a child born outside of a lawful marriage is infamous simply by fact of their birth.[37] More strikingly Aristotelian, a ruler or judge can declare someone infamous by publicly declaring that they are not living a sufficiently virtuous life.[38] Defamation that arises by operation of law also concerns acts, but the basis for making a declaration of infamy is the existence of a written law prohibiting the act, rather than a naturalistic sense of what is right. Thus an adulteress is rendered infamous, as is a widow who enjoys carnal pleasures within a year of her husband's death.[39] In both of these scenarios *infamia* is used to mark out individuals who are on an immoral path. The language deployed, along with the overall function of the label *infamia*, are clearly lifted from Roman law. But they are given an Aristotelian twist in their overriding concern for *honor*. The mixture is completed by a healthy injection of local laws on particularly immoral behaviour, mostly relating to lascivious widows.

A second tract on *deshonras* is a similar hodgepodge of ideas and rules.[40] This idea is linked explicitly to the Roman delict of *iniuria*.[41] *Deshonras* can be caused through words or deeds: verbally, when a person insults someone directly, or mocks him in front of a crowd.[42] The language of mockery draws a close parallel with the *contumelia* of Roman law.[43] The *Siete Partidas* even treats as a distinct form of *deshonras* the creation and dissemination of hurtful songs, in Latin the *malum carmen* of the Twelve Tables.[44] Acts that can constitute *deshonras* include striking, chasing, and even lighting a fire so as to smoke out one's neighbours.[45] This use of a law against defamation to address physical violence is once again reminiscent of Roman law.[46] This is also true of the way in which *deshonras* is redressed: the claimant elects between a claim

37 Ibid., 7.6.2.

38 Ibid., 7.6.2.

39 Ibid., 7.6.3.

40 The intervening two laws elaborate on the way in which *deshonras* is caused, while 7.9 moves on to how it is suffered.

41 Siete Partides, 7.9.1.

42 Ibid., 7.9.1.

43 Ibid., 7.9.4.

44 Ibid., 7.9.3; XII Tables, 8.1 (Crawford), evidenced in Pliny; reference is also made to *famosus libellus*, another distinctly Roman formulation of *iniuria*.

45 Siete Partidas, 7.9.6.

46 A separate law deals with the physical harm caused by violence: ibid., 7.10.

for compensation or entrusting the defendant to the judge for a punishment at his discretion.[47] In cases of compensation, the judge asks the claimant for what sum would he not have experienced the *deshonras*. This acts as an upper threshold for damages, and the judge will decide on an appropriate figure. In all of these rules there is an unmistakably Roman influence, with little sign of an Aristotelian twist

Within homicide the preliminary distinction is between intentional and unintentional killings. Intentional killings are punishable by death unless they can be justified.[48] The main justification offered is self-defence, described as something 'natural'.[49] Most of the other justifications are familiar: it is justifiable to kill a thief who, having been caught in the act, puts up a fight; to kill a man found violating one's wife, daughter or sister; and to kill an arsonist caught in the act.[50] Others are distinctive of the chivalric context of the code: Alfonso writes that it is lawful to kill a knight who has abandoned his lord in the field, provided the killing occurs in an attempt at arresting the knight to take him back to his lord for punishment.[51] This is a clear extrapolation for the circumstances in which it is lawful to kill a thief, but twisted to match a common scenario within chivalry. Presumably, the case needs to be dealt with explicitly as it would be unthinkable to extend the logic behind the killing of thieves to knights, regardless of their cowardice or treachery.

Unintentional killings are divided into two groups. Firstly, some actors simply lack capacity and so do not deserve punishment.[52] Under this heading Alfonso groups the insane, the addled and boys under the age of ten and a half. Secondly, accidental deaths are presumed not to incur liability provided the killer is willing to swear a series of oaths: that the death occurred by accident, that he in no way consented to the death, and that he bore no hostility towards to the deceased.[53] For the third of these, it is preferable for the killer to find compurgators to swear to the good relations that existed between the killer and deceased. If, however, the accident can be attributed to some fault on the part of the killer, he deserves to be punished for it, albeit to a lesser extent than an intentional killer:

47 Ibid., 7.9.21.

48 Ibid., 7.8.2.

49 Ibid., 7.8.2: '*ca natural cosa es et muy guisada que todo home haya poder de amparar su persona de muerte, quieriendo alguno matar á él, et non ha de esperar que el otro la fiera primeramente*'.

50 Ibid., 7.8.3.

51 Ibid., 7.8.3.

52 Ibid., 7.8.3.

53 Ibid., 7.8.4.

Ocasiones acaescen á las vegadas de que nascen muertes de homes, de que son en culpa et merescen pena por ende aquellos por quien avienen, por que non pusieron hi tan grant guarda como debieran, ó ficierorn cosas enante por que avino la occasion: et esto serie como si algunt home cortase arbol o labrase en algunt lugar casa ó la torre que estudiese sobre la Carrera ó sobre la cal pública por do usasen los homes ápasar, et non apercibiese á los que passen por hi en tiempo nine n manera que se pudiesen guardar, et cayese el arbol ó alguna cosa de aquella labor que ficiese, et matase algunt home; ó si alguno corriese caballo en lugar que non fuse costumbrado para correlo, et non apercibiendo los homes que se guardasen, topase con algunt home et lo matase; ó si firiese ó empellase á alguno como en manera de juego, et acaesciese que de aquella ferida ó empujada muriese; ó si algunt home que hobiese costumbrado de levantarse en dormiendo et de tomar cuchiello ó armas para ferir, et sabiendo su costumbre mala non apercibiese della áaquellos con quien dormiese en un lugar que se guardasen, et matase alguno dellos; ó si alguno se embriagase de manera que por la beudez matase áotro: ca por tales ocasiones como estas ó por otras semejantes dellas que aviniesen por culpa de aquellos que las ficiesen, deben seer desterrados por ellas los que las ficieren en alguna isla por cinco años, porque fueron en culpa, non poniendo ante que acaesciese aquella guarda que pudieran poner.[54]

54 Ibid., 7.8.5: 'Accidents happen sometimes which cause the death of men for which those who are responsible for them are to blame, and deserve punishment, because they did not exercise as great care as they should; or have previously been in the habit of doing such things as that from which the accident resulted. This would be the case where a man was cutting down trees, or building a house or tower in some places which was over a highway or public street through which men were passing, and did not notify them in time, nor in such a way that they could protect themselves, and the tree, or any portion of the building which he was erecting, falls and kills someone; or where some person races a horse where he was not accustomed to race him, and did not warn men to take care of themselves; and the horse strikes someone or kills or wounds him; or where one party pushes another, in play, and he dies as a result of the stroke or push. Or it might happen that a man was accustomed to arise during his sleep, and arm himself with a knife, or other dangerous weapon, and being aware of his bad habit, did not warn those who were sleeping in the house to be on their guard, and kills one of them; or where a person becomes intoxicated to such an extent that he kills another because of his drunkenness. On account of accidents of this kind and others similar to them, which happen through the fault of the party who causes them, the latter shall be banished to some island for five years, for the reason that he was to blame for not taking the precautions which he should have done before the accident took place' (Scott).

It is clear that the author of this passage was familiar with the *lex Aquilia*. The five scenarios dealt with are given a common rationale in the last sentence: liability exists because the killer ought to have taken precautions, and his failure to do so caused a death. The first example is clearly inspired by D.9.2.31 ('*si putator*'), and based on the examples chosen seems to be advocating a standard of professional liability. The second example involves doing something that is not of itself inherently dangerous, but that becomes so by virtue of its location. In this respect, it appears to be a Spanish version of Digest texts such as D.9.2.11.pr (playing with a ball and practising barberry in a public place can invite liability) and D.9.2.9.4 (throwing javelins in a suitable location precludes liability).

The third example is a singular event, and something of an anomaly in this list. With each of the other examples, the text gives an example of the expected precautions that could preclude liability. In this text, one party simply playfully shoves another, accidentally causing a death for which the pusher must be punished. It may be that the difference between this and the preceding example is one of inherent danger: riding a horse is not inherently likely to result in a death, but it becomes dangerous when performed in a populated area. Thus when circumstances conspire to increase the risk of death, it is the duty of the risk-taker to warn those who might be affected. Conversely, shoving someone is always going to be dangerous, even if done in jest, and so no precautions are necessary. It is difficult to see any direct link between this scenario and the *lex Aquilia*. Two texts have similar fact patterns. D.9.2.7.3 deals with shoving, but as a text on agency. One person pushes a second person in such a way that the second person causes a death. The first person did not cause the death directly, so he is not liable on the *lex* directly. The second person did not act blameworthily, so he is not liable either. The solution is to grant an *actio in factum* against the first person. In D.9.2.52.4 a small slave is pushed over while retrieving a ball, leading to a broken leg. Here liability did not exist for want of fault: the harm was caused accidentally. Though both these texts resemble Alfonso's third situation, the underlying arguments are quite different.

The fourth and fifth examples approach accidental homicide from a different perspective. Both deal with character flaws and their implications for voluntariness. In his fourth example Alfonso deals with a case quite alien to other treatments of homicide: somnambulism. Liability for stabbing someone while sleepwalking hinges on the killer's awareness of his condition. If the sleepwalker is aware of his penchant for wandering around the house while asleep, he must take precautions against any harm he might cause while unconscious. Fault is ascribed to an oblivious actor on an omissions basis—having created a dangerous situation, it is blameworthy not to guard against obvious consequences. This can be contrasted with his fifth example, a drunkard who kills while in alcohol-fuelled oblivion. Here there is no question of precautions or involuntariness. Unlike somnambulism, intoxication is (according to thirteenth-century psychology) a voluntary decision. Even if it is difficult to say the individual actions performed while drunk are voluntary, the decision to enter a state of intoxication certainly was. There is a clear tonal shift between the first two and last two examples. While the first two have clear and strong civilian influences, the fourth and fifth do not. Instead of asking 'is this blameworthy?' they appear to be asking 'can this man be held responsible for his actions at all?' They are hypotheticals about voluntariness, not fault. This is clear evidence of an Aristotelian influence on the Siete Partidas' content. And although this influence is something that has long been recognised, its significance to specific legal doctrines has, however, been downplayed.[55]

The *Siete Partidas*' treatment of homicide is significant in two respects. The first is its merging of Roman rules on homicide and property damage through the introduction of *culpa*. The influence of the ancient Roman law of homicide can be seen in a number of respects. In the case of intentional homicides, different punishments were meted out to knights (i.e. patricians) and commoners.[56] The former were exiled, the latter executed. This is identical to Roman law.[57] In the context of parricide, the imposition of the barbaric Roman punishment is justified by explicit reference to the jurists.[58] However, the actual substance of the *Siete Partidas*' treatment of homicide owes a greater debt to the *lex Aquilia*. The basic distinction drawn between intentional and accidental homicide is built primarily upon examples of *culpa* under the *lex*, with multiple of the hypotheticals explored being clearly lifted from D.9.2.

Of considerably more importance is the possibility that Aristotelian legal thought had a foothold in Spanish law several centuries before the Thomists began their work, with Spain playing the central role in the reintroduction of Aristotle into Europe from the Arabic world, and its translation into vernacular languages.[59] The *Siete Partidas* is by no means dominated by Aristotelian ideas

55 E.g. Marie R. Madden, *Political Theory and Law in Medieval Spain* (New York: Fordham University Press, 1930), chapter 4.

56 Siete Partidas, 7.8.15.

57 D.48.8.3.5: '*Legis Corneliae de sicariis et veneficis poena insulae deportatio est et omnium bonorum ademptio. Sed solent hodie capite puniri, nisi honestiore loco positi fuerint, ut poenam legis sustineant: humiliores enim solent vel bestiis subici, altiores vero deportantur in insulam*'.

58 Siete Partidas, 7.8.12; J.4.18.6. It is difficult to write off as coincidence the choice of animals to be enclosed in the sack with the killer.

59 Pagden, 'The diffusion of Aristotle's moral philosophy in Spain'.

and constructs in the same way as the works of the Thomists. There are examples of wrongs that are couched primarily in the language of Roman law, or even have no significant influence from either Thomism or the civil law. Rather, it is an early attempt at the reconciliation of Aristotelian ethics and Roman law. This is significant not for the thought of the Thomists but the legal world within which they lived and worked. We know from their own use of sources that the Siete Partidas had very little bearing on their work and thinking. Between an Aristotelian intelligentsia, a quasi-Aristotelian legal system and an education founded on the *Summa Theologiae*, it becomes easier to understand the interests of the Thomists in the sixteenth century.

CHAPTER 7

'Delict' in the *Summa Theologiae*

The Structure of Wrongdoing

The *Summa Theologiae* is divided into three parts, the second of which is further divided into two. The naming of each part is as one would expect: *prima*, *prima secundae*, *secunda secundae* and *tertia*. Each part deals broadly with a theme: the *prima* addresses fundamental questions of theology, the *secunda* ethics and the *tertia* the life of Christ and the sacraments. Ethics, like the *secunda* itself, is divided into two sections. The *prima secundae* constitutes a theory of action and the *secunda secundae* a theory of virtues. Each part is made up of dozens of *quaestiones*, in which Aquinas addresses a point of theological controversy, refuting opposing views in the process. This form of disputation is the hallmark of scholastic learning.

Matters that can be broadly painted as legal arise in two distinct contexts within the *Summa*. The first spans *quaestiones* 90 to 108 of the *prima secundae*, and is typically considered to be Aquinas' treatise on law. The questions dealt with therein are what would today be viewed as matters of jurisprudence and political philosophy. It deals not with questions of doctrine, but matters of legitimacy and authority. What is law? Who can make it? What is the relationship between positive law and natural law? Between law and morality? It is better to view it not as a treatise on law, but on *lex*. Questions of doctrine are matters of *ius*, and are examined elsewhere.[1]

Doctrinal private law is considered under the aegis of justice, the cardinal virtue occupying *quaestiones* 57 to 122 of the *secunda secundae*. The entire *secunda secundae* is spent exploring the cardinal and theological virtues, but as in Aristotelian ethics justice is unique among its peers. The other six virtues are introspective, concerned with self-perfection in the Aristotelian mould. Justice is concerned with shaping harmonious relationships between neighbours.[2] Its doctrines are the rules by which those relationships are given shape, dealing both with the facilitation of communal life and the redress of injustices.

1 A distinction made readily apparent by the Latin but not the English. The language of *lex* permeates Aquinas, *Summa Theologiae* (hereafter ST), I-II, qq.90–108, while *ius* is defined at the outset of ST, II-II, q.57.a.1.

2 ST, II-II, q.57.a.1.

 | DOI 10.1163/9789004344372_008

The result is a wide-ranging set of *quaestiones* that can, for the sake of convenience, be divided into two tracts: the core of justice (*quaestiones* 57–78), and connected issues (*quaestiones* 79–122). The connected issues are of tangential relevance to this book, covering issues such as the overlap between religious observance and justice, internal motivations that might colour relationships but not shape them (e.g. gratitude, vengeance, hypocrisy), and the ephemeral *epikeia*. It is in the core of justice that we identify the kernel of the Thomist theory of delict. This begins with a series of general definitions before examining fifteen individual forms of wrongdoing that are structured in the following way:

Category	Mode	Specific sin
To which the victim does not consent	By deed	*Homicidia* (II-II, q.64) *Mutilatio* and *verberatio* (II-II, q.65) *Furtum* and *rapina* (II-II, q.66)
	By words during a trial	Committed by the *iudex* (II-II, q.67) Committed by the *accusator* (II-II, q.68) Committed by the defendant (II-II, q.69) Committed by a witness (II-II, q.70) Committed by the *advocator* (II-II, q.71)
	By words otherwise	*Contumelia* (II-II, q.72) *Detractio* (II-II, q.73) *Sussurratio* (II-II, q.74) *Derisio* (II-II, q.75) *Maledictio* (II-II, q.76)
To which the victim (prima facie) consents		*Fraudulentia* (II-II, q.77) *Usura* (II-II, q.78)

The way in which the *Summa* is structured, by considering the nature of a virtue through its associated vices, gives a strong bias to injustices caused involuntarily or, by any other name, wrongs. But before these individual forms of wrongdoing can be considered in any detail, it is necessary to first consider the general definitions contained in *quaestiones* 57–62, as it is in these provisions that the mechanics of the Thomist theory of delict are laid down.

Commutative Justice and *Restitutio*

At the heart of Aquinas' account of justice is the familiar distinction between its corrective and distributive forms, though the former is now known as commutative justice. As in Aristotle, Aquinas makes the preliminary point that commutative justice is ultimately subservient to distributive justice—it is, fundamentally, the means of achieving and maintaining distributive justice—before narrowing his focus to issues almost exclusively connected to commutative justice. It is at this point that he introduces a novelty that acts as the foundation for the Thomist theory of delict: *restitutio*.[3] This is the primary remedial concept of the Thomist theory of delict,[4] but its *raison d'être* was straightforwardly theological: '*non remittitur peccatum nisi restituatur ablatum*'.[5] Whatever the mechanical function of *restitutio* within the Thomist theory of delict, within the theology of Thomism it acted as a hurdle to salvation.[6]

Aquinas' concept of *restitutio* can be stated simply:

> [R]estitutio est actus commutativae iustitiae, quando scilicet res unius ab alio habetur, vel per voluntatem eius, sicut in mutuo vel deposito; vel contra voluntatem eius, sicut in rapina vel furto.[7]
>
> [R]estituere nihil aliud esse videtur quam iterato aliquem statuere in possessionem vel dominium rei suae. Et ita in restitutione attenditur aequalitas iustitiae secundum recompensationem rei ad rem, quae pertinet ad iustitiam commutativam.[8]

---

3 Though as has already been seen, canon law already recognised a remedy with the same name: above, pages 77–79.

4 It operated alongside two others: *poena* and *satisfactio*. The former governed the relationship between man and society through punishment; the latter man and God through penance. Thus *restitutio* was the sole remedy concerned with relationships between private citizens, and was a distinct concept: Aquinas, *Super sententiarum*, l.4.d.15.q.1.a.5.

5 Jansen, 'The idea of legal responsibility' (2014) 34 OJLS 221, 226 citing Augustine, '*Epistole CLIII* (*ad Macedonium*)' (1861) 33 Patrologia Latina 653, 662.

6 Hence ST, II-II, q.62.a.2 asking whether *restitutio* is always necessary for salvation.

7 ST, II-II, q.62.a.1: 'So then restitution is an act of commutative justice, namely when one person holds that which belongs to another, whether with the owner's consent, as in a loan or a deposit, or against his will, as in robbery or theft'.

8 ST, II-II, q.62.a.1: 'To make restitution appears to be nothing else than to re-establish a person in possession or of dominion over a thing which is his. Consequently we mark there the equality or balance of justice according to the recompense of thing for thing, which is the concern of commutative justice'. Aquinas defines the verb before the noun, but given the focus of this chapter is on the noun the passages have been reversed.

Distributive justice is used to determine the ideal distribution of wealth across society. Any deviation from that distribution requires justification. Failing that, it is the role of *restitutio* to correct the imbalance. The language used thus far is the language of property. This is equally the case for Aquinas, who talks about restoring '*possessionem vel dominium rei suae*'. Every word in this clause is a term with proprietary implications. This leads to our first question: is *restitutio* a remedy that can be used only to procure the return of property?

Answering this question requires an examination of Aquinas' views on property. These are fairly opaque, with no dedicated treatment to be found within the confines of the *Summa Theologiae*. The most substantial evidence can be gleaned from his analysis of theft.[9] Before examining the sinfulness of theft, he first needs to establish whether private ownership of property is actually compatible with natural law. For Aquinas, property is at heart a dualist concept, based on the contrast between *dominium* and *proprietas*.[10] *Dominium* has a number of meanings. At its most basic, *dominium* refers to the common ownership of the world, and in particular its plants and animals, vested in man by God.[11] *Dominium* also refers to the mastery a person has over aspects of his being, namely his reason, sensitivity, natural strength and his body (*ratio, vires sensitivas, vires naturales, corpus*).[12]

The human institution of private property is named after the position of the owner who has granted a *usufruct* in Roman law. Having given away his rights to use and enjoy the property, he is left with bare ownership: *proprietas*. The use of this term rather than *dominium* to refer to ownership of private property was doubtless intentional, making it clear that property is in no true sense ever 'ours'.[13] Private property is a necessary evil, for some degree of material wealth

9 ST, II-II, q.66.a.1–2.

10 The intellectual origins of this dualism, and in particular the debt owed to feudal models of ownership, are explained in Janet Coleman, 'Property and Poverty' in *The Cambridge History of Medieval Political Thought c.350–1450*, ed. James H. Burns (Cambridge: Cambridge University Press, 1988).

11 ST, II-II, q.66.a.1.ad.1: '*Ad primum ergo dicendum quod Deus habet principale dominium omnium rerum. Et ipse secundum suam providentiam ordinavit res quasdam ad corporalem hominis sustentationem. Et propter hoc homo habet naturale rerum dominium quantum ad potestatem utendi ipsis*' ('God has pre-eminent dominion over all things, and in his providence he ordered certain things for men's material support. This is why it is natural for man to have dominion over things in the sense of having the power to use them'). See also ST, I, q.96.a.1.

12 ST, I, q.96.a.2.

13 References to *proprietas* occur primarily in Aquinas' discussion of *furtum*. E.g. ST, II-II, q.66.a.2.ad.1.

is needed for a virtuous life. It is not something to be hoarded as an end in itself, but rather something to be exploited as an instrument of human flourishing. This emotional detachment that the virtuous ought to foster towards property explains the readiness with which *restitutio* is invoked as the tool of commutative justice. A third term, *possessio*, is sometimes used as a synonym for *proprietas*, and the objects of *proprietas* are regularly called *possessiones*.[14] In passages where, if there was a difference between *possessio* and *proprietas*, we would expect that difference to be made explicit, Aquinas conflates the two.[15] There is nothing to suggest he intended the two words to refer to different ideas.

We return to the initial question: does *restitutio* apply only to possessions? And the answer must be no. It is clear that possessions are the focus of *restitutio*. Examples of *restitutio* invariably involve displaced or damaged things, and in his definition Aquinas tellingly uses the phrase '*possessionem vel dominium*'.[16] This reversal of *dominium* and *possessio* must be an intentional deviation from the traditional method of referring to these concepts. But *dominium* includes *corpus*—the body. This does not extend so far as to allow a man *dominium* over his own life, which is vested in society at large.[17] But so long as matters are confined to mere injuries, affronts to *corpus* as opposed to *vita*, *restitutio* ought to operate to uphold the victim's *dominium*.

This is a conclusion with which Aquinas appears unhappy. If I take your property, I can be forced to restore it to you in kind. If I destroy your property, I can restore it to you by paying its value. But if I wound you, what can be done to restore the injury? Although the conclusion that the body is one's own is inescapable, it does not fit comfortably with the operation of *restitutio*. As has already been mentioned, Aquinas' primary tactic is to avoid the issue. Whenever an example is needed to illustrate how *restitutio* works, it involves property. When mention of injuries is unavoidable, as in his *quaestio* on mutilation, he opts to speak not of *restitutio* but *recompensatio*.[18] Though this is a term left undefined, an earlier reply to an argument makes it clear that *recompensatio* is the non-proprietary equivalent of *restitutio*.[19] It would appear that the application of *restitutio* to the body is an unavoidable consequence of

14 ST, I, q.98.a.1.arg.3.

15 E.g. ST, II-II, q.66.a.2.arg.1 on the legitimacy of private property, refers to '*poessessionum proprietas*'.

16 ST, II-II, q.62.a.1.

17 ST, II-II, q.64.a.5.

18 ST, II-II, q.62.a.6.

19 ST, II-II, q.62.a.1.arg.3.

the definition of *restitutio*, but also a poor fit for Aquinas' conceptualisation of the remedy.

The next task is to uncover what things could constitute property. What did Aquinas mean by *rei suae*? Anyone with any familiarity with Latin will know all too well the problems that arise in translating *res*. Fortunately *res* is given a technical meaning in Aquinas' definition of a second term that might be thought to refer to property: *bona*. This is subdivided into three categories: *bona animae, bona corporis* and *bona exteriorum rerum*.[20] It should surprise no one that spiritual goods are of paramount importance, far above the other two categories. Generally *bona corporis* rank above *bona exteriorum rerum*, and consequently sins affecting them are more serious. Thus murder and adultery are more serious than theft. Within the category of *bona exteriorum rerum* there is a further division. *Fama*, a person's good name, occupies a position above mere property, but below *bona corporis*.[21] *Fama* needs to be viewed as property because it is external to oneself. A man who lives in isolation for all his life does not have a name, as it can only be conferred by the opinions of others. How I behave can shape my reputation, but it exists only in the eyes of society. Because of this externalisation, it is a thing—a *res*—like any other piece of property.

From this it can be seen that from its inception *restitutio* was a concept with two faces. Its roots were firmly entrenched in the language and concepts of property. It is in such cases that it makes sense to speak of restoration rather than compensation. But compensation was equally a facet of *restitutio*, albeit one that Aquinas does his best to suppress through parallel terms such as *recompensatio*. Nevertheless, this duality is reflected in the 'triggers' for *restitutio*. Towards the end of his account of the topic Aquinas introduces a further distinction. A person can demand *restitutio* for one of two reasons: because someone else has his property (*ratione rei*) or because of what that person did (*ratione acceptionis*). It is tempting to think of the latter as allowing *restitutio* in response to how the defendant came by the property, literally how they received it, so as to provide a direct link to the language of *acceptio*. But Aquinas also calls *restitutio ratione acceptionis* by another name: *restitutio ratione iniuriosae actionis*.[22] The two forms of *restitutio* will often coincide. The archetypal situation used to delineate the two forms is where a thief steals another person's property, then sells it on to a third party. The victim cannot demand *restitutio* from the thief *ratione rei*, as he no longer has it. So he focuses on how the

20 ST, II-II, q.73.a.3.
21 Following Proverbs 22:1.
22 ST, II-II, q.62.a.6.

thief came by the property, or what he did. It is relatively unimportant whether we say that his receipt of the property was wrongful, or whether he committed a wrong in obtaining the property. But the language of *iniuriosae actionis* is far broader than mere *acceptionis*, and allows *restitutio* where the defendant did not receive (*acceptio*) any gain himself, but nevertheless caused loss.

It is important to separate out these two species of *restitutio*. As will be seen in due course, different analytical frameworks are required when examining in what circumstances *restitutio* ought to be available. Crucially, it will be argued that *restitutio ratione acceptionis* (or *restitutio ratione iniuriosae actionis*) is only available where someone voluntarily causes loss. *Restitutio ratione rei*, on the other hand, needs no justification for its operation other than the mere fact that a person has in their possession property belonging to another. Under the watch of the later Thomists these two ideas would grow further apart, with *restitutio ratione rei* providing a basis for the law of property and the reversal of unjust enrichment, and *restitutio ratione acceptionis* grounding delict.

Individual Sins

Proceeding from the general to the specific, Aquinas moves from *restitutio* to a series of individual sins. Sinfulness is a matter of tangential (if any) relevance to *restitutio*, instead determining whether a *poena* is due. But it is worth considering in outline how each wrong is defined and detailed by Aquinas, for it is these wrongs that will form the foundations of the developed Thomist account of delict. Given the enormous amount of information contained within Aquinas' account of justice, attention will be paid primarily to those sins that were juridified by the sixteenth century commentators on the *Summa*. Matters which proved to be of solely theological relevance, or which were considered under a legal category other than delict, shall be dealt with at only a cursory level.

Homicide

The starting point of any Christian conception of life must be its value. This is true not only of human life, but of plants and animals. Thus humans may exploit nature's bounty only insofar as it is necessary for their own flourishing.[23]

23 ST, II-II, q.64.a.1. Aquinas frames this rationale in terms of purpose: '*nullus peccat ex hoc quod utitur re aliqua ad hoc ad quod est*' ('To use a thing for the purpose for which it exists is not a sin'). This has clear biblical authority in Genesis 9:3: '*omne quod movetur et vivit, erit vobis in cibum*' ('everything that lives and moves about will be food for you').

Even matters such as hunting caused theological controversies, with Vitoria arguing centuries later that it was permissible only insofar as it procures some benefit. Life is fundamentally God's, and its continued preservation was of paramount concern to the Thomists. For a legally minded theologian the problem is how best to reconcile this conception of life with the practical necessities of a legal system. Legal systems inevitably recognise situations in which the taking of life is permissible, both within society (e.g. killing in self-defence) and on behalf of society (e.g. the execution of criminals, or killing enemies in war). This reconciliation was achieved primarily through the manipulation of self-defence, though the Aristotelian core of Thomist ethics is reflected in a continuing emphasis on homicide's effects on the political community.

Self-defence is the sole exculpating factor for private citizens that Aquinas recognises, building on canon law authority that self-defence is an aspect of natural law.[24] There are two constraints placed on the use of force in self-preservation. Firstly, the force used must be in proportion to the threatened violence.[25] More importantly, the actual death cannot be an intended outcome of the defender's actions:

> [N]ihil prohibet unius actus esse duos effectus, quorum alter solum sit in intentione, alius vero sit praeter intentionem. Morales autem actus recipiunt speciem secundum id quod intenditur, non autem ab eo quod est praeter intentionem, cum sit per accidens, ut ex supradictis patet. Ex actu igitur alicuius seipsum defendentis duplex effectus sequi potest, unus quidem conservatio propriae vitae; alius autem occisio invadentis.[26]

As will be seen in due course, Thomist voluntariness is a considerably broader concept than mere intention, though Aquinas often uses *intentio* as a synonym for voluntariness. It is easy to think of situations in which concomitant ignorance (i.e. where the actor was unaware of the full implications of acting, but would have acted in the same way if he had been fully aware) could lead to a

24 X.5.12.18: '*vim vi repellere omnes leges et omnia iura permittant*' ('all statutes and all laws allow force to be repelled with force').

25 ST, II-II, q.64.a.7.

26 ST, II-II, q.64.a.7: 'A single act may have two effects, of which one alone is intended, whilst the other is incidental to that intention. But the way a moral act is to be classified depends on what is intended, not on what goes beyond such an intention, since this is merely incidental thereto, as we have seen already. In the light of this distinction we can see that an act of self-defence may have two effects: the saving of one's own life, and the killing of the attacker'.

killing in self-defence. Such acts of self-defence would be voluntary for the purposes of establishing sinfulness, and so result in responsibility for homicide.

Having established the limits of the individual's capacity for lawful homicide, Aquinas mapped it onto society. On the legality of killing sinners, he claims:

> occidere malefactorem licitum est inquantum ordinatur ad salutem totius communitatis. Et ideo ad illum solum pertinet cui committitur cura communitatis conservandae, sicut ad medicum pertinet praecidere membrum putridum quando ei commissa fuerit cura salutis totius corporis.[27]

The common good is an interest that can be protected at the expense of a sinner's life.[28] But the common good is not something that can be ascertained and protected by just anyone. Only those responsible for its maintenance and advancement can justifiably kill in its name.[29] The power to kill a sinner is an aspect of sovereignty. The actual act of killing does not need to be carried out by the relevant authority figure, but it does need his authorisation.

Aquinas does not consider how homicide might be remedied. It is clearly beyond the scope of *restitutio*, with life constituting a *bonum corporis* and not a *bonum rerum exteriorum*.[30] But there is no discussion of the consequences of homicide at all. The implication behind this silence is that such consequences are a matter for doctrines unrelated to natural law, such as *poena*. It would hardly be surprising to find homicide being dealt with punitively rather than through compensatory doctrines.

Mutilation and Beating

It has already seen that Aquinas was willing to justify the sacrifice of a part for the sake of the whole, and used the example of an amputation to illustrate the point.[31] Consequently, there can be little doubt that there are situations

27 ST, II-II, q.64.a.3: '… the killing of malefactors is legitimate in so far as it is ordered to the well-being of the whole community. And so this right belongs only to those who are charged with the care of the whole community, just as it is the doctor who has been entrusted with the health of the whole body who may amputate a gangrenous limb'.

28 ST, II-II, q.64.a.3. That an innocent life can never be expended in this way is made abundantly clear in ST, II-II, q.64.a.6.

29 ST, II-II, q.64.a.3.

30 ST, II-II, q.73.a.3.

31 ST, II-II, q.64.a.2.

in which he would allow for interference with a person's body. The first scenario he explores involves the body as a threat to itself. As with homicide, a distinction is drawn between each part and the whole they make up.[32] Here the whole is the *corpus*, while the parts are *membra*. Where the part is healthy and capable of fulfilling its purpose, it is inviolable.[33] It can only be excised when it poses a threat to the whole.

Far more interesting for present purposes is Aquinas' second line of inquiry: can *membra* be violated in the interests of anything other than the *corpus*? Again, the correspondence of society:citizen and *corpus:membrum* is central to Aquinas' reasoning:

> Sed quia ipse totus homo ordinatur ut ad finem ad totam communitatem cuius est pars, ut supra dictum est; potest contingere quod abscisio membri, etsi vergat in detrimentum totius corporis, ordinatur tamen ad bonum communitatis, inquantum alicui infertur in poenam ad cohibitionem peccatorum.[34]

As with homicide, the power to dismember is vested in those with authority over society. Lesser forms of injury are dealt with more flexibly. The mere infliction of pain, as by striking or beating, is lawful when performed within a power relationship (*dicio*, having *potestas*).[35] Such infliction must still be performed with a permissible intention, such as a desire to correct bad habits.[36] The sinfulness of violence may also be escalated according to the victim. It is particularly grievous to assault a political leader, as it effectively harms all of society.[37] Widows and orphans also receive particular protection, '*quia non habent relevantem*'.[38] As has already been seen, wounds to the body were remedied through the *recompensatio*, an idea left undefined and unexplained. Nevertheless, they were capable of remediation.

32 ST, II-II, q.65.a.1.

33 ST, II-II, q.65.a.1.

34 ST, II-II, q.65.a.1: 'At the same time the whole man himself is ordered to the whole community of which he is a part as to his end, as we saw above, and this is why, even though his body may thereby suffer some loss, the community as a whole may benefit from the removal in so far as the penalty is inflicted on him to restrain him from sinning'.

35 ST, II-II, q.65.a.2.

36 ST, II-II, q.65.a.2.ad.1.

37 ST, II-II, q.65.a.4.

38 ST, II-II, q.65.a.4.ad.2.

Theft and Robbery

As the only wrongs to property on Aquinas' list of sins, theft and robbery are of surprisingly little relevance to the later formulations of delict within Thomism. As such they merit only a brief overview. Both theft and robbery consist in the asportation of another's property against his will.[39] The language used in relation to both sins is the verb *accipere*, meaning 'to receive'. This implies a level of passivity that is not borne out by the substance of Aquinas' discussion of *furtum* and *rapina*. The two are differentiated in the way in which the criterion of involuntariness on the part of the property's owner is manifested. In cases of theft, the owner does not consent to the asportation because he is unaware of it. Theft is the secret asportation of another's property.[40] Robbery attacks the will of the owner directly and overwhelms it through violence in order to deprive him of his property.[41] To speak of receiving property violently seems to be a nonsense, and so both sins are typically translated as involving the active deprivation of property. The defining elements of each sin—stealth and violence—are described by Aquinas as two similar but distinct manifestations of involuntariness.[42] They are sufficiently different to give each sin its own brand of wrongfulness. As discussed above, property is restricted only to things. Aquinas makes it clear that neither kidnapping nor dismemberment can properly be construed as theft.[43]

Aquinas' views of property as a means to the furtherance of human fulfilment causes difficulties in describing the 'defences' to the sins of theft and robbery. If property is not something to be hoarded, but rather something to further a human life, can theft be justified by extreme circumstances? Aquinas addresses this problem directly. It is true that the precept that inferior things (i.e. property) can be repurposed according to exigency under natural law, and that natural law overrides any positive rule of human law.[44] Where a person has more than they need, natural law dictates that their surplus be expended on behalf of the needy. Aquinas ameliorates this insecurity by claiming that given the sheer number of people who are in a state of need, we ought to respect the individual stewardship of property produced by distributive justice. It is only when there is a manifest and urgent need ('*urgens et evidens necessitas*'), some imminent danger, that a person can take property belonging to another

39 ST, II-II, q.66.a.3, 4.

40 ST, II-II, q.66.a.3.

41 ST, II-II, q.66.a.4.

42 ST, II-II, q.66.a.4.

43 ST, II-II, q.66.a.3.

44 ST, II-II, q.66.a.7.

without it constituting a sin.[45] This expressly does not include hunger.[46] However, the use of violence is itself inherently sinful and can only be justified through sanctioned authority in the public interest.[47] As such necessity can only bar the sinfulness of theft, and not robbery.

Wrongs Committed During a Trial

Aquinas deals with a long list of verbal wrongs that can arise in the course of a trial. These were mostly ignored by the later Thomists, and so will only be discussed briefly in outline so as to see the full shape of wrongdoing laid down in the *Summa Theologiae*. Aquinas groups the individual wrongs according to the role played within the trial by their actor. There are five such roles: judge, accuser, defendant, witness and the defendant's representative or lawyer. The rules expounded within these five *quaestiones* are primarily procedural norms, with questions of sinfulness arising only rarely.

A judge cannot exercise jurisdiction over anyone other than those subject to the authority delegated to him.[48] He cannot judge a man unless an accusation is brought against him.[49] Once an accusation has been made, he can only reach his decision on the basis of evidence presented to him in his capacity as a judge, and not knowledge gained as a private citizen.[50] And, upon finding a defendant guilty, he must impose a sentence in accordance with the relevant laws rather than his own feelings.[51] Aquinas does not describe breaches of these norms as sins. Rather a failure to comply

45 ST, II-II, q.66.a.7. The logic behind this claim is confusing. Theft is the secret asportation of another's property. This is always a sin, according to ST, II-II, q.66.a.5. For it not to be a sin, Aquinas must make the claim that it is not actually theft. So which element of theft is it that is not proven? Property belonging to another has been taken by stealth. We cannot deny that it is property, nor that it has been taken. Presumably it is the criterion of stealth, itself a manifestation of involuntariness, that can be circumvented by assuming (whether in the spirit of Christian ethics or else fictitiously) that no man would deny another use of his property in the face of such danger.

46 ST, II-II, q.66.a.7.ad.1, claiming hunger is not an urgent need.

47 ST, II-II, q.66.a.8.

48 ST, II-II, q.67.a.1.

49 ST, II-II, q.67.a.3.

50 ST, II-II, q.67.a.2.

51 ST, II-II, q.67.a.4. Concessions can be made when the judge is exercising an undelegated authority (i.e. where the sovereign is acting as a judge), but an ordinary judge cannot remit a sentence according to personal sympathy because he lacks the authority to do so. He ought to mechanically apply the law according to the authority that has been delegated to him.

colours the judgment itself as unjust, but does not stain the conscience of the judge.

A person who suffers a wrong must make a formal accusation where the wrong is one that harms society at large.[52] Aquinas draws a distinction between denunciation, which seeks to show the wrongdoer the error of his ways, and accusation, which aims to punishment meted out by the state. Under all circumstances the wronged party must denounce the wrongdoer, so as to set him on the right path. But where there is a societal interest in the wrong, the wronged party must bring a formal accusation as well. Thereafter Aquinas considers the form of the accusation. Must it be made in writing?[53] Should an accuser be punished for failing to prove his case?[54] Again, this is far removed from questions of sinfulness, lest it be deemed a sin to fail to submit the proper paperwork when bringing a case.

A witness is bound to give evidence when so commanded by a person whose authority he is bound to obey.[55] That authority ought first to determine whether the evidence is necessary or not. And even if there is no official command for a witness to give evidence, he is naturally bound to do so where the evidence will spare a man from an unjust penalty or unjust harm to his reputation.[56] To give false evidence is a sin on three fronts.[57] Firstly, it breaches an oath to tell the truth that all witnesses make in court, and so constitutes perjury. Secondly, it is directly contrary to the demands of justice, and so is the sin of injustice. Thirdly, as a falsehood false evidence can be a sin in the same way as any other lie. As such, although false evidence can be sinful in a variety of ways, once again there is nothing unique about the sin within this specific context.

It goes without saying that a defendant must tell the truth.[58] This is no different from any other context in which a person is under a duty to tell the truth. A breach of this duty is a sin, but it is not a sin unique to this context. This duty to tell the truth justifies the defendant in ruining the reputation of another (e.g. a co-conspirator).[59] His representative does not sin in defending an unjust cause, unless he knows that it is unjust.[60] And there is nothing sinful

52 ST, II-II, q.68.a.1.
53 ST, II-II, q.68.a.2.
54 ST, II-II, q.68.a.4.
55 ST, II-II, q.70.a.1.
56 ST, II-II, q.70.a.1.
57 ST, II-II, q.70.a.4.
58 ST, II-II, q.69.a.1.
59 ST, II-II, q.69.a.2.
60 ST, II-II, q.71.a.3.

about charging for a service rendered unless one is naturally compelled to render that service.[61] The services of an advocate are not naturally available and lawyers can bill their clients with impunity, although the demands of mercy mean that they ought to adapt their terms to the capabilities of their clients.[62]

In relation to every other sin discussed in this chapter, Aquinas needs to address the degree of sinfulness, to show whether the sin under examination is mortal or venial. Such questions do not arise in the five *quaestiones* dealing with verbal wrongs that arise in the course of a trial. There are but two sins discussed—a witness who gives false evidence, and a defendant who lies—but neither of these is a unique sin. Rather, they are permutations of broader prohibitions against lying and breaking oaths. It is perhaps the absence of sinfulness that explains why later Thomists found little of interest in this section. Aquinas was seeking to lay down something akin to a natural law of procedure, rather than a further category of substantive wrongs.

Contumelia, detractio *and Other Injurious Words*

Contumelia is a sin against *honor*. Like *fama*, the interest harmed by the sin of *detractio*, this was an extremely important interest within the Thomist hierarchy. The pair of personality interests rank below the *bona* of the soul and the body, but above all other external *res*.[63] This is hardly surprising if a good name really is worth more than gold and silver.[64] *Honor* as used by Aquinas stems from Aristotle's *Nicomachean Ethics*, where it occupies an extremely important position as one of the prime indicators of a virtuous lifestyle.[65] Book IV of the *Nicomachean Ethics* is filled with references to honour as the 'prize of virtue' and 'the greatest of external goods'.[66] It is considered as one of the contenders for the ultimate good achievable by humans, being rejected for *eudaimonia* (human flourishing) only because it relies on the opinions of others, and in valuing the opinions of others above self-opinions, one places their lifestyles above one's own.[67] Aristotle's conception of *honor* is not solely concerned with moral righteousness. Life's lotteries in looks, lineage, power and wealth all have their role to play, primarily as shortcuts to honour which might then be undone by moral turpitude. For example, a nobleman is by virtue of his

---

61 ST, II-II, q.71.a.4.
62 ST, II-II, q.71.a.4.
63 ST, II-II, q.73.a.3.
64 Proverbs 22:1.
65 Aristotle, *Nicomachean Ethics*, 4.3.
66 Ibid., 4.3.
67 Ibid., 1.5.

position in society deserving of honour, but this might be undone by crassness, pride or other vices associated with honour. When the term is used by Aquinas he intends to narrow its scope to the purely virtuous core of the Aristotelian conception.[68]

Following Romans 1:30 *contumelia* can be committed by words or deeds. Deeds are injurious *per se*, meaning that there are no requirements for sinfulness beyond voluntarily performing the action. Words, however, are ambiguous. To determine sinfulness one needs to look beyond the words themselves at the significance attached to them by the speaker.[69]

> Cum igitur convicium, seu contumelia, de sui ratione importet quandam dehonorationem, si intentio proferentis ad hoc feratur ut aliquis per verba quae profert honorem alterius auferat, hoc proprie et per se est dicere convicium vel contumeliam ... Si vero aliquis verbum convicii vel contumeliae alteri dixerit, non tamen animo dehonorandi, sed forte propter correctionem vel propter aliquid huiusmodi, non dicit convicium vel contumeliam formaliter et per se, sed per accidens et materialiter, inquantum scilicet dicit id quod potest esse convicium, vel contumelia.[70]

Detractio is a sin against *fama*. The origins of Aquinas' use of *fama* are less easy to discern than his use of *honor*. It is used twice in the title of the Digest on *iniuria*. Firstly, in relation to *iniuria* committed against a deceased person.[71] Such insults are described as harming the *fama* of the heir. Secondly, where the disrespect is couched in writing it also harms the subject's *fama*.[72] Though both of these situations could fall within Aquinas' use of the word, they are far too narrow to be seen as his sole source. Whenever the term *fama* is defined in a scholastic text reference is consistently made to Proverbs 22:1: '*melius est*

68 ST, II-II, q.103.a.1, a.1.ad.1.

69 ST, II-II, q.72.a.2.

70 ST, II-II, q.72.a.2: 'Since the notion of insult or defamation implies a certain taking away of a person's character, words uttered with the intention of taking away another's character amount to insult or defamation in the strict sense ... If, on the other hand, somebody has spoken to another in an insulting or defamatory manner, though without intending to take away his character, but, say, to admonish him or the like, he is saying something which amounts to insult or defamation not in a formal and strict sense, but only in an accidental sense and from the point of view of content, for he does say something that could amount to insult or defamation'.

71 D.47.10.1.4.

72 D.47.10.15.29.

nomen bonum quam divitiae multae, super argentum et aurum gratia bona'.[73] It is this idea of a person's good name that is at the heart of *fama*—it is a composite of opinions one can hold about another made up of matters unrelated or tangentially related to virtue. Thus attributes such as nobility which would fall under *honor* in Aristotle become matters of *fama* in scholastic texts. Aquinas was not the first to use *fama* in this sense. Albertus Magnus' *Summa Theologiae*, written just years before Aquinas' version, uses the term in a similar sense.[74]

Detractio differs from *contumelia* in its need for secrecy. Aquinas draws a parallel with theft and robbery.[75] Robbery is a direct and brazen affront, whereas theft is a sneaky deception. To insult a man to his face shows complete contempt for his *honor*. To do it behind his back at least implies a degree of respect. This requirement appears to be an innovation of Aquinas'—Albertus Magnus defined *detractio* simply as *alienae famae denigratio*.[76] It is only in the interest harmed and the need for secrecy that *contumelia* and *detractio* differ. Its sinfulness when constituted in words is determined in the same way, though it is implied that *detractio* committed without a positive intent to harm *fama* is likely to be sinless instead of venially sinful.[77] In both sins, where the risk of harm is particularly great, the threshold for intention appears to be lowered.[78] Presumably this is because a greater risk of harm implies a more offensive statement, and the greater the level of offense the lower the chance of misinterpretation.

Sussurratio (whisperings or gossip) is identical to *detractio* in all respects but one: it targets not *fama* but *amicitia* (friendship).[79] Later scholastic authors simply merged this with other forms of injurious words, as *amicitia* was not legalised in the same manner as *honor* and *fama*,[80] or else they dropped it altogether. As such, there is nothing more of interest to say about the sin. The same is true of *derisio* (mockery), which is only considered a distinct form of wrong because it aims not at *honor*, *fama* or *amicitia*, but at shame.[81] *Maledictio* (curses), the final form of injurious words, has two meanings. The first

73 E.g. ST, II-II, q.73.a.3.

74 Albertus Magnus, *Summa Theologiae*, II, q.117.m.2.a.1.

75 ST, II-II, q.73.a.1.

76 Albertus Magnus, *Summa Theologiae*, II, q.117.m.2.a.1.

77 ST, II-II, q.73.a.2.

78 ST, II-II, q.72.a.2, q.73.a.2.

79 ST, II-II, q.74.a.1.

80 E.g. Soto, *De Iustitia et Iure*, 5.11.

81 ST, II-II, q.75.a.1. No noun is used, only the verb '*erebusco*'. Given the etymological link with reddening, shame seems to be the most appropriate translation, despite the confusion this might cause with the overwhelmingly Roman concept of *pudor*.

simply encompasses the first four forms, and the second is of purely theological relevance.[82]

Fraudulentia *and* usura

The final two *quaestiones* within the first tract of Aquinas' treatment of justice consider sins that arise within voluntary transactions. This is the closest Aquinas comes to considering questions of contractual doctrine. There are two such sins. The first arises within the contract of sale. Referred to as fraud (*fraudulentia*), this sin can arise in a number of ways. It is a sin to use deceit to sell a thing for more than it is worth, though a buyer may knowingly pay over the odds without turning the seller into a sinner.[83] It is similarly sinful to knowingly sell defective goods.[84] From these we can extract a straightforward proposition: it is a sin to deceitfully make a gain by causing another loss in a contractual context. From this bedrock an entire Thomist theory of contract was generated, but that is beyond the scope of this book.[85]

The second sin of this kind arises within monetary loans: usury. It is inherently unjust to sell something that does not exist, and so to charge interest for money lent.[86] The logic is compelling: each man is accorded his due according to distributive justice. A loan for £100 creates an imbalance of £100, but the imbalance can readily be corrected by returning £100. To return £110 creates a further imbalance of £10 that skews the just distribution of assets. The charging of interest by its very nature distorts justice. It is equally sinful to ask for a favour in lieu of interest, if said favour can be measured in monetary terms.[87] This relies on a statement by Aristotle that anything that can be measured in money ought to be thought of as money.[88] Usury by its very nature is incompatible with the Thomist approach to justice, and so is a sin in all circumstances.

Sexual Wrongdoing

The list of sins considered under the aegis of justice excludes anything sexual. The closest thing to a list of sexual offences in the *Summa Theologiae* is to be

82 ST, II-II, q.76.

83 ST, II-II, q.77.a.1.

84 ST, II-II, q.77.a.2.

85 Gordley, *The Philosophical Origins of Modern Contract Doctrine*; Decock, *Theologians and Contract Law*.

86 ST, II-II, q.78.a.1.

87 ST, II-II, q.78.a.2.

88 Aristotle, *Nicomachean Ethics*, 4.1.

found under the virtue of temperance, in Aquinas' discussion of the parts of the sin of lust (*luxuria*).[89] Lust is the pursuit of sexual pleasure that is at odds with right reason.[90] Such acts take two forms: sex that has an object other than its natural end (i.e. procreation), or where the relationship itself is illicit (e.g. incest).[91] From this general definition, Aquinas turns to a number of specific instances of sinful sexual behaviour: fornication, seduction (*stuprum*), rape (*raptus*), adultery, nocturnal pollution, incest, sacrilege and 'the unnatural sins' (*vitia contra naturam*). These are organised into a hierarchy of severity according to the degree of their deviation from natural order. Consequently, the unnatural sins are the most grievous sin of the bunch, followed by incest.[92] The remaining sins are largely interchangeable in severity according to the presence of aggravating factors, such as violence or assaulting someone subject to another's authority (as in adultery).

Two of these sins, nocturnal pollution and sacrilege, were given no further thought by later Thomists, and so do not merit discussion here. Fornication, or impermissible intercourse, is the most basic of the lust-based sins, of which seduction (*stuprum*) and *raptus* are variants.[93] Seduction is the '*illicita virginum defloratio sub cura parentum existentium*'.[94] Aquinas emphasises the need for the victim to still be under the care of her parents, as it is this that differentiates it from other sins. Seduction is a sin both against the daughter (for obvious reasons) and the father, who is supposedly turned into a laughing stock by the offence.[95] If the daughter is not under her parents' care, the offence is more likely to be *raptus* instead of *stuprum*.[96] *Raptus* is the forceful violation of a virgin.[97] Force should be interpreted broadly, and need not be against the virgin. The example given is where a man takes a virgin away from her father's house. This would constitute both *stuprum* and *raptus*, even if the virgin consented.[98]

Adultery is defined by a suspect etymology: '*ad alienum torum*'.[99] This is sinful on multiple fronts: it either goes agains the natural end of sex, or else

89 ST, II-II, q.154.
90 ST, II-II, q.154.a.1.
91 ST, II-II, q.154.a.1.
92 ST, II-II, q.154.a.12.
93 ST, II-II, q.154.a.2.
94 ST, II-II, q.154.a.6.
95 Relying on Sirach, 42:11.
96 ST, II-II, q.154.a.7.
97 ST, II-II, q.154.a.7.
98 ST, II-II, q.154.a.7.
99 ST, II-II, q.154.a.8.

subjects any progeny to the wrong of being raised outside of marriage. It deprives any existing children of the adulterous parties of their parents, and corrupts the adulteress. For a relationship to be adulterous at least one of the parties must be married; sex outside of marriage is merely fornication.[100] Incest is also based on the violation of a relationship, consanguinity.[101] The unnatural sin is a composite of behaviours that Aquinas saw as contrary to the essence of human nature. It is little more than a catch all for sexual behaviour at odds with Aquinas' characterisation of human and divine order. There are four basic categories:

> Uno quidem modo, si absque omni concubitu, causa delectationis venereae, pollutio procuretur, quod pertinet ad peccatum immunditiae, quam quidam mollitiem vocant. Alio modo, si fiat per concubitum ad rem non eiusdem speciei, quod vocatur bestialitas. Tertio modo, si fiat per concubitum ad non debitum sexum, puta masculi ad masculum vel feminae ad feminam ... Quarto, si non servetur naturalis modus concumbendi, aut quantum ad instrumentum non debitum; aut quantum ad alios monstruosos et bestiales concumbendi modos.[102]

In plain English these can be rendered as masturbation, bestiality, homosexuality, and non-vaginal intercourse. As mentioned earlier, because of their deviation from divine order these four categories of wrong are the most serious sins associated with lust. The underlying theological rationale—that as the natural end of sex is procreation rape comes closer than masturbation—is absurd when transformed into a legal rule. The distance between the sexual offences and the sins against justice in the *Summa Theologiae* accurately reflects the chasm between theological and legal ideas on sexual impropriety.

---

100 ST, II-II, q.154.a.8.

101 ST, II-II, q.154.a.9.

102 ST, II-II, q.154.a.11: 'First, through being contrary to right reason, and this is common to all lustful vices; secondly, because, in addition, it is contrary to the natural order of the venereal act as becoming to the human race: and this is called "the unnatural vice." This may happen in several ways. First, by procuring pollution, without any copulation, for the sake of venereal pleasure: this pertains to the sin of "uncleanness" which some call "effeminacy." Secondly, by copulation with a thing of undue species, and this is called "bestiality." Thirdly, by copulation with an undue sex, male with male, or female with female ... Fourthly, by not observing the natural manner of copulation, either as to undue means, or as to other monstrous and bestial manners of copulation'.

Voluntariness

What would become the Thomist theory of delict is grounded in a list of individual sins (*peccatae*). As has just been seen, each of these sins is dealt with at length in the *Summa Theologiae*, but within each consideration there is barely a single *quaestio* that raises the question of *mens rea*. Each sin is described in purely external terms, focusing on the physical manifestation of sinfulness. Murder is the taking of another human's life without just authority. Defamation is the blackening of another's reputation. This might lead to speculation that Aquinas posited a strict liability theory of wrongdoing, justified by focusing on the loss suffered by the victim over the defendant's state of mind.

This belief seems to be supported by the unfamiliar treatment of words which, when used by a lawyer, would lead to fault considerations. *Culpa* is one of the two descriptors of the ways in which evil (*malum*) affects voluntary behaviour. Evil is straightforwardly the deprivation of what is good.[103] This is a far broader concept than sinfulness.[104] A sin is a particular type of evil performed with a particular goal in mind: it is the coalescence of evil and voluntariness. Goodness has two aspects, form and operation, that are mirrored in evil. Thus sight is a formal good, and blindness is its corresponding formal evil.[105] Operational good is simply doing good deeds (e.g. charitable behaviour), and operational evil is a failure to do what is good.[106] Formal evils are known as *poenae*, while operational evils are *culpae*. In plain English, we might think of *culpa* as 'doing something wrong'. *Culpa* and *poena* are deviations from natural order, but they are not themselves judgemental terms. Describing a blind man as afflicted by evil is not to say that he is himself evil, but that he has been deprived

---

103 ST, I, q.48.a.1: '*unum oppositorum cognoscitur per alterum, sicut per lucem tenebra. Unde et quid sit malum, oportet ex ratione boni accipere. Diximus autem supra quod bonum est omne id quod est appetibile, et sic, cum omnis natura appetat suum esse et suam perfectionem, necesse est dicere quod esse et perfectio cuiuscumque naturae rationem habeat bonitatis. Unde non potest esse quod malum significet quoddam esse, aut quandam formam seu naturam. Relinquitur ergo quod nomine mali significetur quaedam absentia boni*' ('One opposite is known through the other, as darkness is known through light. Hence also what evil is must be known from the nature of good. Now, we have said above that good is everything appetible; and thus, since every nature desires its own being and its own perfection, it must be said also that the being and the perfection of any nature is good. Hence it cannot be that evil signifies being, or any form or nature. Therefore it must be that by the name of evil is signified the absence of good').

104 ST, I-II, q.21.a.1.

105 ST, I, q.48.a.5.

106 ST, I, q.48.a.6.

of something good. *Culpa* comes closer to a term of moral censure than *poena* insofar as it describes behaviour instead of wholeness, but it does not carry the inescapable connotations of fault attached to *culpa* in Roman law without an additional ingredient through which sinfulness is born: voluntariness.

Voluntariness determines at the very outset of an inquiry whether an action is actually one which can have certain moral (and, insofar as we are concerned with natural law, legal) consequences.[107] Actions can be attributed to causes either within or outside the actor.[108] A cause is only truly internal when there is a clear end or purpose for that action, though the performance of an action can be an end in itself. If an act is performed without a specific end in mind, it is attributed not to the actor but to outside influences. The former types of action are labelled 'voluntary', while the latter are 'involuntary'. Furthermore:

> Dicendum est ergo quod iniustum, per se et formaliter loquendo, nullus potest facere nisi volens, nec pati nisi nolens. Per accidens autem et quasi materialiter loquendo, **potest aliquis id quod est de se iniustum vel facere nolens**, sicut cum quis praeter intentionem operatur; vel pati volens, sicut cum quis plus alteri dat sua voluntate quam debeat.[109]

From this it is clear that a person only acts unjustly if he acts voluntarily, which for Aquinas requires knowledge of the injustice that would result from the action in question.[110] The second part of the quotation appears to confuse things, but is simply repeating an earlier passage that establishes that acts can be unjust even if the actor himself does not commit an injustice. Such an outcome would in practice be very common, arising whenever a well-intentioned act causes harm.[111]

The meaning of knowledge is convoluted. In most contexts Aquinas uses the term to signify 'actual' knowledge. His treatment of ignorance and

107 ST, I-II, q.18.a.6: '*actus exteriores habent rationem moralitatis, nisi inquantum sunt voluntarii*' ('Nor have external actions any measure or morality, save in so far as they are voluntary').

108 ST, I-II, q.6.a.1.

109 ST, II-II, q.59.a.3 (emphasis added): 'It is to be declared, then, that in the essential and formal sense of the term no one can do an injustice except willingly or suffer one except unwillingly. Incidentally, however, and materially as it were, someone can do what is of itself an injustice unwillingly, as when he acts unintentionally, or suffer one willingly, as when he chooses to give to another more than he should'.

110 Aquinas is essentially paraphrasing Aristotle at this point: Aristotle, *Nicomachean Ethics*, 3.1.

111 ST, II-II, q.59.a.2.

voluntariness suggests that knowledge can be 'constructive'. He argues that ignorance comes in three strains: concomitant, consequential and antecedent. Concomitant ignorance is where the actor was unaware of what he was doing, but would have acted in the same way if he had possessed the requisite knowledge. Such ignorance renders the act neither voluntary nor involuntary:

> Et talis ignorantia non facit involuntarium, ut philosophus dicit, quia non causat aliquid quod sit repugnans voluntati, sed facit non voluntarium, quia non potest esse actu volitum quod ignoratum est.[112]

It is extremely unclear what concomitant ignorance *is* if it is neither voluntary nor involuntary.[113] Consequential ignorance describes ignorance which is itself voluntary—where the actor expressly kept himself in the dark, whether to provide an excuse for sin (*ignorantia affectata*) or where one ought to know something but refuses knowledge (*ignorantia malae electionis*). Both forms of consequential ignorance are sufficient to make an action voluntary:

> Consequenter autem se habet ignorantia ad voluntatem, inquantum ipsa ignorantia est voluntaria. Et hoc contingit dupliciter, secundum duos modos voluntarii supra positos. Uno modo, quia actus voluntatis fertur in ignorantiam, sicut cum aliquis ignorare vult ut excusationem peccati habeat, vel ut non retrahatur a peccando, secundum illud Iob *XXI*, scientiam viarum tuarum nolumus. Et haec dicitur ignorantia affectata. Alio modo dicitur ignorantia voluntaria eius quod quis potest scire et debet, sic enim non agere et non velle voluntarium dicitur, ut supra dictum est. Hoc igitur modo dicitur ignorantia, sive cum aliquis actu non considerat quod considerare potest et debet, quae est ignorantia malae electionis, vel ex passione vel ex habitu proveniens, sive cum aliquis notitiam quam debet habere, non curat acquirere; et secundum hunc modum, ignorantia universalium iuris, quae quis scire tenetur, voluntaria dicitur, quasi per negligentiam proveniens. Cum autem ipsa ignorantia sit voluntaria aliquo istorum modorum, non potest causare simpliciter involuntarium.[114]

---

112 ST, I-II, q.6.a.8: ('And ignorance of this kind, as the Philosopher states, does not cause involuntariness, since it is not the cause of anything that is repugnant to the will: but it causes "non-voluntariness," since that which is unknown cannot be actually willed').

113 The reference to Aristotle suggest consonance with his reluctant conclusion that such acts are voluntary.

114 ST, I-II, q.6.a.8: 'Ignorance is "consequent" to the act of the will, in so far as ignorance itself is voluntary: and this happens in two ways, in accordance with the two aforesaid

Antecedent ignorance is the absence of knowledge which would have caused the actor to act otherwise, but which he was not expected to know or learn. Such ignorance is straightforwardly involuntary. Drawing these strands together, an act is only voluntary if it is performed with positive malicious intent or out of ignorance that ought not to have existed. Voluntariness needed to be able to deal with every sin, and so its boundaries could prove elastic. This is emphasised in a highly entertaining discussion of the sinfulness of 'nocturnal pollution'.[115] Though the discharge itself is involuntary, Aquinas felt that it could still be sinful if the '*humor seminalis superabundat in corpore*' because of sinful conduct such as gluttony, or if prior sinfulness invited the devil to encourage '*phantasmata*'.[116] Though absurd to modern sensibilities, Aquinas' treatment here does provide a valuable insight into how voluntariness works. From his analysis of homicide it seems that exposing yourself by adopting a position likely to result in sin can constructively provide volition.[117] However, this passage shows just how broadly that can be interpreted, with even past sins providing a basis for the imputation of blameworthiness to an activity which by any other metric must be deemed involuntary.

Voluntariness and *Restitutio*

As in Aristotle, Aquinas' theory of delict is silent on a matter of fundamental importance: what is the relationship between responsibility and justice, voluntariness and *restitutio*? This issue is made all the more complicated by the addition of a further consideration: sinfulness. Voluntariness is an element of

modes of voluntary. First, because the act of the will is brought to bear on the ignorance: as when a man wishes not to know, that he may have an excuse for sin, or that he may not be withheld from sin; according to Job 21:14: "We desire not the knowledge of Thy ways." And this is called "affected ignorance." Secondly, ignorance is said to be voluntary, when it regards that which one can and ought to know: for in this sense "not to act" and "not to will" are said to be voluntary, as stated above. And ignorance of this kind happens, either when one does not actually consider what one can and ought to consider; this is called "ignorance of evil choice," and arises from some passion or habit: or when one does not take the trouble to acquire the knowledge which one ought to have; in which sense, ignorance of the general principles of law, which one to know, is voluntary, as being due to negligence. Accordingly, if in either of these ways, ignorance is voluntary, it cannot cause involuntariness simply'.

115 ST, II-II, q.154.a.5.

116 ST, II-II, q.154.a.5.

117 ST, II-II, q.64.a.8.

every sin, and so is a necessary precondition for responsibility for murder, theft and every other individual sin examined in this chapter. The stain of sin can only be removed, and salvation achieved, through *restitutio*.[118] So as long as we remain concerned with sinfulness, there is a clear link between voluntariness and *restitutio*.

Can *restitutio* operate in the absence of sinfulness, or is it by its very nature a response to sin? These questions have tended to be answered in the same legalistic manner with which they were resolved in relation to Aristotle: that the mechanical nature of commutative justice trumps its ethical context. Nevertheless, Aquinas provides a sufficient basis for showing that this understanding of voluntariness and *restitutio* is only a half-truth. In fact, it is important to consider the relationship between the different types of *restitutio* and voluntariness individually. So long as the focus is *restitutio* in relation to property and its displacement, there is no need to resort to questions of voluntariness. But in relation to *restitutio ratione acceptionis*, these considerations are unavoidable as an aspect of Aquinas' theory of action.

Restitutio, as the tool of commutative justice, responds to inequalities.[119] The principal form of *restitutio* is *ratione rei*. This is clear both from the definition of *restitutio*, which deals with restoring a person to ownership or possession of their property, and the scenarios used to illustrate this: loaned and deposited property, theft and robbery.[120] All concern property. Within *restitutio ratione rei* we need to be able to distinguish between two scenarios: where I make a gain, and where I cause a loss. The two will often coincide, but not always in a proportionate fashion.

Where I make a gain is straightforward: I must return so much of my gain as is required to restore equality.[121] Where I innocently come by £n of your money, and invest it so as to end up with £2n, commutative justice only requires me to restore £n. The profit is mine to keep, unless I obtained it through an injustice (or, put another way, a sin).[122] In such cases (e.g. theft), the profit can be stripped away through a *poena*, but this has nothing to do with *restitutio*.[123] The *poena* will often go beyond the demands of mere equality, but unlike *restitutio*

118 ST, II-II, q.62.a.2.

119 ST, II-II, q.62.a.1.

120 ST, II-II, q.62.a.1.

121 ST, II-II, q.62.a.3.

122 ST, II-II, q.62.a.3: voluntarily causing a state of *iniustitia* (an imbalance of assets or deviation from distributive justice) is clearly a sin: ST, II-II, q.59.a.1.

123 ST, II-II, q.62.a.3.ad.1.

this is a demand that can only be made through a judicial sentence, a matter for positive rather than natural law.[124]

Within this context there is no need to think in terms of sinfulness or voluntariness. If I have your property, there is no need for any justification for its return other than the mere fact that it belongs to you and not me. Suppose a magpie swipes your shiny jewellery, flies off with it, and later drops it into my lap. There needs to be no reason for me to return your property other than the fact that I have what is yours. We do not need to question how I came by the property, or whether I caused your loss or am otherwise responsible for it, so long as it remains in my possession.

Where I cause a loss, I am bound to make *restitutio* according to the degree of that loss.[125] A distinction is drawn between actual loss and loss of a chance.[126] The meaning of actual loss is obvious. It means to deprive a person of something they actually have. This sort of loss needs to be restored in kind. Loss of a chance means preventing a person from acquiring something they might have acquired. This loss of potential property is to be restored according to its condition, meaning that the proportion of the full value that needs to be paid will correspond to how close the potentiality was to being realised.

Between these two notions of gain and loss, it is clear that it is the loss that determines the measure of *restitutio* required. This is made clear by Aquinas' citation of a passage of the *Nicomachean Ethics* in which Aristotle discusses the meaning of 'gain' and 'loss', only the latter of which is referenced by Aquinas.[127] It can also be seen in those scenarios where the gain and loss are unequal. As has already been seen, where the gain is more significant than the loss, a portion of the gains might be retained provided they were made without sinfulness. Implicit in his approach, though not expressly stated by Aquinas, is that where the loss is greater than the gain, the defendant is expected to go out of pocket in order to restore the loss.

Difficulties arise where there is no gain at all, where I simply cause you loss, to have less than you ought to have. It is in this context that Aquinas distinguishes between *restitutio* owed on account of possession of another's property (*ratione rei*), and on account of the action by which an imbalance in wealth was caused (*ratione acceptionis*). On the latter, he says:

124 ST, II-II, q.62.a.3.ad.3.

125 ST, II-II, q.62.a.4.

126 ST, II-II, q.62.a.4.

127 ST, II-II, q.62.a.4.

> Sed ipsa acceptio rei alienae potest tripliciter se habere. Quandoque enim est iniuriosa, scilicet contra voluntatem existens eius qui est rei dominus, ut patet in furto et rapina. Et tunc tenetur ad restitutionem non solum ratione rei, sed etiam ratione iniuriosae actionis, etiam si res apud ipsum non remaneat. Sicut enim qui percutit aliquem tenetur recompensare iniuriam passo, quamvis nihil apud ipsum maneat; ita etiam qui furatur vel rapit tenetur ad recompensationem damni illati, etiam si nihil inde habeat; et ulterius pro iniuria illata debet puniri. Alio modo aliquis accipit rem alterius in utilitatem suam absque iniuria, cum voluntate scilicet eius cuius est res, sicut patet in mutuis. Et tunc ille qui accepit tenetur ad restitutionem eius quod accepit non solum ratione rei, sed etiam ratione acceptionis, etiam si rem amiserit, tenetur enim recompensare ei qui gratiam fecit, quod non fiet si per hoc damnum incurrat. Tertio modo aliquis accipit rem alterius absque iniuria non pro sua utilitate, sicut patet in depositis. Et ideo ille qui sic accepit in nullo tenetur ratione acceptionis, quinimmo accipiendo impendit obsequium, tenetur autem ratione rei. Et propter hoc, si ei subtrahatur res absque sua culpa, non tenetur ad restitutionem. Secus autem esset si cum magna sua culpa rem depositam amitteret.[128]

This article deals with three distinct situations, of which the first is the most significant for present purposes. The second and third can be dealt with briefly. Both can be seen as contractual doctrines connected with loss. The second scenario introduces the straightforward rule that where a person has another

128 ST, II-II q.62.a.6: 'Next as to the taking. This may affect the issue in three ways. First, sometimes it is injurious, that is, against the will of the owner, as appears with theft and robbery. Then a man is bound to restitution, not only because of the thing he takes, but also because of this injurious action, even though it is no longer in his possession. For as one who strikes another, though gaining nothing thereby, is bound to compensate the injured person, to, too, one who commits a theft or robbery, though becoming no better off, is bound to compensate for the damage he has done. Furthermore he must be punished for it. Secondly, when a man receives another's property for his own use but without committing an injury, that is, with the consent of the owner, as in a loan. Then the receiver is bound to restore that property, not only because of the thing itself, but also because of the taking of it, even if he has lost it. For he is bound to recompense the one who did him a favour, and this debt would not be met were the latter to suffer loss by his lending. Thirdly, when a man receives another's property without doing him an injury and without profit to himself, as in a deposit. Here an obligation is incurred, not on account of the taking, for a service rather is rendered, but on account of the thing itself. If this be taken from him without a fault on his part, he is not bound to restitution. It would be otherwise were he gravely to blame for losing possession'.

person's property under a voluntary transaction, he will be required to restore that property even if he loses it provided the transaction was in his favour. The third scenario envisages a situation like deposit in which the depositee is actually doing the depositor a favour—there is no gain to be made in receiving the deposit. In this situation, in the absence of a gain, only *restitutio ratione rei* applies by default. In other words, the depositee can only be compelled to return the property so long as it remains in his possession. The only deviation from this is where he commits a '*magna culpa*' in losing the property. In such cases, *restitutio ratione acceptionis* is triggered. This is the first hint of a connection between questions of *mens rea* and voluntariness.[129]

This leaves the first scenario, which covers involuntary transactions such as theft. Here *restitutio* is owed '*ratione iniuriosae actionis*'.[130] Does such an action necessarily entail voluntariness? There are two paths towards an answer. One can either engage directly with the arguments of the *Summa*, or else superimpose the Roman taxonomy of *dolus*, *culpa* and *casus* onto the individual situations discussed in the *seconda secundae* in order to get closer to an answer. Aquinas' own account can give the impression of being fundamentally inconsistent, and so aspects of recent scholarship have favoured the latter approach.[131] This section will seek first to explain the problem using Aquinas' own analysis, before turning to the civilian superimposition.

The language of *iniuria* in the label '*ratione iniuriosae actionis*' is unhelpful, as it arises only rarely in the *Summa Theologiae* and always without definition. It is typically used to describe a sin such as adultery or theft, and there can be no sin without voluntariness.[132] But this link is far from clear, and it may well simply reflect the likely frequent coincidence of wrongfulness and sinfulness. However, its combination with the word 'action' might be significant. Under Aquinas' theory of action, much like Aristotle's, moral consequences are

129 Though one should bear in mind the complicated meaning of *culpa* within the *Summa Theologiae*. It is worth noting that in relation to voluntariness and culpability, Aquinas simply mashes together the ideas of evil, sin and blame in ST, I-II, q.21.a.2: '*Unde relinquitur quod bonum vel malum in solis actibus voluntariis constituit rationem laudis vel culpae; in quibus idem est malum, peccatum et culpa*' ('For an action is said to deserve praise or blame, from its being imputed to the agent: since to praise or to blame means nothing else than to impute to someone the malice or goodness of his action').

130 ST, II-II, q.62.a.6.

131 Chiefly Gordley, *Foundations of Private Law*, 159–284.

132 E.g. ST, II-II, q.61.a.3: '*Sed adulterium et servi seductio sunt proprie iniuriae circa has personas*', wherein *servi seductio* would meet the requirements for theft; ST, II-II, q.61.a.3 also deals with violence and defamation as examples of *iniuriae*: '*sicut cum aliquis in ipsam personam hominis iniuriam facit, puta percutiendo vel conviciando*'.

attached only to voluntary actions.[133] Involuntary actions in their purest form, such as spasms, are not to be seen as human actions but rather something primal.[134] Without reflection and consideration as to the purpose of an action, there is no point in embarking on an inquiry into its moral qualities. Ethics, that most distinctly human endeavour, is only to be applied to human actions. Does labelling an action as injurious (*iniuria*) imply moral censure? Certainly for an act to be *iniustum* it must be performed voluntarily.[135]

This suggests that voluntariness is an integral part of *restitutio ratione acceptionis* (or, to give it another name found in the *Summa*, *restitutio ratione iniuriosae actionis*). But it relies on *iniuria* and *iniustum* being synonymous concepts. This is a difficult position to support. *Iniustitia* is a term of art within the *Summa*, a specific sin against justice involving the voluntarily creation of an imbalance of wealth.[136] *Iniuria* holds no such importance. It is an ordinary adjective, without technical significance. Moreover, *iniustum* describes a state of affairs, an inequality between two people, whereas *iniuria* describes an action.[137] It may be that the two are performing the same function within these two contexts: an action is wrongful (*iniuria*) precisely when it causes an injustice (*iniustum*). But it is not at all clear whether this is the sense in which Aquinas intended *iniuria* to be understood.

Aquinas seems to be suggesting a link between *restitutio ratione acceptionis* and voluntariness, but it cannot be shown with certainty. In the wake of this uncertainty, there has been a tendency towards examining the *Summa* through a civilian lens. The scenario is simple: I cause you loss, with no corresponding gain to myself. The question of my liability within the civil law would depend on whether I acted intentionally (*dolus*), blameworthily (*culpa*) or blamelessly (*casus*). With this framework in mind, we can examine the *Summa* for clues as to how these situations would be dealt with, testing the argument discussed above that *restitutio* is only available for voluntarily caused loss. The first situation, where loss is caused intentionally, is trivial. Causing an imbalance in wealth is the sin of *iniustitia*, this sin can only be committed voluntarily, and

133 ST, I-II, q.6.a.5; ST, I-II, q.18.a.6.

134 ST, I-II, q.1.a.1.ad.3.

135 ST, II-II, q.59.a.3: '*Dicendum est ergo quod iniustum, per se et formaliter loquendo, nullus potest facere nisi volens, nec pati nisi nolens*' ('It is to be declared, then, that in the essential and formal sense of the term no one can do an injustice except willingly or suffer one except unwillingly').

136 ST, II-II, q.59.a.1.

137 ST, II-II, q.59.a.1.

the stain of the sin can only be removed through *restitutio*.[138] There is a clear link between voluntariness and *restitutio* in this context.

Blameworthily caused loss is far harder. As seen above, voluntariness uses the language of will and ignorance to decide whether an action ought to have moral consequences. Ignorance will only count as voluntariness where the actor knowingly kept himself in the dark, or where he ought to have known something but refused knowledge.[139] Refusing knowledge is very different to simply lacking it: the foolish man might be *culpa* for not knowing the obvious in Roman law, but he is not necessarily acting voluntarily in Thomist ethics. Within this model, there is relatively little room for blameworthiness, let alone splinter doctrines reliant on a failure to take due care (e.g. *negligentia*, failures of *diligentia*).

Against this, Gordley has put forward two arguments that Aquinas would have allowed compensation for loss caused through fault less than intention.[140] The first relies on a sin against prudence known as *negligentia*:

> According to Aquinas, a person was responsible for negligence [*negligentia*] because it was a voluntary act depriving another person of what belonged to him, and therefore a violation of commutative justice. It was a voluntary act because it was a failure to exercise prudence.[141]

It is certainly true that *negligentia* is a sin against prudence.[142] But Gordley's argument here is mistaken on two fronts. Firstly, it gives *negligentia* a meaning akin to that held by negligence in modern legal lexicons. As used by Aquinas, *negligentia* means a failure to exercise reason. But this failure must still be intentional. For it to be a sin, as Gordley acknowledges, it must be voluntary. But, as has just been seen, an action is only performed voluntarily when it is intentional, or the product of ignorance that ought not to exist, whether because the actor intentionally kept himself in the dark, or knowingly refused knowledge. Secondly, it conflates the dimensions of sinfulness that would arise in the

138 Sin of *iniustitia*: ST, II-II, q.59.a.1; only capable of being performed voluntarily: ST, II-II, q.59.a.3; stain of sin only removable through *restitutio*: ST, II-II, q.62.a.2.

139 ST, I-II, q.6.a.8.

140 Gordley, *Foundations of Private Law*, 196, 201. The language of compensation is extremely unhelpful, as both *restitutio* and *poena* could fulfil this function. Presumably he is referring to *restitutio*, as the precise content of *poena* is to be determined within a given legal system, not imposed by natural law, and so might not entail compensation.

141 Gordley, *Foundations of Private Law*, 196. Presumably 'compensation' refers to *restitutio*.

142 ST, II-II, q.54.a.1.

typical case of modern negligence. If I fail to take due care and cause you loss, I have sinned on up to two fronts. The first is a sin against prudence, *negligentia*, for which I must make *satisfactio*. But *negligentia* is not itself a sin against justice, and so cannot invoke the mechanism of commutative justice, *restitutio*.

The second means by which it can be argued that negligence (or a similar fault standard less than intention) was sufficient for compensation arises in relation to Aquinas' discussion of accidental homicides.[143] In this context, Aquinas claims that the sin of homicide might be proven even where a person does not act intentionally, provided they failed to take due care:

> Hoc autem contingit dupliciter, uno modo, quando dans operam rebus illicitis, quas vitare debebat, homicidium incurrit; alio modo, quando non adhibet debitam sollicitudinem. Et ideo secundum iura, si aliquis det operam rei licitae, debitam diligentiam adhibens, et ex hoc homicidium sequatur, non incurrit homicidii reatum, si vero det operam rei illicitae, vel etiam det operam rei licitae non adhibens diligentiam debitam, non evadit homicidii reatum si ex eius opere mors hominis consequatur.[144]

It is the final passage, in which Aquinas accepts the possibility of lapses in diligence founding responsibility for homicide even where they occur in lawful contexts that provides Gordley with evidence for his claim. Again, arguments founded on this passage ought to be viewed with suspicion. It takes the criteria for establishing a single sin and extends them wholesale. Aquinas is very conservative in his articulation of this possibility, and his comments are contained only to homicide: '*non evadit homicidii reatum si ex eius opere mors hominis consequatur*'. Given the cagey tone of the passage, and the failure to find similar ideas elsewhere, it would be an unwarranted extension of the article to use it to say that negligence (or, more accurately, failures of diligence) were sufficient to establish sinfulness.

In this one scenario dealing with accidental homicide sinfulness could be established using a fault standard less than the ordinary requirements of voluntariness. In recognising this, it should be borne in mind that Aquinas did

143 Gordley, *Foundations of Private Law*, 201.

144 ST, II-II. q.64.a.8: 'This can come about in two ways—when a person engages in nefarious activities which he should not have engaged in, or when he does not take due care. This is why the law lays down that if a man engages in legitimate activities and uses due care, he is not guilty of any homicide that may ensue; if, on the other hand, he engages in illicit activities, or even fails to take due care in some legitimate enterprise, he is guilty of any homicide that may occur'.

not consider life something capable of being restored.[145] The slackening of the fault standard for homicide affects the imposition of *poenae*. This might include compensation, but that is a matter for a given system of positive law to determine. The apparent link between involuntary accidents and the sin of homicide has no bearing on the availability of *restitutio*.

In other situations, the link between *restitutio* and blameworthiness is unsupported by the *Summa*. Consider the following scenario: a thief sells a merchant a watch owned by the victim. The victim would like to recover his watch from the merchant, but it has already been sold to a stranger who has wandered off never to be seen again. *Restitutio ratione rei* is not an option. Should the victim be able to recover the value of the watch from the merchant? Suppose the merchant notices that the watch has the victim's name carved into it, but decides it is easier to pretend he never saw the engraving so that he doesn't have to make inquiries as to the true owner of the watch. This is wilful blindness, a form of ignorance recognised as voluntariness. The merchant has, in a state of wilful blindness, caused a person to have less than he is due under the requirements of justice. This is the sin of *iniustia*, and *restitutio* must be made to cleanse the merchant's soul. What if the merchant was simply operating a business, and the stolen watch simply passed through his store like any other product without raising suspicions of theft? We could make the argument that he *ought* to have checked the watch, or inquired into its origins. Such logic might lead to an accusation that the merchant sinned against prudence by failing to exercise proper reason, but without a sin against justice there can be no invocation of *restitutio*, the tool of commutative justice. There is nothing in the *secunda secundae* that appears to link blameworthiness less than intention to *restitutio ratione acceptionis*. Only voluntary actions that cause loss must be restored.

So long as it is the action and not the consequent state of affairs that dictates the availability of *restitutio*, inquiries into voluntariness are inescapable. And this seems to be precisely the manner in which Aquinas thought of *restitutio ratione acceptionis*, or *restitutio ratione iniuriosae actionis*. This logic appears to feed backwards into Aquinas' discussion of *restitutio ratione rei*. An example given in an earlier passage is the liability of a person who destroys a house belonging to another.[146] He must make good the loss he has caused by paying the value of the house in full. But who is 'he'? So long as we are dealing with *ratione rei* this is obvious—it is the person who has the property now. But once there is

145 Simply because your life is not actually your own: ST, II-II, q.64.a.5.

146 ST, II-II, q.62.a.4.

no gain to counterbalance the loss, we need a means of attributing responsibility. Is it the person who stood closest to the house when it was destroyed? The crowd who stood by and watched? The answer is obvious: it is the person who *caused* the house to be destroyed. But destruction is an action, and for actions to have moral consequences they need to be performed voluntarily. Although Aquinas groups this situation alongside *restitutio ratione rei* scenarios, the focus is on the way in which the loss was caused, making it a matter of *restitutio ratione acceptionis*.

The bifurcation of *restitutio* according to its triggers—on the one hand, the mere fact of holding property, on the other, the performance of an injurious action—necessitates two approaches to the remedy. The view that Aquinas was advocating a model of strict liability responsibility can only be true of *restitutio ratione rei*. To apply it to *restitutio ratione acceptionis* is to divorce Aquinas' account of justice from his broader theory of moral agency. However, the route by which the link between voluntariness and *restitutio ratione acceptionis* is shown is far from straightforward. More importantly, there is no opportunity within the confines of the *secunda secundae* for a commentator to deal with issues of voluntariness. Consequently, regardless of the truth of Aquinas' original position, in the works of the later Thomists that took the *secundae secundae* as a source separate from the rest of the *Summa*, *restitutio* can take the form of a strict liability remedy in all circumstances. Whether this is an appearance, reflecting a belief on the part of the author that the reader would be familiar enough with Aquinas to recognise the central role played by voluntariness, or a legitimate departure from Aquinas, will be explored in a later chapter.

Responsibility and Agency

One final difficulty remains within Aquinas' account of delict. So far as *restitutio ratione acceptionis* is concerned there is a latent concept of causation. When translated into English, the discussion cannot avoid recourse to terms such as 'causing loss'. This is a concept that needs substantiating. How involved in wrongdoing does a defendant have to be before he is bound to make *restitutio*? This is not a question that can be answered from first principles. The principle of equality that underpins *restitutio* means that the net compensation cannot exceed the loss caused, but where there are multiple causative factors how is the obligation to restore divided? And by what principles are causative factors to be identified?

The Thomist idea of causation is extremely inclusive. Besides the actual wrongdoer, individuals who participate in a number of ways can be viewed as causally significant. Aquinas divides such secondary causes into direct and indirect factors:[147]

Direct or indirect?	Genus	Species	Automatically demands *restitutio*?
Direct	Setting the sinner into motion	By command	Yes
		By counsel	No
		By consent	Yes
		By flattery	No
	Assisting the sinner, e.g. by providing shelter		Yes
	Participating in the sin directly		Yes
Indirect	Omitting …	To command or advise against committing a sin	Possibly
		To act so as to prevent the sin	Possibly
		To deprive the sinner of assistance after the fact	Possibly

Restitutio is only demanded where it can be shown that as a matter of fact the causal contribution was actually effective. Certain contributions are always viewed as effective. For a command to be so named, it must be authoritative. Where such an authoritative directive is issued, its issuer takes on responsibility for any wrongs committed in its performance. So too with consent, assistance and participation. Each of these causal factors is treated as identical to 'the' cause; there is no differentiation between principal and accessorial causes. Flattery and counsel may be causally significant, but only when it is actually proven that the sinner listened to the counsellor or flatterer. The only deviation from this rule is the position of indirect causes. Here *restitutio* is demanded automatically if the indirect cause was under a duty to safeguard societal justice. Who such individuals are is not clear, but the mention of a salary for their duties implies Aquinas is restricting his comments to individuals with official responsibility for public order. As the obligation to make *restitutio* demanded nothing more than the restoration of equality, the net liability of the various causes of the injustice was capped at the value of the loss experienced by the wronged party.

147 ST, II-II, q.62.a.7.

A final problem raised by the strictures of Thomist doctrine is the inability of the framework to deal directly with the problem of liability for another, as in vicarious or noxal liability. The theological focus on sinfulness is extremely individualistic. For *restitutio ratione acceptionis* to be owed, it is first necessary to stain the conscience of the defendant by forcing on him the label of sinner. This is a label that can only be removed through *restitutio*.[148] From a legalistic perspective, this provides an excellent rationale for the father of a child who commits a wrong to make *restitutio*: if he does not, he will be blocked from salvation.[149] But Aquinas was a theologian before a lawyer, and to expose the souls of otherwise innocent parties to the threat of damnation for such a practical end was clearly an impossibility. For a lawyer, the consequences of the father being destitute and so unable to pay are unfortunate but transient. For a theologian, until *restitutio* is made and the injustice persists the father, through no wrong of his own other than questionable parenting, is a lost soul. Rather than any automatic doctrine akin to the noxal liability of Roman law, it is instead necessary to treat the father as a cause using the principles discussed above. In particular, it should be relatively straightforward to treat the father as a cause for providing shelter for the wrongdoer, or for failing to properly instruct his son against sinfulness.[150] But this is a different approach to the automatic responsibility recognised in Roman law through noxal liability.

Conclusion

The model of delict found in the *Summa Theologiae* is unlike any that came before it. The general part presents in *restitutio* a remedy that is fundamentally proprietary, and whose primary form, *ratione rei*, would form the basis of the Thomist law of property.[151] It is only in the peculiar twist to its orthodox form found in *restitutio ratione acceptionis* that it becomes something more recognisably delictual. This second limb to the remedy, underdeveloped in the *Summa*, never strays far from its proprietary core, as evidenced by the language of *recompensatio* employed whenever Aquinas considers non-proprietary

148 ST, II-II, q.62.a.2.

149 The language of father and son is used, but the same reasoning would apply to any situation of noxal or vicarious liability.

150 ST, II-II, q.62.a.8. Were it possible to say that a father was always under a duty to instruct his son against sinfulness, then Aquinas would be far closer to having a general principle of noxal liability.

151 Jansen, *Theologie, Philosophie und Jurisprudenz*, 34.

wrongdoing. But it provided the kernel of a delictual regime, a restorative remedy that responded to wrongdoing in the abstract.

Three features of Aquinas' treatment of delict deserve emphasis. Firstly, though the detail of its applications reveal *restitutio ratione acceptionis* to be a proprietary remedy, Aquinas explores the recovery of non-proprietary harm. The language of *recompensatio* is hardly a far cry from *restitutio*, especially when the definition of the latter includes the former.[152] This would provide the gateway for later commentators to consider extending *restitutio* to other forms of wrongdoing. Secondly, the way in which matters of fault are dealt with, though mystifying, is important. Two possibilities exist. If the argument presented above is correct, Aquinas was pushing for a single fault standard applicable across the full range of injurious actions. If it is wrong, he was instead arguing for a strict liability model of delict. Both outcomes are remarkable. Thirdly, the structure adopted by Aquinas would prove highly influential. This was certainly not adopted for any other reason than the scholastic progression from the general to the specific, but it results in a model of delict where isolated wrongs are united through a common remedy and a common fault standard, however incomplete they might be at this stage.

152 ST, II-II, q.62.a.1: '*Et ita in restitutione attenditur aequalitas iustitiae secundum recompensationem rei ad rem, quae pertinet ad iustitiam commutativam*' ('Consequently we mark there the equality of balance of justice according to the recompense of thing for thing, which is the concern of commutative justice').

CHAPTER 8

The Mechanics of *Restitutio*

To carve a law of delict out of Aquinas' account of justice it was first necessary to refocus *restitutio*. Aquinas' own formulation of the remedy principally played a proprietary function, with the consideration of individual wrongs arising out of discussions of sinfulness. The earlier Thomists of the sixteenth century maintained the focus of their source material, but increasingly in the last years of the sixteenth century *restitutio ratione acceptionis* was emphasised and *restitutio ratione rei* elided. By the early seventeenth century Lessius was formulating *restitutio* almost entirely in terms of wrongdoing, its proprietary dimension having been largely marginalised. Parallel to this was an increasing emphasis on viewing *restitutio* as a compensatory remedy, a development readily observable in the remediation of wrongs affecting non-proprietary interests.

Wrongdoing as the Primary Source of Inequality

Restitutio is a proprietary concept that can be triggered by wrongdoing. Does this make it a part of the law of property or the law of obligations? Such taxonomical questions are irrelevant so long as one is looking at the concept through the virtue of justice. Categorisation only becomes problematic when one attempts to reinterpret Aquinas' views on natural law and justice through a legal lens. This is precisely the undertaking we find in the works of several Thomist authors in the late sixteenth century. The majority of their writings on justice and law typically take one of two forms: a gloss on the *Summa Theologiae*, *quaestio* by *quaestio*, or a restructured version of the *Summa* that slots Thomist ideas into a legal skeleton (typically called *De Iustitia et Iure*). It is only in the latter type of work that the author is forced to categorise theological ideas under legal headings, though the former works often provide detailed analysis of how theological concepts ought to be interpreted so as to be compatible with the law.

A pioneer of the latter approach is Domingo de Soto. In his *De Iustitia et Iure*, *restitutio* is discussed in the final pair of *quaestiones* in book four. They are thus located in the following position:

 | DOI 10.1163/9789004344372_009

Book 4	Q.1	*De dominio in genere*
	Q.2	*De rebus quarum homo est dominus*
	Q.3	*De rerum divisione*
	Q.4	*De peculiari quorundam dominio*
	Q.5	*De translatione dominiorum*
	Q.6	*De restitutionis substantia* (ad ST, II-II, q.62)
	Q.7	*De circumstantiis restitutionis* (ad ST, II-II, q.62.a.5)
Book 5	Q.1	*De homicidio* (ad ST, II-II, q.64)
	Q.2	*De mutilatione membrorum* (ad ST, II-II, q.65)
	Q.3	*De furto*
	Q.4	*De iniustitia iudicis*
	Q.5	*De iniustitia accusatoris* (ad ST, II-II, q.68)
	Q.6	*De iniustitia rei*
	Q.7	*De iniustitia testis*
	Q.8	*De iniustitia advocatorum* (ST, II-II, q.71)
	Q.9	*De contumelia* (ad ST, II-II, q.72)
	Q.10	*De detractione* (ad ST, II-II, q.73)
	Q.11	*De sussurratione et derisione* (ad ST, II-II, qq.74–75)
	Q.12	*De maledictione* (ST, II-II, q.76)
Book 6 (in part)	Q.1	*De usura* (ST, II-II, q.78)
	Q.2	*De generali ratione contractus emptionis et venditis*
	Q.3	*De iniustitia quae in emptione et venditione committitur* (ad ST, II-II, q.77)
	Q.4	*De emptione credito pretio*

The divisions drawn by Soto are interesting. Considered as a whole, it is no stretch to characterise book four as a work on property, book five as delict, and book six as contract. *Restitutio* sits on the boundary between property and delict. It is firmly rooted in the former, but leads into the discussion of the latter. This introductory function is similar to the role it played in the *Summa*.

But its surrounding material is unfamiliar to the Thomist environment. Note how none of the first five *quaestiones* in book four are treated as commentaries on specific provisions within the *Summa*. This is in stark contrast to book five, which follows the structure of *quaestiones* 64–76 of the *Secunda Secundae* slavishly, even if the references to Aquinas are sometimes omitted. The decision to associate *restitutio* with this novel treatment of property over the sins with which it was grouped in the *Summa* was no doubt intentional, and accurately reflects the basic thrust of the remedy.

Similarly important is the boundary drawn between books five and six. Again, the division introduced between '*de maledictione*' and '*de usura*' is novel. Within the *Summa* the two are part of the same tract, separated only by the wrongs that affect sale.[1] Usury and contractual fraud are the only two sins from the *Secunda Secundae*'s analysis of justice that are omitted from book five of Soto's treatise. Moreover, their order is reversed, a noticeable departure from the structure of book five which faithfully adheres to the ordering of the *Summa*. *Quaestiones* four through thirteen of book six are on the law of contract proper. It is only the introductory *quaestiones* that are related to wrongdoing. Just as *restitutio* is treated as a proprietary doctrine that ought to be located near to wrongdoing, usury and fraudulence are treated as contractual doctrines that share a border with wrongdoing. Through drawing this boundary, Soto has effectively carved out the territory of wrongdoing: homicide, mutilation, theft and the various judicial and extrajudicial verbal wrongs of the *Summa*.

One of the first authors to associate *restitutio* primarily with wrongdoing was Covarruvias, although he did not move far beyond proprietary wrongdoing. Despite acknowledging both *ratione rei* and *ratione acceptionis* as triggers for *restitutio*, and initially placing them on equal footing, he argues that *ratione rei* is subsumed by *ratione acceptionis*.[2] Mere possession of someone else's property is not enough to force *restitutio*, lest contracts such as pledge be rendered useless. Even where one party is demanding the return of property still in the hands of the defendant (which is the very definition of *restitutio ratione rei*), it is still necessary to point to some underlying injustice in either the means by which they came to possess the property, or the basis on which they continue their possession. In light of this, the rest of his treatment of *restitutio* considers only *restitutio ratione acceptionis*.

1 Dealt with by Aquinas in ST, II-II, q.77, and Soto, *De Iustitia et Iure* in 6.3.

2 Covarruvias, *Opera Omnia*, 598 ('*Regula de illicita acceptione: de restitutionis origine, et usursis restituendis*').

When discussed in relation to property, *restitutio* is only mentioned when there is clear bad faith.[3] It is a marginalised doctrine in this context. By contrast, many of his delictual inquiries expressly consider *restitutio*, such as express inquiries into its application to theft[4] and gambling.[5] These are instances of wrongdoing with obvious proprietary implications: the sinfulness of the action directly relates to the possession of illicit gains. When Covarruvias considers types of wrongdoing that simply 'take' from the victim with no material gain to the defendant, *restitutio* is not mentioned.[6] The same impasse is found in the works of Covarruvias' teacher, Navarrus. In his *Enchiridion*, a commentary on the Ten Commandments, *restitutio* is discussed at great length in his analysis of the seventh commandment ('*non furtum facies*').[7] By contrast, his treatment of the sixth commandment ('*non occides*') is silent on the matter. The only mention of *restitutio* in this section is his discussion of the remedy owed when a person kills a slave or child, which contains a straightforward reference to chapter one of the *Lex Aquilia*.[8] Given the content of his treatise, Navarrus cannot help but discuss *restitutio* in relation to wrongdoing. But the context he selects, the sole form of wrongdoing affecting property, shows that it is still a proprietary concept. Covarruvias has no such limitation, and his decision to associate *restitutio* with wrongdoing despite any shackles of structure represents a clear move towards the intertwining of the two ideas. Nevertheless, the detail of his analysis shows that *restitutio* rarely moved beyond the proprietary implications of wrongdoing.

Even though Navarrus and Covarruvias thought of *restitutio* as a remedy limited to the restoration of property, their association of it with wrongdoing laid the groundwork for Lessius to complete its transformation into a generalised delictual remedy. From the outset of his treatment of wrongdoing, *restitutio* is a necessary element of his definition. The section in question is titled '*de iniuriis, et damnis in omnibus humanorum bonorum generibus, et necessaria restitutione*'. The very first chapter within the section again pairs the two concepts, dealing with '*de iniuria et restitutione in genere*'.[9] '*Restitutio*

3 Ibid., 580.

4 Ibid., 600.

5 Ibid., 613.

6 Ibid., 688 ('*De vulneribus*').

7 Navarrus, *Enchiridion*, 17.7–93, and passim thereafter.

8 Ibid., 15.22. A second possible reference, 15.15, refers only to the restoration of property taken in an unjust war.

9 Lessius, *De Iustitia et Iure*, 2.7.

in genere' is discussed in relation to *iniuria*—this can only be the *restitutio ratione acceptionis* of earlier Thomists, but it has lost its qualifiers.[10] This new form of *restitutio* is said to be triggered not *ex acceptione* but *ex iniusta acceptione*, making considerations of wrongfulness unavoidable.[11] For these purposes, *iniustam acceptionem* is defined so as to include all *damnum*, explicitly bringing all the wrongs to be discussed, and even homicide, under the mantle of *restitutio*.[12] This generalisation brings to the fore an idea that had been lurking beneath the surface since Aquinas: *restitutio ratione acceptionis* is triggered by the unjust causation of loss.

By contrast, *restitutio ratione rei* retains its earlier name, thereby marking it out as exceptional. It is discussed in an awkward transition chapter, in between the details of specific injustices and how they are to be restored, and the practical details of *restitutio*. The matters dealt with under the heading of *restitutio ratione rei* are particular difficulties one might encounter in the restoration of property: what do you do if property belonging to another has been consumed or alienated in good faith?[13] What if you sell property belonging to another in good faith?[14] In short, the chapter addresses the remedial gap where a person no longer has the property in question, but did not cause loss in an unjust manner. And the answers given are that despite the absence of malevolence, *restitutio* must still be made simply because it is unjust to use or alienate the property of another without his consent. Consistent with his Thomist origins, Lessius maintains that the obligation to make *restitutio ratione rei* is strict; it is neither here nor there whether the possession is just or unjust.[15] These concerns aside, the remainder of Lessius' treatment of *restitutio* focuses entirely on wrongdoing.

It would be wrong, however, to suggest that Lessius treats *restitutio* as a solely delictual remedy. On occasion the word arises in relation to the law of contract. In this context, it is typically referred to as *restitutio in integrum*.[16] When it appears without these tags within the law of contract, it is invariably

10 Ibid., 2.7, 2.7.4.

11 Ibid., 2.7.5.

12 Ibid., 2.7.5. This is achieved by thinking of *damnum* as the infringement of a right, as will be discussed in chapter nine.

13 Ibid., 2.14.1.

14 Ibid., 2.14.5.

15 Ibid., 2.7.5.

16 Ibid., 2.17.9: '*quibus concedatur restitutio in integram, si ex aliquot contractu damnum notabile acceperint*'; 2.17.10: '*utrum in hac in integrum restitutione comprehendatur etiam fructus percepti*'.

in scenarios discussing wrongdoing.[17] The result is a threefold formulation of *restitutio*, with the terminology used denoting the aspect of private law to which it relates. *Restitutio* on its own relates to the law of delict and the redress of injustices; *restitutio ratione rei* belongs to the law of property, and fulfils the basic role of a proprietary claim; and *restitutio in integrum* which rescinds contracts in a manner reminiscent of the praetorian remedy of Roman law. The focus of his analysis is clearly delictual, but the remedial framework he constructs is applicable across private law.

Commensurability

The newfound delictual context of *restitutio* was mirrored in the remedy's content. Increasingly it became more concerned with compensation rather than the vindication of property rights. This can be seen most clearly in the remediation of wrongs that affected interests other than property. The Thomist model of delict encompassed three sets of wrongs that affected interests that were a poor fit for the proprietary conception of *restitutio*: life, limb and personality interests. With the wrongs affecting these interests, there was no obvious way of applying *restitutio*. A lost life cannot be restored, a detached arm cannot be reattached (at least, not through early modern medical techniques), and reputations as composites of opinions held by society at large are not easily changed. Nevertheless, for *restitutio* to function as a general delictual remedy it needed to be able to address each of these wrongs. Some of the work would inevitably be done through punishment (*poena*), but as *restitutio* came to resemble compensation for wrongdoing more than the mechanical restoration of property described in the *Summa* it became less and less justifiable to have no means of redress for the entire gamut of wrongdoing within natural law.

17 E.g. Ibid., 2.20.7: '*utrum licitum sit mutuare alteri cum pacto ut poenam debitam, vel famae honorisve violati restitutionem condonet*' ('Whether it is allowed to make a loan to another with an agreement that a penalty will be owed, or if a reputation or honour are violated whether restitution can be pardoned'). More doubtful, but likely still on the side of wrongdoing, is gambling: 2.26.3: '*Utrum is qui ludo vetito aliquid est lucratus, teneatur ad illius restitutionem*' ('Whether he who plays forbidden games to make a profit is held to make restitution of them'). The association of *restitutio* sans adjective with wrongdoing recurs in other chapters, e.g. 2.30.8: '*Utrum testis teneatur ad restitutionem, si nolit testari, vel si veritatem occulet*' ('Whether a witness is bound to make restitution if he refuses to testify, or hides the truth'); 2.31.2: '*Utrum reus, si impingat accusatori crimen mendacii seu calumniae, peccet, et teneatur ad restitutionem*' ('Whether a defendant who suggests his accuser is guilty of spreading falsehoods or calumnies sins, or is held to make restitution').

Wrongs affecting the body would prove incompatible with this project.[18] Despite its ever more delictual context, it was still the basic function of *restitutio* to restore to a person their lost property, the subject matter of *dominium*. Within the Thomist framework there was no way of viewing life nor limb as property. Lessius, advancing a perfectly orthodox Thomist view, wrote '*hominem non esse dominum, sed solum custodem vitae suae membrorumque*'.[19] Life and limb simply aren't 'things', and so are beyond the scope of *restitutio*. Nevertheless, several Thomists were unhappy with the traditional legal approach of denying compensation, with Navarrus arguing '*esse stultum putare, eum, qui bovem proximi necat, teneri ad restitutionem; non autem, qui proximum ipsum occidit*'.[20] The best that could be done was to allow a remedy focused on the financial consequences of the injury.

The common solution was to have a person responsible for a death make amends through a number of payments.[21] Firstly, he could reimburse any expenses connected to the harm for which he was an effective cause. Secondly, he could restore the deceased's *spes lucri*, where the *spes* could be anchored to some position or skill possessed by the deceased. From this, the defendant could subtract any sum that the claimant-heir had already received by way of inheritance so as to avoid over-compensation. A person's working life was deemed to end at sixty, so the *spes lucri* was multiplied by however many years short of that age the victim was.[22] In so doing, the Thomists turned life into something with a price tag. Non-financial considerations such as a desire for revenge would have to be satisfied by the prevailing local *poena* (in all likelihood capital punishment for culpable homicide) or through the *satisfactio* the killer had to offer to God.

Having taken this step, wrongs to the body are straightforwardly viewed as lesser variations on the theme.[23] Unlike life, the language of *recompensatio* used to describe the remediation of wrongs affecting the body in the *Summa* provided a basis for a monetary remedy for wounds.[24] Nevertheless, the remedy for such injuries is formulated in the same way as the remedy for

18 Jansen, *Theologie, Philosophie und Jurisprudenz*, 112–119.

19 Lessius, *De Iustitia et Iure*, 2.4.10: 'Man is not the owner, but merely the custodian, of his life and limbs'.

20 Navarrus, *Enchiridion*, 15.22: 'It is stupid to think that somebody who kills a cow is bound to make restitution, but not someone who kills his neighbour'.

21 Lessius, *De Iustitia et Iure*, 2.9.19; Navarrus, *Enchiridion*, 15.22.

22 Lessius, *De Iustitia et Iure*, 2.9.20.

23 Ibid., 2.9.23.

24 ST, II-II, q.62.a.2.

homicidia, focusing on the financial consequences of the injury. *Restitutio pro membro* is discussed as an addendum to *restitutio pro vita*. It does not even receive a dedicated *dubitatio*.[25] The only complication is the remediation of sexual wrongdoing.[26] The remediation of *stuprum* is based on the harm done to the victim's marriage prospects. For Lessius such harm is most easily remedied through marrying the wrongdoer to his victim. If the girl or her parents refuse this arrangement, they forfeit any further remedy unless the *stuprum* was forceful rather than fraudulent.[27] Lessius' paradigm case of such wrongdoing involves a virgin being tricked into bed by a false promise of marriage, and so it is easy enough to see why he considered this the best remedy. However, given the range of other behaviours that might constitute fraud, it seems harsh that a refusal to marry a con-artist is treated as tantamount to a failure to mitigate loss. If a girl's marriage prospects are unharmed by her violation, there is no need to make *restitutio*. If, however, *restitutio* is made in anticipation of a less favourable marriage, but the girl ends up marrying as well as could have been expected, '*poterit retinere pro ipso pudicitiae damno*'.[28]

The application of *restitutio* to a wounded reputation provoked a different set of concerns.[29] Unlike a person's life and limb, their reputation had long been considered property. A reputation that has been dragged through the dirt is not lost forever. If peoples' minds have been changed, they can be changed back. The difficulties lie in how this is to be achieved, and if it is even worth attempting. Consequently, the restoration of damaged reputations provoked considerably more discussion than the application of *restitutio* to homicides and wounding. The first substantial discussion of how personality interests might be remedied was provided by Navarrus.[30] Earlier accounts of *restitutio* were general, and the obligation to restore was invoked without any attempt at applying the rules to

25 *Restitutio* for adultery is discussed at slightly more length, but relates mostly to the delineation of sins against justice and sins against temperance. Only the dimension of the wrongdoing that is an affront to justice merits *restitutio*. This will only arise where the financial position of an affected party is made worse, as where an illegitimate son is born from the adultery, thereby costing any legitimate children a share of their inheritance: Lessius, *De Iustitia et Iure*, 2.10.7.

26 Jansen, *Theologie, Philosophie und Jurisprudenz*, 100–106.

27 Lessius, *De Iustitia et Iure*, 2.10.2.

28 Ibid., 2.10.2. Though laudably humane, this seems inconsistent of Lessius. Elsewhere in his discussion of *stuprum* her chastity is essentially valueless.

29 Jansen, *Theologie, Philosophie und Jurisprudenz*, 106–111.

30 Navarrus, *Enchiridion*, 18.42–50.

the unique problems posed by the restoration of intangible concepts.[31] Navarrus' account of the remedy also responds generically to the idea of harm.[32] The basic rule is that anyone who unjustly causes notable harm to the reputation of another is bound to restore it, as is their heir, unless the obligation is pardoned or excused.[33] This is almost identical to the general chapters on *restitutio* found in the *Summa* and Soto, but for the explicit mention of *fama*. It is likely the product of the *Enchiridion*'s structure—as a commentary on the Ten Commandments, there is no opportunity to offer a general account of *restitutio*, forcing instead narrower considerations of how the remedy is applied to each sin.

This structurally imposed atomisation allows Navarrus to examine the difficulties peculiar to the restoration of *fama*. He begins by distinguishing between harm caused by truth and lies.[34] Restoring the damage caused by falsehoods is straightforward. The detractor must go to everyone who heard or read his lies and set the story straight.[35] The most extreme measure that can be expected of the detractor is the swearing of a legal oath that restores his victim's *fama*.[36] Harm caused by the revelation of the truth is trickier. Once Pandora's Box has been opened and its contents have nestled in the minds of strangers it is difficult to see what can be asked of the detractor. One solution, speedily rejected, is to lie—the detractor can claim he was mistaken about the wrongdoing of the defamed, restoring the *fama* of the defamed at the expense of his own.[37] This shifts the inequality, but does not resolve it. To actually restore the wounded *fama* it makes more sense to publicly extol the merits of the defamed to improve his image among honest men.[38] And this is all that can be done. This means that in extreme cases, e.g. the revelation of a secret murder, the reputation will in all likelihood remain stained. This does not seem to trouble Navarrus.

Lessius' treatment of the remediation of *fama* is substantial, taking up almost half of the chapter. The core of *restitutio* is straightforward, and in most respects identical to Navarrus' remedy. The wrongdoer must make every effort to erase the false opinion he has spread.[39] This will involve talking to those who

---

31 E.g. ST, II-II, q.62; Cajetan, *Secunda Secundae Summae Theologiae cum Commentariis*, ad q.62; Soto, *De Iustitia et Iure*, 4.6.

32 Navarrus, *Enchiridion*, 18.44. The idea is also explored in 18.22 and 18.42.

33 Ibid., 18.42.

34 Ibid., 18.45.

35 Ibid., 18.45.

36 Ibid., 18.45.

37 Ibid., 18.45.

38 Ibid., 18.45.

39 Lessius, *De Iustitia et Iure*, 2.11.20.

heard the defamatory comments and setting them straight, with the possibility of swearing an oath as a last resort. The wrongdoer can say he was deceived, mistaken or misled. In the case of the unjust revelation of a true sin, he can honour and praise the defamed to bolster his reputation. He can also claim he spoke unfairly, a solution Navarrus rejected as it did not address the actual inequality.[40] The swearing of an oath is the most powerful method of restoring the damaged *fama*. If this does not work, the wrong ceases to be attributable to the defamatory comments and is instead seen as the product of the ignorance of the listeners. Furthermore, *restitutio* requires the restoration of all loss flowing from the harmed *fama*.[41]

Where the cause of the *infamia* is irreversible, monetary compensation is acceptable.[42] Lessius recognises there are problems with quantifying this sort of loss. Money, he argues, is not the measure of all human activities but the mechanism that makes them possible. There is biblical authority that prevents monetary compensation from being the primary remedy for wrongs to *fama*,[43] but its role as a final resort is justified by reference to the general requirements of commutative justice. As soon as the injustice is caused an obligation is generated, and it will continue to exist until balance is restored. If it cannot be restored, it is better for the obligation to be partially discharged than to be neglected entirely. In the same way, it is better for the man who owes 1000 gold coins but only owns 500 to pay over those 500 than to wash his hands of the debt entirely. Immediate resort to monetary remedies is appropriate in limited circumstances.[44] The first is where charity demands it, such as where a rich man defames a pauper. The second is where the monetary award forms part of a judicial sanction, i.e. where the award is part of *poena* and not *restitutio*. Such a sanction can be imposed even if the *fama* has already been restored, as the penalty for an earlier delict. The third is where the defamed and the defamer agree on a sum as compensation.

This monetisation of *fama* can be seen even in Lessius' formulation of the hierarchy of interests. Though it is still generally true that interests of the soul are more important than interests of the body, and those in turn trump external interests, Lessius injects a degree of flexibility into their boundaries. Asking

40 Navarrus, *Enchiridion*, 18.45.

41 Lessius, *De Iustitia et Iure*, 2.11.19.

42 Ibid., 2.11.16.

43 E.g. Proverbs 22:1: '*melius est nomen bonum quam divitiae multae; super argentum et aurum gratia bona*' ('A good name is worth more than great wealth, valued above silver and gold'); Lessius interprets '*multae*' ('great') as '*infinitae*' ('infinite').

44 Lessius, *De Iustitia et Iure*, 2.11.16.

whether one can ever be asked to put one's life at risk in the restoration of a damaged reputation, he relies principally upon Aquinas' argument: a life is more important than any reputation, and so the answer is no.[45] He then considers the question more generally—can lower ranked goods ever be equivalent to higher goods? It is the boundary between *fama* and property that he focuses on. Though it is unlikely that even a great fortune could offset infamy, he argues that a large enough sum can undo minor blemishes to a reputation.

The Problem of Priorities

At the heart of *restitutio* is the idea that imbalances must be fixed. Translated into legal terms, this is reformulated using the language of indebtedness. For Lessius, who articulated all of private law in terms of *restitutio* and, thus, in terms of debt, this was problematic. Thomist doctrine had long adopted an approach to indebtedness that ranked competing debts according to their source, with certain categories of injustice being inherently prior to others. For some, delictual debts were inherently prior to contractual debts; for others, the reverse was true. Lessius' contribution was to reconceptualise the notion of indebtedness behind *restitutio*, providing a level playing field for the different categories of obligation and their potential to make claims on a person's assets. This is a topic that casts light on Lessius' very different approach to doctrinal problems. This section will first consider the approach of two of the foremost theologians of the fifteenth and sixteenth centuries who dealt with priorities, before turning to the solution offered by Lessius. With the first group of theologians it will become readily apparent that priorities were only a concern insofar as they were the subject of natural law and natural reason. They attempted to show that certain debts were by their very nature prior to other types of debt. In stark contrast to this is Lessius' approach, which establishes first that all debts are fundamentally equal, but goes on to offer a series of principles to guide any legal system through the potential juridical morass posed by priorities.

As a preliminary point it should be noted that priorities were not dealt with by Aquinas. It was, however, treated in an opuscule that was for many centuries believed to be the work of Aquinas, but was in fact written by his student Aegidus de Lessinia (d.1304), himself a prominent thirteenth-century Dominican.[46] He wrote:

45 Ibid., 2.11.15.

46 Steven Epstein, *The Medieval Discovery of Nature* (Cambridge: Cambridge University Press, 2012), 137.

> … maiori iustitia restituenda sunt ablata quam debita sint solvenda, cum in hoc impleatur iustitia tollens iniuriam factam Deo et proximo: sed in solutione debitorum nulla tollitur iniuria, sed tantum solvitur iustitia: quare secundum hoc videntur prius restituenda ablata quam solvenda debita.[47]

The rationale is simple: leaving a debt unpaid is an injustice, and in this respect delictual debts and contractual debts are equal. But if we look at the cause of the debt, we will discover a second injustice behind all delictual debts but not most contractual debts. It is then a simple problem of deciding between two evils. It is better to undo two injustices in one repayment than a single injustice, and so delictual debts are inherently prior to contractual debts. This explanation is tediously orthodox, offering nothing that cannot be found in any other theological work of the central Middle Ages that touched on the subject. Nevertheless, it is the approach attributed to Aquinas.

This line can be traced into the *Summa Angelica* of Angelo Carletti di Chivasso (1411–1495). Moving beyond the somewhat reductive view of the pseudo-Aquinas, Chivasso sought to categorise injustices by their severity, resulting in a hierarchy of priorities.[48] As Chivasso maintained *restitutio* was a straightforwardly proprietary concept, the most serious injustice that could trigger its operation was *rapina* followed by *furtum*. The next most serious injustice was usury. This was followed by debts flowing from onerous contracts, and finally gratuitous contracts. With each it is possible to see a justification stemming from the very nature of the category that justifies its position in the order of priorities. Having already established that the double injustices of delicts ought to be repaid first, it is a simple matter of deciding which is the more serious: *rapina* or *furtum*. As *rapina* includes *furtum* but with the added element of violence, this decision ought to be easy. Usury occupies a curious position between contract and delict. Though it at least has a facade of voluntariness, the parties have consented to an unconscionable arrangement. This is sufficient to set it apart from other contracts. Finally, one must decide which contracts ought to be repaid first: undertakings for which the restorer has received some recompense, or those which he undertook gratis. Again, it is not difficult to see how Chivasso reached his decision.

---

47 Aegidus de Lessinia, *De Usuris in Communi*, c.18: 'It is in the greater interests of justice that losses are restored before debts; for in these there is a wrong to both God and neighbour. But in the payment of debts there is no wrong. Consequently, it seems that losses must be restored before debts are repaid'.

48 Chivasso, *Summa Angelica*, II, 328 (n.18 '*restitutio*').

Juan de Medina (1490–1547) was one of the intellectual foundations of the sixteenth-century revival of Thomism. His treatise on *restitutio* offers a more expansive conception of the remedy, encompassing not only the return of property but also the unravelling of deleterious effects. Instead of imposing a hierarchy on the sources of the obligation to restore he formulated a number of guiding principles, an approach that would be mirrored in later Thomist writings.[49] Firstly, property in which someone else has *dominium* must be returned before any question of debt arises. Secondly, certain debts ought to be preferred to uncertain debts. Thirdly, between certain debts, real debts are to be preferred to personal debts '*quia in realibus maius ius*'. As debts stemming from ownership are dealt with under the first principle, this must refer to secured debts such as hypothecs. Fourthly, between personal debts, delictual debts are to be preferred to contractual debts. The rationale offered is broadly the same as that offered in the Summa Angelica—it is the gravity of the sin that determines priority. Thus it is claimed that '*maius peccatum fuerit in rapina commissum (caeteris paribus) quam in furto, et maius in furto quam in usura*'. Fifthly, where there are several debts of the same type, the first in time is the first to be repaid.

Lessius's approach is for the most part the same as Medina's.[50] However, the point on which Lessius disagrees is significant. Within personal debts there is no meaningful distinction to be drawn between contractual and delictual debts based on their basic nature. When a person commits *furtum* they wrong their neighbour, their community and their God. The injustice that triggers *restitutio* is simply the displacement of property. The wrongfulness of the thief's actions is erased through punishment at the hands of the community and offering satisfaction to God. If the theft is committed violently, which of the three remedial strands seeks to ameliorate the unjustified force? Lessius answers that it has no effect on *restitutio*, which seeks solely to restore the property to its rightful owner. The violence is likely a matter of *poena* instead. Thus the injustice targeted by *restitutio* in *furtum* and *rapina* is identical, and the same is true of every other legal institution that triggers the obligation to restore. Delicts do involve the coincidence of several injustices, but not all of those injustices are the subject of *restitutio*.

By denying that certain categories of obligation are inherently prior Lessius is crafting a remedy that is versatile. All that is needed for the invocation of *restitutio* is the existence of a debt. The remaining principles governing priorities

49 Medina, *De Restitutione et Contractibus Tractatus*, q.2.d.5.

50 Medina was followed closely by several prominent Thomists. E.g. Navarrus, *Enchiridion*, 17.58.

are grounded in natural reason, with a focus not on the source of the debt but on its content. The prime example of such a principle is certainty. The rule is straightforward: certain debts must be paid before uncertain debts.[51] He differentiated between three forms of uncertainty that might affect debts, each having different consequences. The first and most straightforward problem is when it simply can't be satisfactorily proven that a debt is owed at all. In this situation there is no obligation to make *restitutio*. The second type of uncertainty encompasses situations where a debt is clearly owed, but the identity of the true creditor is ambiguous as between a small number of possibilities. Here the just solution is to divide the value of the debt equally across those with legitimate claims to the debt.

The third type of uncertainty proved the most problematic: where there is simply no indication as to whom the debt is owed. Lessius distinguished between two situations: debts over specific goods that are obviously not the property of the possessor and debts over fungible objects. In the case of specific goods there is a clear logical impasse: it is clearly unjust for the possessor to retain the property of another, but what is he to do if there is no one to whom it can be restored? The solution is a charitable donation to the poor.[52] There is no correspondingly clear answer to the problem of fungible goods. Lessius simply claims that certain debts must be paid before uncertain debts. The same logical impasse encountered in the case of specific goods ought to apply here, and there is no reason for the solution to be any different. It may be more readily apparent that an item of clothing does not belong to a possessor than one bushel of wheat out of a hundred, but that does not alter the basic fact that neither is actually owned by the possessor. Even if the true identity of the owner cannot be discovered, the retention of the property is an injustice. This injustice ought to be remediable through a donation to the poor regardless of whether the property is specific or fungible. Nevertheless Lessius treats the two differently.

Beyond this basic maxim that 'certain debts must be repaid before uncertain debts' there are a handful of additional rules that affect the priority of creditors. Between certain creditors, there are a handful of debts that are inherently prior by their nature, but not their origin. For example, debts that affect one's spiritual wellbeing (e.g. funeral expenses) must be restored before other debts, for despite his general neglect of spiritual concerns in his analysis of delict it would hardly be possible for Lessius to deny their inherent superiority to material wealth.[53] Secured debts must also be repaid before unsecured

51 Lessius, *De Iustitia et Iure*, 2.15.1.

52 See also Lessius, *De Iustitia et Iure*, 2.16.10.

53 Ibid., 2.15.4.

debts, lest the very bedrock of the institution be undermined.[54] Where there are multiple creditors of the same type, a second principle applied: '*qui prior est tempore, potior est iure*'.[55] The reason given for this is refreshingly uncomplicated: it is fair and easy to apply. These rules essentially mirror those found in Medina.[56] The only change to Medina's model is the omission of the priority of delictual debts over contractual debts. But this change is of fundamental importance, an omission that allowed *restitutio* to operate as a remedy across the law of obligations.

Actual and Hypothetical Losses

Aquinas stated that *restitutio* was available for both actual losses and failures to make a gain. Actual losses must be restored in full, while failures to make a gain would be restored in proportion to their degree of realisation.[57] But Aquinas failed to take into account the nature of the gain. In a recurring disputation identified by Professor Gordley the Thomists sought to bring their doctrines into line with Roman law by considering whether a distinction ought to be drawn within hypothetical gains founded on the degree of entitlement.[58] This disputation not only reveals the development of a strand of doctrine, as identified by Gordley, but also the changing focus of *restitutio* as it transformed into a primarily delictual remedy. Two situations were differentiated. In the first, a worthy candidate was unjustly prevented from obtaining a benefice.[59] Here Aquinas argued that the unjust actor was bound to make 'some compensation' for the loss he had caused, though said compensation would be worth less than the benefice. The second scenario has a man unjustly dig up another's seeds.[60] For Aquinas this is the same sort of problem—a question of hypothetical loss—differentiated only in the degree of *restitutio* required. In this case the owner of the seeds was virtually certain to make a gain, and so his loss must be almost completely restored.[61] Aquinas' position seems at least compatible with the Roman rules on the recovery of speculative loss. Under chapter three of

54 Ibid., 2.15.4.

55 Ibid., 2.15.6.

56 Medina, q.2.d.5.

57 ST, II-II, q.62.a.3.

58 Gordley, *The Jurists*, 87.

59 ST, II-II, q.62.a.2.ad.4.

60 ST, II-II, q.62.a.4.arg.1.

61 ST, II-II, q.62.a.4.ad.1.

the *lex Aquilia*, costing someone an opportunity to make a gain was certainly recoverable.[62] The question is whether the recoverability of such loss became less likely as the loss became more speculative. The sole text associated with remoteness, D.9.2.29.3, is silent on this point. Unlike Aquinas, there is nothing to suggest that the measure of damages would scale according to how speculative the failure to make a gain was, but the evidence is too slight to rule out the possibility.

The two scenarios were seen as distinct by Cajetan.[63] He argued that unlike the case of the benefice, the owner of the seeds had been denied what was his as of right.[64] Beneath his argument appears to be the Roman distinction between *spes* and *res speratae*. The former are capable of being commercially viable goods even in their embryonic state, whereas the latter are only viable once realised.[65] For *restitutio* to apply in the case of the benefice, the candidate would have had to have lost something that was *his*. But all that was lost was something he hoped for (*res sperata*), rather than something he was actually entitled to despite its embryonic state (*spes*). The absence of a clear *ius*, even a *ius in spe*, was sufficient to deny the would-be holder of the benefice any compensation.

Lessius disagreed with Cajetan's argument and conclusion, but did not return to Aquinas' original reasoning.[66] Regardless of the absence of a right, it could not be denied that a wrong had been committed.[67] It was this wrongfulness that drove the need for *restitutio*. It was still necessary to identify a thing that needed to be restored, and to this end Lessius relies on the idea of a conditional right.[68] But it is clearly the existence of an unaddressed injustice that provides Lessius with the impetus for finding a remedy. In working out the degree of compensation needed to make *restitutio*, Lessius relies on the basic mechanisms of *restitutio*. One simply asks what loss has been caused, and what payment is required to restore the just balance of assets. There is no hint of the approach employed by Aquinas founded on a sum proportionate to the likelihood of the chance being realised. In so doing the Thomist approach became more similar than ever to the solution of the civil law, looking simply at the *damnum* caused.

62 See above; generally, D.9.2.23.1–6.

63 Gordley, *The Jurists*, 87–88.

64 Cajetan, *Secunda Secundae Summae Theologiae cum Commentariis*, ad q.62.a.2.ad.4.

65 Buckland, *Text-book of Roman Law*, 483.

66 Gordley, *The Jurists*, 88.

67 Lessius *De Iustitia et Iure*, 2.12.18.

68 Ibid., cited Gordley, *The Jurists*, 89.

Excusing *Restitutio*: Impossibility and Disproportionate Hardship

Lessius' practical approach to Thomist theory can be further illustrated by his efforts towards making *restitutio* a more legalistic remedy. In a word, Aquinas' conception of *restitutio* was mechanical. It identified an imbalance and demanded it be rectified. To retain property that is not yours is a sin, specifically the sin of *iniustitia*, and it is wrong to remain in sin for even a slither of time.[69] The mere fact that the return is impossible does not affect the sinfulness of unjustly keeping property from its true owner. This is clearly a problem—a person is drowned in an ever more serious state of sinfulness despite having no avenue for escape. Aquinas' solution is to make the retention just. The injustice of the detention stems from the fact that it is against the owner's will. If the owner consents to the detention it ceases to be unjust and, by extension, sinful.[70] The only exception to the obligation is straightforward impossibility, and even then the wrongdoer must ask the wronged for a release from his obligation.[71] Thus it would appear that so long as the wrongdoer has the material wealth to restore the loss he has caused, it would be a sin for him to withhold *restitutio*. Hinging the applicability of an excuse like impossibility on the consent of the claimant is pragmatically difficult to accept. Suppose the property has simply been destroyed, and the claimant does not have the assets to replace it. A system of private law needs some sort of mechanism to deal with this situation. Merely stating repeatedly that the detainer is a sinner does nothing for either party, and expecting the claimant to drop his claim solely out of concern for the best interests of the defendant is naïve.

Covarruvias considers a slightly different question: what if making *restitutio* would cause severe hardship for the wrongdoer? Here Covarruvias would allow the obligation to restore to lapse—the wronged party must allow the wrongdoer sufficient material wealth for his survival.[72] Having established that *restitutio* cannot be demanded where it is tantamount to a death sentence, Covarruvias turns to a different situation: must a wife reveal to her husband that one of his children is the result of adultery? The very phrasing of the question implies an answer in the positive: '*ut hoc modo filium excludat a mariti haereditate, et ea veris haeredibus restituantur*'.[73] But he answers, supported *omnium consensu* (though perhaps tellingly without any specific references) that she is under no

69 ST, II-II, q.62.a.8.

70 ST, II-II, q.62.a.8.

71 ST, II-II, q.62.a.8.ad.3.

72 Covarruvias, *Opera Omnia*, 6.1.2.

73 Ibid., 6.1.4.

obligation to reveal the truth, and consequently to restore the inheritance to its rightful owners. This is because it is impossible for a wife to reveal such a secret without harming her *fama* and putting her life at risk. The justification for this is given as an abstract principle: *restitutio* cannot be demanded where '*maius damnum sequeretur restituenti, quam commodum ipsi, cui restitutio facienda est*'.[74] The inclusion of *fama* provides a path to a quite radical departure from Aquinas—that severe harm to one's private wealth (*bona externum rerum*) can provide an excuse from *restitutio*. Covarruvias does not take his analysis this far, instead emphasising repeatedly the significance of *periculo vitae* for this exception to apply.

Lessius modified Covarruvias' position by arguing that hardship was only sufficient to postpone the obligation to restore, but set the bar for the invocation of this excuse well below the standard of *periculum vitae*.[75] Instead of requiring the endangering of a life, he formulated the excuse in terms of harm broadly construed. The underlying logic is simple: for the claimant to insist on the enforcement of his rights when he knows that it will result in loss (*damnum*) to another is to act contrary to the requirements of charity.[76] This will be the case so long as the threatened loss is equal to or greater than the right to be enforced by the claimant. However, it would be equally uncharitable to extinguish the claimant's rights entirely—as soon as the looming *damnum* has been removed (or lessened to a level below the value of the claimant's right) there is nothing to stop the operation of *restitutio*. This is a typical example of Lessius' manipulation of the requirements of justice and charity to achieve the desired outcome, effectively obfuscating the boundaries of strict justice with the concern man ought to show for his neighbour under charity.

Conclusion

By manipulating the triggers by which it might be invoked, the later Thomists transformed *restitutio* into a remedy that arose primarily in the context of wrongdoing. Of course, the idea that property has to be restored finds a far broader application, but the emphasis placed on *restitutio ratione rei* over *restitutio ratione acceptionis* in the *Summa Theologica* was increasingly inverted. By the time of Lessius *restitutio ratione rei* was only discussed within a broader

74 Ibid., 6.1.4.

75 Lessius, *De Iustitia et Iure*, 2.16.4.

76 Indeed, a threat to '*tua vel tuorum vel proximi*' seems to suffice in cases of extreme necessity—Lessius, *De Iustitia et Iure*, 2.16.1.

consideration of *restitutio* and wrongdoing, with *restitutio ratione acceptionis* having become the primary form of the remedy. These developments were accompanied by an increasing concern for how *restitutio* ought to actually work in practice, though it is only the latest of the Thomists who shared any regard for such issues. In the process *restitutio* was increasingly conceptualised as compensatory rather than vindicatory, and was invoked to redress a wider range of wrongdoing than was possible under Aquinas.

CHAPTER 9

Sins, Wrongs and Rights

Restitutio was the only Thomist remedy that could fulfil the role of compensation. This function was limited by the fact that *restitutio* was at its heart a proprietary notion, concerned with the distribution and redistribution of assets. This was not changed by its ever more delictual context. As the Thomist theory of delict became more sophisticated, it became increasingly apparent that there were significant remedial gaps stemming from this proprietary focus. This was already apparent at numerous points in the *Summa* where a discussion ends with a reference to the inevitability of punishment at a local level, thereby shirking the need for natural law to deal with such issues. To fill these gaps, the Thomists needed to develop a means of analysing the full range of wrongdoing using a common measure. The solution adopted was to first formulate all wrongdoing in terms of interference with a right, and then to commoditise those rights. If successful, the result would be a theory of delict that was truly general, with a single remedy available for any blameworthy interference with a protected right.

From Specific Wrongs to Protected Interests

Before considering how the various interests protected by delict might be rendered remediable, it is first necessary to consider what those interests are. This can be seen in the changing structure of freestanding treatises based around the *secunda secundae*, and in particular the manner in which individual wrongs were enumerated. As has already been seen, Aquinas' account presents fifteen individual sins that cover a wide range of wrongdoing. Under the watch of the sixteenth-century Thomists some of these sins were ignored, and others were introduced from elsewhere in the *Summa Theologiae*. The result is a list of sins that more closely resembles a list of delicts. Once this has been compiled, it is only a small step to extract from this list the various interests protected by the law.

The Fifteen Wrongs

Among the fifteen sins originally discussed by Aquinas in relation to justice, some were clearly not of a legal character, and others were more at home in legal categories other than delict. It has been already seen how from an early date within the neo-scholastic movement *quaestiones* 77 and 78 on usury and

 | DOI 10.1163/9789004344372_010

fraud in sale were moved away from delict towards contract.[1] A similar fate befell the wrongs consisting in injurious words spoken during a trial, though at a later date than the contractual wrongs.[2] Even within Aquinas, these were viewed more as matters of procedure than forms of wrongdoing. Nevertheless, Soto dealt with these issues in book five of his *De Iustitia et Iure*, in a location that corresponds to their place in the *Summa*, and in a way largely indistinguishable from their treatment by Aquinas.[3] The same approach can be seen in Cajetan's commentary on the *Summa*.[4] It was not until Lessius that the five *iniuriae in iudiciis* were separated from the main body of delict, viewed as a *sui generis* species of obligation. They occupy the fourth chapter of his treatment of justice, separated from delict by the entire law of contract.[5] Easily the shortest chapter within *De Iustitia et Iure*, he reduces the number of wrongs to just three disputations: wrongs committed by judges, wrongs committed by accusers and witnesses, and wrongs committed by advocates and defendants. Tellingly for Lessius, the focus in these disputations is not on the interest harmed but the context within which the wrong occurs. As will shortly be seen, though faithful to Aquinas' focus on procedure this is an extremely poor fit for the way in which Lessius deals with delict, and was likely sufficient justification in itself for their removal from the core of wrongdoing.

Injurious words spoken outside the courtroom fared better than their official counterpart, but still survived only in a severely curtailed form. Aquinas dealt with five such wrongs, four of which concerned specific interests and the fifth acting as a residual category.[6] The four interests are *honor*, *fama*, *amicitia* and shame (or whatever name ought to be given to the harm caused by *erebuscere*). The difficulties with treating friendship as a legal right are clear, and shame proved too close a parallel to *fama* to merit separate consideration. Even Soto, who normally deals in full with all questions raised by the *secunda secundae*, conflates *susurratio* and *derisio* into a single *quaestio*, each being discussed in a single article.[7] For Navarrus *sussuratio*, *derisio* and *maledictio* merited little more than a sentence each, couched in language lifted directly from the *Summa*.[8] They are included simply to show how *contumelia* and *detractio*

1 Above, 166. E.g. Soto, *De Iustitia et Iure*, 6.1 and 6.3.

2 I.e. ST, II-II, qq.67–71.

3 Soto, *De Iustitia et Iure*, 5.4–8.

4 Cajetan, *Secunda Secundae Summae Theologiae cum Commentariis*, ad qq.67–71.

5 Lessius, *De Iustitia et Iure*, 2.29–31.

6 Above, pages 144–145.

7 Soto, *De Iustitia et Iure*, 5.11.1–2.

8 Navarrus, *Enchiridion*, 18.13, 15, 16.

differ. Lessius omitted the three extraneous wrongs entirely, leaving only *contumelia* and *detractio*, the wrongs against *honor* and *fama*.

The Development of Individual Wrongs

Thus the fifteen wrongs of the *Summa* were reduced to a list of just five: *homicidia, mutilatio, furtum, contumelia* and *detractio*.[9] Under Aquinas each of these had been defined in fairly expansive terms, and little work was needed to pin down the conduct each prohibited. Instead, the Thomists focused on fringe issues within each sin that might arise in practice, and how they ought to be resolved. In each sin it is possible to see the Thomist structure being opened up to outside influences. These are not exclusively legal in nature. For example, within homicide the Thomists dealt with one of the perennial questions of political thought: is it ever justifiable to kill a sovereign? The overall impression given is a desire to show that Thomism is practical, and that issues of every type can be solved within a Thomist framework. But with each new solution that requires a concrete answer, the abstractions of Aquinas are rooted evermore in certainty, and in the process Thomist doctrine acquired an increasingly legalistic form.

Homicidia

The near-total prohibition on homicide found in the *Summa* unsurprisingly persisted in the writings of sixteenth-century Thomists. The only substantive changes to the sin arose through the slight expansion of the sole category of justifiable homicide recognised by Aquinas, namely where the taking of a life is in the interest of the community at large. This is a power vested in the sovereign to be used sparingly so as to protect the common good.[10] Later commentators focused on one aspect of the common good's protection that Aquinas overlooked. What happens when the one threatening the common good is the one vested with the authority to take a life? In short, is tyrannicide ever acceptable? This is a very common theme in theological treatises, and seems more relevant to political philosophy than delictual doctrine. However, it is through the development of this disputation that the language of rights was injected into discussions about *homicidia*, and so it merits further consideration.

9 This numbering is according to the manner in which they are grouped from the *Summa* onwards. *Furtum* includes *rapina*, and *mutilatio* includes *verberatio*. In each case the former is typically analysed as including the latter.

10 Above, 136–137.

The issue was concisely stated by Lessius: '*utrum homini privato liceat interficere tyrannum*'.[11] The starting point was uncontentious: the power to end a life was an aspect of authority. This power can be delegated directly, such as where a sovereign appoints an executioner. But it can also be delegated in the abstract, through the sovereign's identification of an interest of the community that can be protected by private citizens through lethal force.[12] As such, private citizens can kill enemies of the state and criminals in accordance with laws properly created, explaining local and Roman law rules such as the lawful killing of thieves caught in the act.[13] To allow tyrannicide, all that had to be shown was that killing a ruler was in the state's interest.

So long as the power to take a life remained anchored to the office of sovereign scholars were reluctant to take this step. This can be seen in the writings of the father of Spanish criminal law, Alphonso de Castro (1495–1558).[14] His position was complicated by the exceptionally broad definition he gave to the word '*tyranni*', focusing on the exercise of *dominium*.[15] Husbands are *tyranni* to their wives, and the leaders of the Church are *tyranni* to both their underlings and followers. The word is used without the perjorative connotations of its English translation, meaning nothing more than the exercise of control over another. As such, allowing tyrannicide even as a hypothetical possibility would lead to the inconceivable position that there existed a set of conditions which would allow for the death of the pope: '*possent oves interficere suum pastore*[*m*], *sive ille esset unus simplex parrochus, sive episcopus, sive Pape*'.[16]

The power over life and death needed to be severed from the position of the sovereign. Soto's analysis of tyrannicide considered three possible solutions, one of which took a step in the direction of severability, although he did not follow through. To do this, he used the precedent of the golden calf in Exodus. Unless Moses committed a heinous sin when he told his followers to kill their

11 Lessius, *De Iustitia et Iure*, 2.9.4.

12 Ibid., 2.9.3. Translating *republica* as state is slightly anachronistic, but unproblematic for present purposes. Though its precise conceptualisation in sixteenth-century thought is contentious, the essence of the term is a political community, whatever form that might take.

13 Though some Thomists incorporated these laws within their framework of homicide, e.g. Navarrus, *Enchiridion* 15.5–6.

14 Castro, *Adversus Omnes Haereses*, f.206d.

15 Ibid., f.206b under '*tyrannus*': '*quamvis enim aliquis sit quantumlibet scelestus et criminosus, qui mille mereatur mortes, non potest tamen iuste ab aliquot occidi, nisi ab habente potestatem et iurisdictione*[*m*]'.

16 Ibid., f.206b: '... then the sheep could kill their shepherd, whether he be a local priest, a bishop or the pope'.

kin, there must be circumstances in which homicide is sinless.[17] Soto argues that Moses was acting as the paradigm judge. Authority stems from God, so it would be absurd to argue that Moses when following the very word of God was not exercising legitimate authority. The argument here is almost complete. All Soto had to do was claim that as authority stemmed from God, it was possible for a sovereign to act in defiance of his delegated power, and this justified tyrannicide. But this step was not taken. Instead Soto moves on to two other arguments intended to show that the taking of a life by a private citizen is never justifiable. Firstly, he discusses the merits of comparing sinners to animals that can be slaughtered.[18] The argument draws support from secular laws allowing for the killing of thieves, or enemies in wartime. Nevertheless it is rejected. Even if man degrades himself through sin, his humanity persists, and so he remains above a beast. Soto's third argument, that it is laudable to act in the public good even when acting in private, receives very short shrift. He simply argues that it cannot be in the public good to execute private citizens without the veneer of public authority.

Cajetan also refused to allow private homicides, but seemed to find the theological prohibition difficult to reconcile with practice. What, for example, of the law allowing a father to kill his adulterous daughter?[19] When dealing with tyrannicide, he introduces an important distinction between rulers who are tyrannous because of the origins of their rule, and those who are tyrannous because of the nature of their rule.[20] The former, referring to despots who seize power, is no true *princeps* and so can be killed by the people '*pro liberate populi*'.[21] The citizenry are allowed to kill in this situation because in the absence of a sovereign there is no recognised authority in whom the power over life and death can vest. Covarruvias directly compares the situation to a war between the citizenry and their false leader. Consequently, where the *princeps* is legitimate but behaving tyrannically, there is nothing that can be done.

Lessius followed his intellectual forebears in arguing that a *tyrannus* is not a *princeps* (i.e. a legitimate ruler) but an '*invasor et oppressor reipub*[*licae*] *et singulorum*'.[22] Showing his humanist tendencies, he uses historical evidence in

17 Exodus 32:27.

18 Soto, *De Iustitia et Iure*, 5.1.3: '*corruptum hominem ac perditum cum bestijs: sylvestrem autem bestiam, ac praesertim si nocua sit, unicuiq*[*ue*] *liberum est occidere: pari ergo ratione et brutum hominem*'.

19 Cajetan, *Secunda Secundae Summae Theologiae cum Commentariis*, ad q.64.a.2.

20 Ibid., ad q.64.a.3.

21 Ibid., ad q.64.a.3.

22 Lessius, *De Iustitia et Iure*, 2.9.4.

place of theological authority, citing the historical approval of the tyrannicide of Julius Caesar. He places particular emphasis on Aquinas' praise for Cicero: '*pro sententia adducit* [referring to Aquinas] *Ciceronem laudente[m] eos, qui Caesarem, quamvis familiarem et amicum occiderunt*'.[23] This is somewhat peculiar, as Aquinas makes sparing use of Cicero in his account of justice, and does not refer to him in relation to homicide at all. It seems Lessius was uncomfortable departing so radically from Aquinas' teachings, and sought to link his own theories to the *Summa* using whatever pretext he could find. Faced with an *invasor*, the community can repel force with force.[24] By stripping away the authoritative trappings of the *tyrannus*, Lessius turned tyrannicide into a matter of self-defence, which he considered to be a natural right.[25] But this approach could only work where the *tyrannus* could be described as an *invasor*. This has been interpreted as applying solely to usupers of power, as in Cajetan.[26] However, a later passage suggests that even a legitimate *princeps* can be rebranded a *tyrannus* and killed:

> Quia Princeps, etsi tyrannice regat, tamen manet Superior … ergo non potest a subdito interfici, nisi forte ob necessarium vitae suae defensionem, de quo infra. … si tantum excrescat tyrannus, ut non videatur amplius tolerabilis, nec ullum aliud remedium super sit, primum a Repub[lica] vel comitiijs regni, vel alio havente auctoritatem, esse deponendum, et hostem declarandum, ut in ipsius personam liceat quidquam attentare.[27]

It is difficult to describe self-defence without using a term like 'right'. Thus we find in the Decretals of Gregory IX the phrase '*vim vi repellere omnes leges et omnia iura permittant*'.[28] But in the latter stages of sixteenth-century Thomism emerged a positively formulated right of self-defence, making use of the

23 Ibid., 2.9.4: 'In support of this opinion he [Aquinas] uses Cicero's praise for those who killed Caesar, even though they were his friends and family'.

24 Ibid., 2.9.4.

25 E.g. Lessius, *De Iustitia et Iure*, 2.9.7: '*defensionem iure naturae*'.

26 Harro Höpfl, *Jesuit Political Thought: The Society of Jesus and the State, c.1540–1630* (Cambridge: Cambridge University Press, 2004), 316–318.

27 Lessius, *De Iustitia et Iure*, 2.9.4: 'Because a prince, even if he rules tyrannically, remains superior … therefore he cannot suddenly be killed, unless it becomes necessary for the defence of one's own life, as discussed earlier … If the tyranny continues to grow, to such an extent that it seems it can be tolerated no longer, and no other remedy is available, the leaders of the state or the counts of the king or others with similar authority, must depose him and declare him an enemy, so that anybody is allowed to interfere with his person'.

28 X.5.12.18.

more powerful *fas* or divine right. Lessius ultimately defined self-defence as '*fas esse occidere iniustum invasorem ob defensionem vitae suae et integritatis membrorum*'.[29] The language of *fas* could then be used to sculpt the boundaries of homicide, providing a justification wherever a *fas* could be identified. Thus it is *fas* for a father to kill his adulterous daughter, though the exercise of this particular *fas* was permissible only at the end of a trial. The language of *fas* was important insofar as it provided a link to God's authority—executions by authorities were justified because the authorities had a divine decree to minister over life and death, but the authority was ultimately God's. If private citizens could show a parallel divine imperative to kill, it could be theologically justified. This use of a divine right to sculpt the contours of a wrong that is otherwise left undefined is without precedent.

Mutilatio and *vulneratio*

In the *Summa* Aquinas used the dramatic language of dismemberment to illustrate the lofty level of protection afforded to the body, although it certainly seems to be the implicit in his treatment that lesser harm was sinful. His discussion adopts the surgical tone found in relation to *homicidia*, asking whether a part can be removed for the sake of the whole.[30] Given Aquinas' focus on the more severe forms of injury to the body that can constitute a sin, some of the later Thomists concerned themselves with lesser forms of injury so as to cast light on the limits of sinfulness. Cajetan asked whether digits are protected, prompting a comparison with early Roman law and contemporary canon law.[31] The former protected only the limb, the latter '*coniunctim*' body parts. Cajetan aligns himself with canon law on the basis that even fingers have a function, and the loss of that function is still a serious injury, though not as serious as the loss of a limb. From this, Cajetan constructs a four-tiered hierarchy of wrongs to the body: homicide, mutilation, wounding and imprisonment.[32] The sinfulness of the first two is beyond doubt. Like Aquinas, Cajetan argues that wounding is prima facie sinful, with important exceptions for discipline within and beyond the family.

Lessius largely deals with mutilation by extrapolating from his thoughts on homicide. If killing can be justified by public authority and the common good, why should mutilation be any different?[33] Consequently the content of the sin

29 Lessius, *De Iustitia et Iure*, 2.9.8.

30 ST, II-II, q.65.a.1.

31 Cajetan, *Secunda Secundae Summae Theologiae cum Commentariis*, ad q.65.a.1.

32 Though this is little more than extracting the key words from ST, II-II, qq.64 and 65.a.1–3.

33 Lessius, *De Iustitia et Iure*, 2.9.14.

receives just one *dubitatio* of consideration. Aquinas' *corpus:membrum* correspondence refigures, with Lessius claiming *''licitum esse se mutilare, quando id necessarium est ad corporis salute, ut si cancer membrum occupet'.*[34] He perceives only two difficulties specific to mutilation. Firstly, can a person mutilate himself in the interests of salvation? Secondly, can a person cut off their own hand at the behest of a *tyrannus* if the alternative is death?[35] Neither hypothetical casts much light on the nature of wrongs to the body.

Furtum, rapina and *iniustitia*

Amongst the sins against justice of the *secunda secundae, furtum* and *rapina* had perhaps the most discriminating conduct element: asportation. These two were the only sins against property discussed by Aquinas, and so had to develop so as to cover the entire range of proprietary wrongdoing. The simple causation of loss, whether purely economic or consequent on property damage, did not fit neatly into the Thomist framework, existing only as the general sin of *iniustitia*. This gave *iniustitia* an awkward duality, representing both the nexus of all sins against justice, and a specific form of wrongdoing. Moreover, Aquinas' own discussion of *iniustitia* does not make it clear whether the sin could be used as a blanket means of reversing the causation of loss. A handful of cursory comments in this direction were made in relation to *restitutio* itself, though these seem to have been intended only to show how *restitutio* worked at a mechanical level.[36] The task of the Thomists was to find a way of making such loss remediable within the confines of *furtum* and *rapina*, or else to innovate and create a new category of wrongdoing separate from the generalities of *iniustitia*.

The probems caused by Aquinas' discussion of the basic causation of loss did not escape the notice of the later Thomists. As has already been seen, Cajetan latched onto Aquinas' discussion of the causation of actual and hypothetical losses.[37] This discussion can only take place if such loss is recoverable, but like Aquinas Cajetan does not address how it arises in relation to the various nominate sins of the *secunda secundae*. Presumably voluntarily causing a person to have less than their due is the sin of *iniustitia*, and so *restitutio ratione*

---

34 Ibid., 2.9.14.

35 Lessius, *De Iustitia et Iure*, 2.9.14: '*Utrum ob animae salute, v.g. ad carnis tentationes vitandas aut superandas liceat se mutilare ... Utrum iubente tyranno possis tibi manum abscindere, si aloquin mos esse intericiendus*'.

36 E.g. ST, II-II, q.62.a.2, discussed in Gordley, *The Jurists*, 87–88; Gordley, *Foundations of Private Law*, 268. The general sin of *iniustitia* also loomed as a residual source of liability.

37 Above, pages 178–179.

acceptionis can operate to correct the imbalance. But this is not an issue that is adequately explained, and relying on the general sin of *iniustitia* rather than a distinct nominate sin is a somewhat clumsy solution. Nevertheless, it is the best that can be done in a work that seeks only to comment on Aquinas.

By contrast, Cajetan's discussion of *furtum* represents a departure from Aquinas:

> ... furtum est contrectatio rei alienae mobilis corporalis, invito domino animo lucrandi sive ipsius rei, sive usus, sive possessionis.[38]

The ambiguous language of *accipere* used by Aquinas has disappeared. Instead Cajetan opts for a definition ripped from the Digest.[39] That *furtum* applies only to movable property has no foundation in Thomist thought, but a clear link to Roman law.[40] Similarly without precedent is the idea of '*animus lucrandi*'. The inclusion of this element is significant: by defining *furtum* along Roman lines, the sin could not perform the function carried out by the *lex Aquilia* in Roman law. The straightforward causation of loss would have to find another home. The only element Cajetan omits from the Roman law definition of the delict is *fraudulosa*, no doubt because the same job was performed by the notion of voluntariness in Thomism. A second fault standard would be a redundant addition. It should be noted that despite the clear link to Roman law, Cajetan provides no authority for his definition. Given his lack of subtlety it is difficult to believe this is an attempt at subterfuge, but it is nevertheless telling that Cajetan did not think it necessary to indicate that he was deviating from his source material. Given the wholesale conversion to Roman law found in Cajetan's definition of *furtum*, it is surprising that *rapina* is given an orthodoxly Thomist definition.[41] It seems that Cajetan, like most scholars who have examined delict throughout history, had little to say about *rapina*. Barely one hundred words are given to the topic before he returns to *furtum*.

---

38 Cajetan, *Secunda Secundae Summae Theologiae cum Commentariis*, ad q.66.a.3: 'Theft is interference with another's movable property, without the consent of the owner and with an intention to gain, whether from the thing itself, its use or possession of it'.

39 D.47.2.1.3 (Paul): '*furtum est contrectatio rei fraudulosa lucri faciendi gratia vel ipsius rei vel etiam usus eius possessionisve*'.

40 D.47.2.25.pr (Ulpian).

41 Cajetan, *Secunda Secundae Summae Theologiae cum Commentariis*, ad q.66.a.4. In Roman law the use of force is a criterion additional to those required for showing *furtum*. In Thomism violence is an alternative to secrecy, which is used to define *furtum*.

Not all Thomists were so eager to abandon their roots. Soto's account of *furtum* is entirely orthodox, following Aquinas to the letter: '*furtum est occulta acceptio rei aliene*'.[42] There is not a hint of Roman law to his treatment of the sin. Instead, his focus is on what property can be stolen, carefully drawing the boundary between *furtum* and *detractio*. Both involve causing a person to have less property than they are due, so *furtum* applies only to *bonorum temporalium* while *detractio* deals solely with *fama*.[43] Adopting the language of temporality instead of tangibility avoids giving *detractio* a broader ambit than it has in the *Summa*. *Rapina* is defined in precisely the same way as in the *Summa*, using force instead of secrecy to undermine the will of the property's owner.[44]

Navarrus walked the middle path between these two extremes. He adopted the language of *contrectatio*, making it clear that *furtum* involves an action and not just receipt of another's property, but also retained Aquinas' focus on the will of the property's owner.[45] The generic language of *invito domino* serves to unify *furtum* and *rapina*. The manner in which the two sins are distinguished within Thomism is through the way in which the will of the owner is circumvented: secretly in the case of *furtum*, and forcefully in the case of *rapina*. By grouping these two facets together as '*invito domino*' Navarrus skirts around the need for a separate discussion of *rapina*. As his goal is to explain the Commandment '*non furtum facies*', this is to be expected.

More significant than the merger of *furtum* and *rapina* is a further consequence of striking a path between the Roman and Thomist approaches to proprietary wrongs. As a consequence of omitting the language of *animus lucri faciendi* adopted by Cajetan, Navarrus attempted to bring together all three of the property delicts of Roman law:

> … non solum prohibetur contrectatio occulta, vel voluntas eam faciendi, quae proprie furtum dicitur: sed etiam omnis illa, qua aliquid ab aliquot iniuste accipitur, et iniuste retinetur, et omnis iniusta damni illatio …[46]

Furtum, already defined so as to encompass *rapina*, is now extended to cover *damnum iniuria datum*. This unprecedented unification of the wrongs to

42 Soto, *De Iustitia et Iure*, 5.3.1.

43 Ibid., 5.3.1.

44 Ibid., 5.3.2.

45 Navarrus, *Enchiridion*, 2.17.1.

46 Ibid., 2.17.1: 'Not only is stealthy interference prohibited, when done intentionally, which is properly called theft, but also unjust receipt of what belongs to another, or its unjust rentention, and the causation of unjust loss'.

property is presented as an addendum to the definition of *furtum*, and discussed no further. Its significance is unmistakable: the causation of loss now fits comfortably within the nominate sins of the *secunda secundae*. The Thomist framework now has a clear means of dealing with this scenario, and a clear link is drawn between bare *damnum* and *restitutio*.

Lessius takes a step back from Navarrus, and identifies three distinct wrongs to property: *furtum*, *rapina* and *damnum illatum*. *Furtum* and *rapina* are dealt with separately from *damnum illatum*. Acknowledging the tendency towards defining *furtum* in Roman law terms exhibited by his predecessors, Lessius defines *furtum* as '*occulta res aliena acceptio invito domino*'.[47] *Rapina* differs only in the use of force rather than secrecy.[48] Both of these are the paradigm of Thomist orthodoxy. It is surprising that Lessius does not say more about the civilian definitions of *furtum* employed by Navarrus and Cajetan. Lessius does not normally shy away from brazenly identifying mistakes in his predecessors. But with *furtum* he simply offers the civilian definition of *furtum*, mentions that it can be found in Navarrus, and then moves on to consider the three elements of the Thomist doctrine: *occulta*, *res aliena* and *invito domino*.[49] Even if Lessius' approach to *furtum* and *rapina* is uncharacteristically conservative, he makes up for it with his introduction of a new form of wrongdoing affecting property: *damnum illatum*.[50] Unlike Navarrus, he sees this as a type of wrongdoing distinct from *furtum*, rather than a subspecies of that wrong. It is in this context that he discusses issues relating to the nature of recoverable loss examined earlier. In the creation of *damnum illatum* Lessius overcame one of the final hurdles separating the Roman and Thomist approaches to wrongdoing by providing a means of analysing the *lex Aquilia* through a Thomist lens.

Contumelia and *detractio*

Perhaps the most radical changes within the surviving sins of the *secunda secundae* can be seen in relation to *contumelia* and *detractio*, the sins against *honor* and *fama* respectively. *Honor* occupied a peculiar position within Thomist thought. As the badge of virtue, by which a person's worth ought to be known, it was too important to be discarded. But it was not a concept that leant itself to juridification. *Honor* is a notion internal to the individual—it can only be harmed where a person makes a victim think

47 Lessius, *De Iustitia et Iure*, 2.12.1.

48 Ibid., 2.12.2. It is telling that for the definition of *rapina* Lessius cites Cajetan, but not for *furtum*. He clearly disagreed with Cajetan's shift to a civilian definition of the wrong.

49 Ibid., 2.12.1.

50 Ibid., 2.12.18.

worse of themselves. At an analytical level, who is it that actually causes harm to *honor*: the insulter or the insulted? And how can such harm be restored—are we to compel the insulted party to think better of themselves? *Fama*, on the other hand, had long been considered ephemeral property, and so lent itself to a legal context. These concerns reflect the first major shift in relation to *contumelia* and *detractio*, the ascendancy of the latter at the expense of the former.

A second strand of development relates to the way in which these harms occurred. Aquinas' sole requirement for *contumelia* was that a person's *honor* was harmed, and for *detractio* that *fama* was harmed through secret denigrations. The later Thomists sought to define the boundaries of both sins more rigorously, with particular attention paid to the newly dominant *detractio*. Finally, in relation to *contumelia* and *detractio* there is a curious exploration of a plurality of fault standards. Within the *Summa* virtually all sins against justice share a fault standard: voluntariness. This requirement is typically left unspoken. There are just two exceptions to this. The first is *homicidia*, in which accidents that ought to have been avoided appear sufficient for sinfulness. This is the sole deviation from the Thomist imposition of liability for only intentional wrongdoing. The second is *contumelia* and *detractio*, wherein the injuriousness of words is to be gauged according to the intention with which they were uttered.[51] Though intention is of course an aspect of voluntariness, this is the only context in which Aquinas explicitly demands an inquiry into the state of mind of the wrongdoer. This explicit reference to *intentio* clearly caught the eyes of many Thomists, and led to a third line on inquiry exploring, in typical scholastic style, the boundaries of intentions in this context.

All three of these strands can be seen to differing degrees in Soto's *De Iustitia et Iure*. Soto follows the structure of Aquinas' analysis of injurious words to the article. In the case of *contumelia*, both the sin and *honor* are defined in familiar terms. A handful of examples of contumelious actions are given but the form of the sin remains much as Aquinas left it.[52] *Detractio* is defined as *occulta denigratio alienae famae*, which omits only the *verba* of Aquinas' definition.[53] This likely reflects Aquinas' own inclusion of actions in his discussion of *detractio*.[54] Otherwise his outline of the sin is identical.

51 ST, II-II, q.72.a.2; ST, II-II, q.73.a.2.

52 Soto, *De Iustitia et Iure*, 5.9.1.

53 Ibid., 5.10.1; ST, II-II, q.73.a.1.

54 ST, II-II, q.72.a.1.ad.1.

The first major departure from Aquinas is Soto's definition of intention:

> Non censetur formaliter contumelia nisi quae ex animo convitiandi procedit, vel ex crassa ignorantia et negligentia.[55]

And for *detractio*:

> Quare ille proprie dicitur detractor qui ex intentione vel crassissima negligentia rumorem hominis absentia disseminit, cuius famam obscurat.[56]

The fault standard is more demanding in the case of *detractio*. Not only will *ignorantia* not suffice, the superlative *crassissima* is used to describe the required degree of *negligentia*. This is effectively the same in content as Aquinas' discussion of intention in relation to the two sins, but its transition to a more legal range of terminology is significant. In particular, the use of *animus* instead of *intentio* in the case of *contumelia* seems to be an effort to associate that form of sin with the Roman *iniuria*.[57] The association of *contumelia* with *iniuria* then serves to push *detractio* to the fore as an exclusively theological form of injurious words.[58] There are other signs of Soto's efforts to bring *contumelia* in line with the Roman *iniuria*. It is now possible for the sin to be aggravated where there is a risk of 'corruption'. The examples given are familiar: where the wronged party is a father, prelate or someone of high birth. As such a rule has no counterpart in the *Summa*, it is hard not to see this as Soto bringing the Thomist version of *iniuria* into line with Roman law's *atrox iniuria*. This can also be seen in a small number of explicit references to the Roman law of *iniuria* that pepper the text, and the alternative title of '*convicium*' given to *contumelia* in the title of the chapter.[59] These measures are necessary precisely because it would otherwise be unclear how *contumelia* fits into a Thomist model of delict.

55 Soto, *De Iustitia et Iure*, 5.9.2: 'Something should not formally be considered contumelious unless it stems from an intention to insult, or from crass ignorance or carelessness'.

56 Ibid., 5.10.2: 'It is proper to call a detractor he who intentionally or through crass carelessness spreads rumours about someone who is absent, harming his reputation'.

57 It is likely that Aquinas made a similar attempt through his very description of the sin. Labels like *convicium* and *contumelia* are hardly technical legal terms, but their preponderance in such a small section of the *Summa* is telling. And though it is difficult to know how familiar Aquinas was with the technicalities of Roman law, as an educated Italian in the thirteenth century it is almost inconceivable that he would be entirely ignorant of the subject.

58 There is not a single reference to Roman law to be found in Soto, *De Iustitia et Iure*, 5.10.

59 E.g. references to Labeo and Ulpian in Soto, *De Iustitia et Iure*, 5.9.1.

Identifying *contumelia* with Roman law was not a solution universally adopted. Navarrus' considers wrongs to *fama* and *honor* under the aegis of the eighth commandment: '*non sis falsus testis*'. The first section of this rushes through the gamut of relevant sins.[60] The remainder of the chapter considers *detractio* under two headings: '*de detractione sive murmuratione* and *de detractione sive revelatione secreti*'.[61] It is not difficult to see where his interests lie. *Contumelia* is dealt with in less than a hundred words, several of which are references to Aquinas.[62] In this space Navarrus identifies it as intentional harm to the *honor* of another.[63] *Honor* is an *exhibitio reverentiae*.[64] This is safely Thomist in content, and shows that Navarrus had no interest in straying from the content of the *Summa*.

By contrast, Navarrus' treatment of *detractio* is substantial and goes far beyond the *Summa* in several respects. It is characterised by three novel aspects: the division of *detractio* into two distinct forms, a wide array of factual examples and a concern for the unique difficulties encountered in the restoration of *fama*. The first two will be discussed here, the third having already been seen in relation to the development of *fama* as a commensurable interest. The two forms of detractio are *murmuratio* and *revelatio secreti*. The core of *murmuratio* is simultaneously familiar and alien. The basic definition of *murmuratio* is illustrative of this dissonance: an attack, whether direct or indirect, which harms another's *fama* or *gloria*.[65] The mention of direct and indirect attacks is a reference to an aspect of the *Summa* which Soto had glossed over relating to the vast number of ways in which a reputation can be harmed.[66] The reference to *gloria* is soon forgotten, with most of the passage referring to *fama* exclusively. But the core elements of the Thomist *detractio*, the need for secrecy and the primacy of malicious intentions, are absent. This is followed by seven factual examples of *murmuratio:* spreading falsehoods, revealing secrets, revealing secrets under torture, revealing secrets out of a sense of justice, authoring defamatory literature, listening to *detractio*, and the judge who forces the revelation of secrets during a trial.[67] Several of these might more naturally

60 Navarrus, *Enchiridion*, 18.1–16, and in particular 18.10, 18.13, 18.15.

61 Ibid., 18.17, 18.51. Herein the former will be referred to as *murmuratio* and the latter as *revelatio secreti* to avoid confusion. *Detractio* refers to both forms together.

62 Ibid., 18.10.

63 Ibid., 18.10.

64 Ibid., 18.11.

65 Navarrus, *Enchiridion*, 18.17.

66 ST, II-II, q.73.a.1.ad.3.

67 Navarrus, *Enchiridion*, 18.24–41.

be thought of as *revelatio secreti*, but are nevertheless dealt with as forms of *murmuratio*.

The second form of *detractio*, *revelatio secreti*, is considered separately. However, as the remedy discussed under *murmuratio* details the restoration of *fama* harmed by the revelation of the truth, it seems likely that the two sections are to be read together. A secret is simply something known only to a handful of people, which is *nec famosus nec notorius*.[68] Secrets have two forms: those knowable only to one person (i.e. thoughts) and those knowable to many (i.e. actions, including revealing thoughts through speech).[69] There are three instances where actions must be kept secret. Firstly, where the parties know, without the need for any explicit promise of secrecy, that they are obliged to keep the act a secret because its discovery would harm the interests of another, the revelation of the secret would be a sin.[70] Secondly, it would be a sin where there was an explicit or tacit promise to keep the secret.[71] Thirdly, in some situations divine law demands the secret be kept, such as secrets learnt through confession.[72]

This heavily casuistic analysis of *detractio* is a departure from Aquinas and Soto. However, by far the biggest difference is the omission of intention in most of the situations discussed. It appears as *mortifera intentione* in a discussion of the sinfulness of accusing someone of a crime; where the accuser had just motivations the accusation is sinless, whereas accusations motivated by a thirst for destruction are mortal sins.[73] Harm is used instead of intention to aggravate or reduce liability. Harm can be said to be *levis* or *notabilis*.[74] Loss is *notabilis* when it harms an interest of the soul, body or the loss is measurable in money.[75] Loss is *levis* when it is not *notabilis*. In drawing this boundary, Navarrus has to rely on the language of intention. *Fama*, as a *bonum exteriorum rerum* that is not measurable in money, falls outside all three of these categories. So Navarrus reintroduces intention to determine the severity of the sin:

68 Ibid., 18.51, relying on ST, II-II, q.70.a.2.ad.2.

69 Ibid., 18.52.

70 Ibid., 18.52. The interests listed are *animae, corpori, honori, vel famae, vel fortunis alicuius*—the straightforward hierarchy seen in Navarrus, *Enchiridion*, 18.47.

71 Ibid., 18.52.

72 Ibid., 18.52. See also Ibid., 18.51.

73 Ibid., 18.3[illegible].

74 Ibid., 18.20.

75 Ibid., 18.20.

> Est autem mortale, quoties sit animo famam proximi notabiliter laedendi: aut absque tali animo, eam notabiliter laedit ... Veniale tantum est, quoties sit animo laedendi parum, aut sine male animo parum nocet, aut notabiliter, sed ignoranter, vel sciens, sed inadvertenter, quam non teneretur advertere.[76]

This tautology effectively returns the content of the analysis to that found in the *Summa*. But Navarrus' flight to intention is clearly a last resort. If he thought it was possible to conceive of *fama* as an interest of the soul or body, or measurable in money, he would have tried to dispense with intention entirely, thereby harmonising Thomism's approach to fault across the entire range of wrongdoing.

Lessius' definition of *fama* is considerably more legalistic than that found in earlier authors. This can be seen in a text discussing whether a man commits a mortal sin when he defames himself.[77] The actual issue is whether a man can in any sense be understood to be the owner of his reputation. After all, a man who exists in isolation from birth to death will never have a reputation as defined by Thomism, and so it cannot be said to be a natural right. He attributes this line of thought to Cajetan.[78] He disagrees because 'man is the owner of his reputation, just as he is the owner of his own accomplishments'—natural rights can include what is earned through praiseworthy efforts.[79] Lessius even tries to articulate the sort of factors that contribute to a person's good name: eloquence, nobility, strength, beauty, power and wealth.[80]

Detractio is defined as '*alienae famae occulta et iniusta denigratio seu violatio*'.[81] *Contumelia* is not positively defined, but distinguished from *detractio* through the interest harmed. The title of the *dubitatio* does not even mention *contumelia*, showing by just how much the wrong had been marginalised by

76 Ibid., 18.21: 'This can be mortal, such as where a person intentionally harms the reputation of a noteworthy neighbour; or even where done unintentionally, if it does harm someone noteworthy ... It can be venial, when done with the intention of harming someone less important, or where the reputation of such a person is unintentionally harmed, or where the reputation of a noteworthy person is harmed through ignorance, or knowingly but inadvertently, in circumstances where there was no expectation to think of the harm'.

77 Lessius, *De Iustitia et Iure*, 2.11.6.

78 Referencing Cajetan, *Secunda Secundae Summae Theologiae cum Commentariis*, ad q.71.a.2.

79 Lessius, *De Iustitia et Iure*, 2.11.6: '*homo est Dominus suae famae, sicut suarum opum*'.

80 Ibid., 2.11.1.

81 Ibid., 2.11.2: 'The secret and unjust denigration or violation of another's reputation'.

this point.[82] After this, *contumelia* and *honor* are ignored until the very end of the chapter. Intention is used to determine the degree of sinfulness in a manner reminiscent of Navarrus.[83] *Detractio* is a mortal sin when intended with a direct desire to harm the *fama* of another. Other forms of intention are likely to result in a venial sin unless the harm inflicted is particularly grievous, which can justify the aggravation of liability.

The remainder of the first half of the chapter is a long list of situations, mostly addressing perceived difficulties in the accounts of earlier authors. The most noteworthy aspect in most is the incorporation of charity that was seen in Soto, but on a larger scale. Most of the situations discussed are familiar from Soto and Navarrus, but a few are novel. For example, can I defame someone who has built their reputation on false virtues? [84] The substance of the answer is predictable given the requirements of charity: where this false reputation poses a risk of harm to another, the revelation is justified. Where there is no risk of harm the deception must be kept secret. However, Lessius discusses the matter in terms of the fraudster's right to his reputation. He identifies a line of argument stemming from Adrian of Utrecht that differentiates between falsehoods grounded in error and outright hypocrisy.[85] In the former situation there may be some capacity in which one can be said to have a right to the continued existence of the falsehood, if only because the falsehood may one-day result in a criminal trial, to which the fraudster has a right. Hypocrisies are intended to deceive, and while morally reprehensible will never result in judicial proceedings. As such, there is no right to the maintenance of hypocrisy, and the revelation may be permissible regardless of the innocuousness of the deception.

From Aquinas through Soto and Navarrus to Lessius it is possible to trace an increasingly legal idea of wrongs to *fama* and *honor*. The latter interest, though never ignored, is paid markedly less attention in successive treatises, while *detractio* and *fama* are pushed to the fore. Intention, which in the *Summa* is necessary to determine whether a sin exists at all, performs the additional task of determining the severity of a sin already proven to exist. And the abstract definition of *detractio* provided by Aquinas—the secret denigration of a reputation—was substantiated through discussions of myriad fact patterns and their wrongfulness. These factors combined served to transform *detractio* and

82 Ibid., 2.11.2

83 Ibid., 2.11.3.

84 Ibid., 2.11.10.

85 Adrian of Utrecht, *Quaestiones in Quartum Sententiarum ubi Sacramentorum Materia Exactissime Tractatur*, 11.q.1.

fama, and to a lesser degree *contumelia* and *honor*, into wrongs that slotted neatly into the emerging Thomist model of delict.

Sexual Wrongdoing

The separation of sexual offences from matters relating to justice was problematic for the later Thomists. Their output can be broadly divided into two types of work: *quaestio* by *quaestio* glosses on the *Summa Theologiae* and restructured commentaries on the demands of justice (inevitably called *De Iustitia et Iure*). The former genre allowed their authors to consider the sexual offences, and they proved fertile ground for legal thinking. For example, Cajetan's gloss on *quaestio* 154 on lust runs to twenty pages, ten times the length of his gloss on *quaestio* 65 on mutilation and five times the length of his gloss on *quaestio* 64 on homicide. However, those authors who chose to write exclusively on justice had to make a difficult decision to either omit the sexual offences as a topic irrelevant to justice, or break from Aquinas' structure.

The decision may seem like an easy one to modern eyes. However, the reverence with which Aquinas was viewed by his followers cannot be underestimated. Thus it should come as no surprise that otherwise comprehensive commentaries like Soto's *De Iustitia et Iure* omit sexual wrongdoing entirely out of fealty to the content of Aquinas' analysis of justice.[86] The number of Thomists who actually attempted to deal with sexual wrongdoing can be counted on one hand. In addition to Cajetan, Navarrus, following the structure of the Ten Commandments, discussed it in relation to the sixth commandment: *non maechaberis*.[87] Of the authors of restructured commentaries, only Lessius included sexual wrongdoing as a distinct type of injustice. He categorised such wrongs as offences to *corpus*. There are just two: *stuprum* and adultery.[88] Though lip service is still paid to lust contrary to termperance as the underpinning sinful concept, the very fact that *restitutio* is possible shows that these offences have been relocated to the domain of justice.[89]

The paucity of authors dealing with sexual wrongdoing makes it possible to give a comprehensive analysis of how the Thomist treatment of such wrongs developed. The first substantial treatment is Cajetan's gloss. His thoughts on

86 See also Covarruvias, who discusses only bigamy as an aspect of conversion: Covarruvias, *Opera Omnia*, 669ff ('*de bigamis et neophytis*').

87 Navarrus, *Enchiridion*, 16.1–50.

88 Lessius, *De Iustitia et Iure*, 2.10.

89 It will be remembered that *restitutio* is defined as an act of commutative justice: ST, II-II, q.62.a.1. Lessius was not the first to suggest *restitutio* was available after sexual wrongdoing: Navarrus, *Enchiridion*, 16.16–19.

nocturnal pollution are indistinguishable from Aquinas', and are equally devoid of legally interesting material.[90] Considerably harder to navigate was the boundary between fornication, seduction and *raptus*. Aquinas said that fornication is simply sex outside of wedlock, *raptus* is the forceful violation of a virgin, and *stuprum* is the violation of a virgin under her parents' care. Aquinas conceded that there was a great deal of overlap between these three sins, but maintained that there was enough content sufficiently unique to *stuprum* and *raptus* to differentiate them from each other and from fornication. These doubts were redoubled by Cajetan. *Stuprum* caused particular difficulties, as revealed through a number of hypotheticals posed without a clear answer. For example, if a virgin masturbates does she commit *stuprum*? Cajetan thinks she probably does, as '*virginitas non perditur irreparabiliter et illicite nisi per stuprum*'.[91] This is a possibility not explored by Aquinas, but is in line with his reasoning on *stuprum*. In this and a number of other hypotheticals Cajetan shifts the focus of *stuprum* away from the violation of a parent's guardianship and onto the taking of a person's virginity. This process is completed through an examination of the sinfulness of a person who has consensual sex with a virgin who has no parents. The lack of force means it cannot be *raptus*. They are not related, so it is not incest, nor are they married, ruling out adultery. Yet a virginity has been taken, so it cannot be '*simplex fornicatio*'.[92] Three options remain: it is not sinful activity, deflowering a virgin is no different to *fornicatio*, or it is *stuprum*. Cajetan chose the latter, arguing that the loss of virginity made it vital that this wrong be viewed more seriously than fornication.

Having rebranded *stuprum*, he turns to *raptus*. His account of *raptus* is in line with Aquinas', his primary concern being the effects of *raptus* on marriage. This has two aspects: firstly, can a man who has committed the sin marry before he has made penance? Secondly, what effect does *raptus* have on a marriage?[93] Neither question has any bearing on the delictualisation of lust, and need not be considered further. However, in the examples explored Cajetan clearly places the focus on *raptus* on the use of force, not the taking of virginity. In so doing *stuprum* and *raptus* are given clearer identities than they had under Aquinas: *stuprum* is the violation of a virgin, regardless of consent, while *raptus* is using force to have sex, regardless of the victim's status. The remaining sins are largely underdeveloped. Adultery remains much as it was in Aquinas, with most of Cajetan's commentary given to hashing out the different requirements for

90 Cajetan, *Secunda Secundae Summae Theologiae cum Commentariis*, ad q.154.a.5.

91 Ibid., ad q.154.a.6: 'Virginity isn't irreparably and illicitly lost except through *stuprum*'.

92 Ibid., ad q.154.a.6.

93 Ibid., ad q.154.a.6.

sinfulness for each gender.[94] His discussion of incest is dedicated to the degree of consanguinity permissible before a relationship enters sinful waters, and whether incestuous relationships are inherently sinful.[95] Taken as a whole, Cajetan's discussion of the sins of lust are concerned exclusively with when the sin exists. The discussion is founded entirely on Aquinas, though with biblical support where appropriate. Cajetan clearly viewed sexual wrongdoing as a matter disconnected from justice and, by extension, law. Consequently, there is no discussion to be found of the secular consequences of any of the sins of lust, whether compensatory or penal.

Navarrus' exploration of adultery and related sins begins by paying lip service to Aquinas and Cajetan, setting out six types of sin identified in their works:

> [P]rima est fornicatio simplex, quae est inter solutos, solutos, inquam, non solum a vincula matrimoniali ... Secunda species est adulterium; sciliciet, cum alter vel uterque est coniugatus. Tertia est incestus, quando scilicet, ambo sunt consanguinei, vel affines ... Quarta stuprum; quando scilicet, femina est virgo est: est enim peccatum speciale ratione fractionis sigilli virginalis ... Quinta est raptus; quando scilicet violenter aliqua contra voluntatem ipsius, vel partis eius extrahitur a domo sua ... et etiam quando violenter extorquetur copula, sive sit virgo, sive non ... Sexta est contra naturam, quando non solum peccatur contra rationem naturalem...[96]

This lengthy quotation, despite making constant reference to Aquinas and Cajetan, contains several important departures from their works. Firstly, the number of sins has been decreased from eight to six. Navarrus omits nocturnal pollution and sacrilege, notably the two sins of lust that would be the most difficult to reframe in legal terms. Of the remaining sins, two have altered definitions. Navarrus departs from Aquinas by following Cajetan's definition of *stuprum*, with no mention of guardianship. But unique to Navarrus is the

94 Ibid., ad q.154.a.6.

95 Ibid., ad q.154.a.9.

96 Navarrus, *Enchiridion*, 16.3: 'The first is simple fornication, which takes place between singles, being those unbound by marriage ... The second species is adultery, namely, where one or both of the parties is married. The third is incsent, where both are related by blood, or affinity. The fourth is *stuprum*, where the woman is a virgin, a sin by special virtue of the breaking of the seal of virginity ... The fifth is rape, which is violent and against the other's will, or dragging a girl from her home ... and this is so whether she is a virgin or not ... Sixth are the sins against nature, which go against natural reason...'.

definition of *raptus*, which associates violence with the absence of consent. This focuses the violence of *raptus* firmly on the victim, unlike Aquinas who was satisfied to combine 'violence' (i.e. disrespect) towards a father and consensual intercourse with a daughter to find *raptus*.[97] Moreover, by explicitly making it irrelevant whether or not the victim was a virgin, Navarrus like Cajetan gave both *stuprum* and *raptus* clear identities as unique offences.

Though these definitional tweaks are clearly of significance to the juridification of lust, his most important contribution was to lay the groundwork for the remediation of such sins. His thoughts on the matter are fairly insubstantial, considering only how *restitutio* might be made to virgins, or those believed to be virgins. He requires *dolo et deceptione* for such liability, regardless of the truth of their virginity.[98] However, regardless of bad intentions a person who takes a virginity is required to take his victim as his wife. In so doing the harm to her marriage prospects are purportedly restored. Like Cajetan and Aquinas before him, Navarrus makes no use of legal sources. However, his altered definitions and the introduction of remedial concerns paved the way for Lessius to turn lust into something legally recognisable.

Lessius' account of lust is a departure from his predecessors. Though the full title of his treatise is *De Iustitia et Iure Caeterisque Virtutibus Cardinalibus*, lust is divided between his treatments of temperance and justice. Those aspects of lust which can be given a legal form are treated both in his sections on temperance and justice, which makes them the subjects of *restitutio*. Only two sins are handled in this way: *adulterium* and *stuprum*. These, he argues, are the two sins of lust that cause harm to another with consequences that can be restored. The remainder of lust's sins are dealt with exclusively in temperance.[99] This division allowed Lessius to delineate between the secular and theological issues that arise out of lust, as well as their legal and theological consequences.

Lessius defines *stuprum* as '*defloratio virginis*', an affront both to the virgin and her parents.[100] Unlike Cajetan, Lessius places consent at the fore. The relevant consent is typically not the virgin's but that of her parents or guardian. The virgin's views on the matter are relevant only if she is *sui iuris*.[101] The result is a conception of *stuprum* narrower than its predecessors, greatly limiting the

97 ST, II-II, q.154.a.7.

98 Navarrus, *Enchiridion*, 16.16.

99 Lessius, *De Iustitia et Iure*, 4.3.7–15.

100 Ibid., 2.10.1.

101 Ibid., 2.10.1: '*si puella non est sub potestate parentum vel tutorum, vel si illis consentientibus se pariatur violari, illud stuprum non continent specialem malitiam mortalem supra fornicationem*'.

significance of virginity to legal evaluations of an action's wrongfulness. This is further illustrated by a later passage on the sinfulness of '*corruptor virginis*'. Lessius simply states: '*si puella libere consensit, ipse ad nihil ei tenetur*'.[102] Significantly, this conclusion is built not on theological grounds, but legal principle: '... *quia volenti non fit iniuria*'.[103] The question then becomes the meaning of *volenti*. Consent can be overwhelmed through force or through fraud.[104] Using force in this way is, Lessius argues, the defining feature of *raptus*. Thus *raptus* is a subspecies of *stuprum* in Lessius' framework, not a distinct sin against justice. The most common form of fraud in this context is an empty marriage proposal, though any other deceit will suffice.

Lessius' discussion of adultery focuses narrowly on illegitimate progeny, which he views as the only real *damnum* to stem from adultery.[105] An adulterer is only liable to the husband of his paramour where it can be claimed with absolute certainty that the child is his.[106] However, when this can be proven the extent of the adulterer's liability is impressive, tracing into any financial loss attributable to the illegitimate child's existence. This includes not only the cost of raising the child, but the harm done to any legitimate progeny's inheritance.[107] The position of the adultress is less clear, with Lessius imposing a fairly nebulous liability: '*tenetur quantum fieri potest, sine famae dispendio et vitae periculo procurare, ne legitimi heredes ratione huius illegitimae prolis aliquid detrimenti capiant*'.[108] The underlying assumption appears to be that the adulterer would make right any loss caused, excusing the adultress from *restitutio* as double recovery is itself an injustice. Her liability is more of a failsafe for the cuckolded husband, and she is presumably liable to the same extent as her paramour.

It is clear that sexual wrongdoing was not a significant part of the Thomist theory of delict. Structurally isolated from the outset, most authors simply ignored its existence. The explanation is simple: wrongful behaviour is so because it exists in relation to a single sin, contrary to a single virtue. Though justice governs relationships between people, the defining feature of sexual wrongdoing must be its sexuality, a factor which instantly links it to temperance and lust in the Thomist mindset. Conjoined in this way, there is no room

102 Ibid., 2.10.2.

103 Ibid., 2.10.2.

104 Ibid., 2.10.2.

105 Ibid., 2.10.5.

106 Ibid., 2.10.6.

107 Ibid., 2.10.6.

108 Ibid., 2.10.7.

for discussions grounded in justice. It cannot be true that the Thomists did not realise that sexual wrongdoing raised legal questions. Instead those questions did little to illuminate the nature of justice and the perfect form of law.

Nevertheless, some authors could not leave the topic alone. Cajetan and Navarrus both used their adopted structures to facilitate discussion. Navarrus, in addressing the Ten Commandments, was free to address the problem of adultery and cognate wrongs. Cajetan simply looked at the entirety of the *Secunda Secundae*, while many of his peers paid lip service to the cardinal virtues other than justice. But it is only with Lessius that we find the argument that sexual wrongdoing can be wrongful in two distinct senses. The result is a severely scaled back version of the sins against lust found in Aquinas, but with clearly articulated considerations of the legal consequences of *stuprum* and adultery.

From Wrongs to Rights

Within the *Summa* wrongdoing is primarily defined through prohibited conduct. Although *restitutio*, the remedy that binds everything together, is triggered by a state of affairs, the nominate sins all focus on conduct. These sins are invariably formulated in extremely expansive terms. Homicide is any voluntary causation of death other than acts in self-defence where death is not the intended consequence of the defender's actions. Theft is the secret asportation of another's property, while robbery is violent asportation. *Contumelia* is an attack by words or deeds on another's *honor*. *Detractio* is secretly harming another's *fama* through the spread of gossip or rumours.

With a handful of exceptions, the sins enumerated in the *Summa* have fairly relaxed conduct requirements. Most focus on the causation of the prohibited harm, with additional requirements used to differentiate one sin from another. Theft is secretive and robbery violent simply so that it is possible to identify which sin has been committed when property is taken.[109] *Detractio* is secretive to prevent overlap with *contumelia*.[110] Thus while the sins are discussed in the language of conduct, Aquinas' model of wrongdoing is not far removed from a rights-centric approach to delict. There is not a terribly large gap between

109 ST, II-II, q.66.a.4.

110 ST, II-II, q.73.a.3.

defining *homicidia* as 'causing death by any means whatsoever' and 'the infringement of the right to life'.

Nevertheless, the conduct-centric approach to wrongdoing survived into the earlier Thomists of the sixteenth century. Sometimes this was an inevitable product of each author's adopted structure. So long as Cajetan was writing an article-by-article commentary on the *secunda secundae*, the discussion of individual sins was unavoidable. So too for Navarrus, lest his *Enchiridion* rewrite the Ten Commandments. But even the likes of Soto, who adopted his own structure for his treatises, dealt conservatively with his source material.[111] The transition to a rights-centric model of delict was only made by Lessius. The means by which this was achieved was extremely simple, through a very slight abstraction from the existing categories of wrongdoing recognised by Thomism. '*De homicidio*' and '*de mutilatione*' became '*de iniuria in corpus proxima per homicidium vel mutilationem*'.[112] '*De contumelia*' and '*de detractione*' became '*de iniuriis fame et honoris per detractionem et contumeliam*'.[113] The content was very similar, the scope of the wrongdoing examined largely unchanged. All that was required for a rights-centric model of delict was a basic inversion, from 'murder: a wrong against life' to 'wrongs against life, such as murder'.[114] This inversion was applied to every type of wrong against justice.

Having identified the rights protected by the individual wrongs of the *secunda secundae*, Lessius reorganised Aquinas' sins to reflect the hierarchy of interests:

111 Hence '*de homicidio*' (Soto, *De Iustitia et Iure*, 5.1), '*de mutilatione membrorum*' (Soto, *De Iustitia et Iure*, 5.2), etc.

112 Lessius, *De Iustitia et Iure*, 2.9.

113 Ibid., 2.10.

114 A more difficult question to answer is why this inversion happened so late in the life of Thomism. Thomists were accustomed to using the language of rights in legalistic arguments: Brian Tierney, *The Idea of Natural Rights: Studies on Natural Rights, Natural Law, and Church Law, 1150–1625* (Atlanta, Ga.: Scholars Press, 1997), 255–315. Moreover, Aquinas' categorisation of *corpus* as an aspect of *dominium* (ST, I, q.96.a2) ought to have provided an easy path to a rights-centric model of delict. The answer likely lies in a reluctance to depart from the *Summa Theologiae*. Although a rights-centric approach would necessitate departing from the structure of the *secunda secundae*, this is likely more than a problem of mere taxonomy; viewing life as an individual right, an aspect of *dominium*, runs counter to Aquinas' view that human life is ultimately vested in the community (ST, II-II, q.64.a.5).

TABLE 9.1 *Lessius' conversion of sins into rights*

Order of sins in the *secunda secundae*	Order of wrongs in Lessus' *De Iustitia et Iure*
Homicidia (ST, II-II, q.64)	*De iniuria in bonis spiritualibus* (2.8)
Mutilatio (ST, II-II, q.65)	*De iniuria in corpus proxima per homicidium vel mutilationem* (2.9)
Furtum et rapina (ST, II-II, q.66)	*De iniuria in corpus proximi per adulterium et stuprum* (2.10)
Contumelia (ST, II-II, q.72)	*De iniuriis fame et honoris per detractionem et contumeliam* (2.11)
Detractio (ST, II-II, q.73)	*De iniuriis fortunarum per furtum, rapinam, damnumve illatum*

This table 9.1 records the location of those sins dealt with by Aquinas that survived the transformation from theology to law. That Lessius is organising his treatise around the Thomist hierarchy of *bona* is unmistakable. He begins with the soul, despite there being nothing of legal significance to say about it. *Bona animae* had been absent from Thomist examinations of wrongdoing up until this point, but are reintroduced here for the sake of completeness. Below *bona animae* rank *bona corporis*. These are divided into two categories. Within the first the deprivation of life comes before mere physical injury, as the greatest affront the body can suffer. The second category deals with sexual wrongdoing, as the quality of the wrong is different as an affront both to temperance and justice. Turning to *bona exteriorum rerum*, Lessius makes the conscious division to reverse the order of wrongs to physical and intangible property. After all, '*melius est nomen bonum quam divitiae multae; super argentum et aurum gratia bona*'.[115] As a result, the entire structure of the Thomist theory of delict is redefined according to the interest harmed.

This distillation of wrongs into interests allowed Lessius to make one further generalisation. In saying that *restitutio* responds to any *iniusta acceptio*, defined as *damnum* including life, honour and other rights other than property, Lessius was advancing an approach to delict remarkably close to that which would be found two decades later in Grotius' *De Iure Belli ac Pacis*: it is the infringement of a right that constitutes *damnum* and thereby triggers *restitutio*.[116]

115 Proverbs, 22:1.

116 Lessius *De Iustitia et Iure*, 2.7.5.

A single remedy covering all wrongdoing, being compelled into action by the diminution of what a person naturally has, all wrapped up in the language of *damnum*. By this point the Thomist model of delict had been transformed into an almost entirely independent system of rules for establishing liability in the wake of wrongdoing. All that remains is the question of fault as a means of attributing responsibility.

CHAPTER 10

Roman Law and Thomism

The last strand of delict within Thomism that requires attention, fault, provides a basis for the examination of a broader theme: the degree to which the Thomists drew upon civil law sources in creating their conception of delict. The interactions between the two traditions thus far has been fitful. The Thomist remedy, *restitutio*, bears almost no relation to anything civilian, and was developed only through a concern for practicality. The individual formulations of wrongs, on the other hand, borrowed heavily from the *Corpus Iuris Civilis* and the later civil law, sometimes to the complete exclusion of Thomist doctrine.[1] In relation to the Thomist approach to contract, Decock described the approach of the Thomists indicative of a 'syncretic legal culture', bringing together civil law, canon law, humanism and scholasticism.[2] Is this a claim that holds true within delict?

The Rise of Fault within Thomism

The Thomist theory of delict described thus far is missing one crucial element: a fault concept. This gap was filled through one further conceptual shift: the voluntariness precondition put forward by Aquinas was transformed into a positive element of liability, namely *culpa*. The significance of this development to the later life of *restitutio* outside of Thomism cannot be understated. As a delictual remedy *restitutio* was attractive. As understood by the early seventeenth century it covered any loss that could be assigned a monetary value, and required nothing more than the infringement of an interest. Unlike its Roman law analogues, it was a remedy that could be simply stated and universally applied. This would make it extremely attractive to natural lawyers seeking simple and all-encompassing legal principles.

The only hurdle to the applicability of *restitutio* outside of Thomism was the language of injustice. *Iniuria* had come to be used as a synonym for *peccatum*, with both words referring to an untenable state of affairs rather than conduct. The more legally interested within the Second Scholastic repeated a juristic

1 E.g. Cajetan on *furtum* above, 191.

2 Decock, *Theologians and Contract Law*, 40.

 | DOI 10.1163/9789004344372_011

interpretation innovated centuries earlier: the reinterpretation of *iniuria* as *culpa*. In addition to the benefits wrought by this shift when employed within the civilian tradition, the Thomist transition to *culpa* shed *restitutio* of its theological baggage and brought the concept in line with the civilian method of analysing wrongdoing.

The contribution of the sixteenth-century Thomists would be to twist Aquinas' foundations into something legally acceptable. Even if substantively his theory of action could fulfil the same function as a fault element through the notion of voluntariness, it required one to subscribe to a particular view of the world and its relationship with God that would be unattractive to many. The role of voluntariness in Aquinas' ethics would be problematic for anyone disposed towards determinism, a particularly thorny issue in sixteenth and seventeenth-century theology and philosophy across Europe. By repackaging the concept as a discrete legal ingredient, just one of many, the theory of action was shorn of any necessary moral or theological implications. For Grotius, who was looking for an uncontroversial and universal formulation of liability for wrongdoing, the value of this severability is difficult to overstate. These changes were made tentatively, with individual Thomists making small advances in discrete areas of overlap between *culpa* and *restitutio*. Clearly the sharp distinction between *restitutio* and fault in the *Summa* loomed large. But by the turn of the seventeenth century the distinction had been sufficiently undermined for Lessius to draw the individual strands together into a coherent exposition of the relationship between *restitutio* and *culpa*.

The shift in terminology from *culpa* to *iniuria* had a further important benefit: the point at which responsibility crystallises. Sinfulness is determined according to the subject's state of mind—the actual manifestation of his desires and intentions in the physical world are of surprisingly little significance within Thomism.[3] Physical realities only affect sinfulness insofar as they enhance the praiseworthiness or sinfulness of the will (*voluntas*). The implications of this for juridified Thomism were significant, forcing all liability to be conceived of as inherently inchoate. Merely formulating an intention to kill, wound, steal or defame was sufficient to impose sanctions, though *restitutio* would only react to manifested imbalances in the physical world. In practice, without any physical wrong to undo the only remedy available would be *satisfactio*. It goes without saying that basing liability solely on a person's state of mind would be wildly impractical, both for its effects on litigation rates and on matters of evidence. Wrongs, on the other hand, typically need to have some physical

3 ST, I-II, q 20.a.4.

manifestation before they are actionable. By redefining the existing range of *peccata* as wrongs the Thomists could force them into the *forum externum*, turning them into something legally acceptable.

The juridification of voluntariness into *culpa* is convoluted.[4] At the beginning of his section on the topic, Lessius laments the terminological morass posed by legal and theological usages of the term *culpa*. Few of his predecessors were as sensitive to the confusion the term could cause, and unravelling the various strands of thinking is no easy task. Not only does *culpa* mean different things to lawyers and theologians, even within Thomism its role is ambiguous. Aquinas' conception of voluntariness was functionally similar to fault in Roman law, insofar as it prescribes a threshold of blameworthiness needed for sinfulness (liability) to be inferred. It did, however, stand somewhere between *dolus* and *culpa*, ascribing sinfulness for direct intentions and wilful blindness. However, *culpa* itself also refers to the state of affairs whereby one person has voluntarily harmed the property interests of another, the end product of the juridification of *peccatum* just alluded to.[5] Depending on the Thomist, *culpa* could be used both as an ingredient of, and a synonym for, liability.

The absence of a clear path through this terminological thicket led to a wide variety of interpretations of *culpa*. The conjoining of Roman *culpa* with *restitutio* was actually one of the earliest solutions explored. The *Summa Angelica* offered a cursory overview of the term's legal connotations, referencing Bartolus instead of the Church Fathers.[6] Explicit reference is made to Bartolus' discussion of *culpa* in relation to the contract of deposit, presumably a reference to his comments on D.16.3.32.[7] Using the writings of the commentators, and in particular Bartolus, Chivasso recreates the civilian gradation of *culpa*. In total he provides three forms of *culpa*. The first, *culpa lata*, is equivalent to *dolus*.[8] The second, *culpa levis*, is failing to act as the diligent man (*diligens homo*) would.[9] The third, *culpa levissima*, is failing to act as an extremely diligent man

4 This chapter will consider only those Thomists used by Grotius, who together present a sufficiently tangled development in themselves. For the contributions of other Thomists, and in particular Gabriel Vasquez, see Jansen, *Theologie, Philosophie und Jurisprudenz*, 127–136.

5 ST, I, q.48.a.6: *'Malum vero culpae opponitur proprie ipsi bono increato, contrariatur enim impletioni divinae voluntatis, et divino amori quo bonum divinum in seipso amatur'*; ST, I-II, q.21.a.2: *'Ex hoc enim dicitur aliquis actus culpabilis vel laudabilis, quod imputatur agenti, nihil enim est aliud laudari vel culpari, quam imputari alicui malitiam vel bonitatem sui actus'*.

6 Di Chivaso, *Summa Angelica*, 97 ('*de verbo culpa*').

7 Ibid., 97 ('*de verbo culpa*').

8 Ibid., 97 point 1.

9 Ibid., 97 point 2.

(*dilligentissimus*) would.[10] The latter two forms of fault are explicitly viewed as contractual concepts, with the former being anchored to *pignus* and the latter *commodatum*. Within the *Summa Angelica culpa* is a legal concept, but one isolated from wrongdoing.

By far the most interesting aspect of the *Summa Angelica*'s cursory overview of *culpa* is the link drawn between *culpa* and *restitutio*. It is claimed that *restitutio* can only be demanded for '*omni damno ex quacumque culpa*'. Later generations interpreted this as a reference to *culpa levissima*.[11] Chivasso's intentions are not quite so clear cut. Though it is perfectly natural to link 'any fault whatsoever' with the most inclusive gradation of *culpa*, the remainder of the passage relies entirely on the language of *negligentia* and *diligentia*. In so doing Chivaso draws together the canonist strands on these specific notions, uniting them under the umbrella of *culpa*, leaving the latter loosely defined so as to include the fault concepts of all who came before him.[12] This brief discussion represents the first association of *restitutio* with fault. This is particularly significant if the fault standard being used was the same as that used by contemporary canonists. But even if the standard incorporated is the lesser *culpa levissima*, it is nevertheless significant that *restitutio* was given a *de minimis* fault requirement. In arriving at his position Chivaso provides little in the way of discussion—the purpose of the *Summa Angelica* was to expound rules, not to justify them. Nevertheless, it was this passage that would provide a foundation for the handful of Thomists who sought to further analyse the Thomist theory of delict in terms of fault.

Chivasso's approach was carried into the Second Scholastic by Cajetan, who also analysed questions of voluntariness through terms such as *diligentia* and *negligentia*. This can be seen in his commentary on Aquinas' article on accidental homicides. Aquinas said that accidents cannot be sinful unless the accidental cause is one which ought to have been avoided.[13] This means that a person is only responsible for an accidental death where he was engaged in an unlawful activity, and in so doing displayed less care than was owed. Aquinas then suggests that a failure to take due care might also result in responsibility for a death even when pursuing a lawful activity.[14]

10 Ibid., 97 point 3.

11 E.g. Lessius, *De Iustitia et Iure*, 2.7.6.

12 Thus he manages to encompass the fault concepts of Gratian (*prima*, D.50.c.37), the Decretals (X.5.36.9) and '*multi doctores*': Lessius, *De Iustitia et Iure*, 2.7.6.

13 ST, II-II, q.64.a.8.

14 ST, II-II, q.64.a.8. It is this claim that founds the argument that Aquinas had a standard of negligence. It would be unwise in the absence of any further evidence to take his

Cajetan links this article to a scenario identified by Gordley as having been lifted from Gratian.[15] It discusses the liability of a person who falls asleep in their bed with an infant child, and as a result the child dies:

> Si autem honestatur circumstantiis, puta quia lectus est ex extensis, et non habetur prope se, et nutrix consuevit semper invenire in eodem loco et situ, quo se incipiendo dormire posuit, et implicabilitas infantis hoc exigat, excusari videtur: quia non est rationale his concurrentibus, periculum timere.[16]

The terminology Cajetan relies upon in this scenario is the language of rationality. The *nutrix* acted according to a logic that was impliedly acceptable. The bed was big, the child wouldn't go to sleep unless she acted as she did, and she was not accustomed to moving while asleep. She had no reason to fear a fatal accident. Elsewhere in his commentary on the same article Cajetan uses words like *prudentia, diligentia* and *negligentia* to describe the boundaries of culpable accidents. That he is drawing on canonist texts in order to understand Aquinas on this topic points quite strongly towards a civilian basis for his thought. However, like Aquinas, there is no indication that this sort of analysis extended beyond responsibility for homicide.

Less radical was the analysis exemplified by Soto, who persisted in defining *culpa* along theological lines. He argues that it is essentially the stain of sin on man's conscience, and can be removed only by making *restitutio*.[17] Rather than being an ingredient of a moral or legal theory of responsibility, it is a state of being akin to indebtedness. A person remains a sinner until they have made their peace not only with God but also with the wronged party. This leads to a convoluted analysis of the sinfulness of the accidental killer.[18] He haphazardly weaves together three ideas: voluntariness, intention and *culpa*. Voluntariness and intention perform the same function in parallel worlds, the former

comments as applying to any wrong other than homicide. The wording of the article certainly does not support a broader application: '... *non evadit homicidii reatum si ex eius opere mors hominis consequatur*'.

15 Gordley, *Foundations of Private Law*, 201 n.122, citing C.2.q.5.c.2.

16 Cajetan, *Secunda Secundae Summae Theologiae cum Commentariis*, ad q.64.a.8: 'If, however, they were honest in the circumstances, thinking for example that bed was bigger, and the child isn't beside them, and the nurse always finds themselves in that very spot when she goes to sleep, and she has no choice because the child is implacable, then she seems to be excused, because it is not rationale in these circusmtances to fear the danger'.

17 Soto, *De Iustitia et Iure*, 4.7.2.

18 Ibid., 5.1.9: '*utrum qui casu alterum occiderit, fiat homicidii reus*'.

determining the existence of sin, the latter wrongdoing.[19] The occasional references to *culpa* are confusing and seemingly tautological. He writes that '*si ex intentione illum tam grauiter vulnerasset, eadem culpa inficeretur ac si esset homicida*'.[20] In this passage *culpa* does not appear to add anything to *intentio* other than the 'staining' (*inficeretur*) of the wrongdoer, obliging him to make amends. Given Soto's proprietary conception of *restitutio* and the lack of further explanation, it is not at all clear how, if at all, Soto intended for this stain to be removed.

Navarrus represents yet another approach to the problem. For him, *culpa* was first and foremost a contractual concept.[21] Bound by the structure of the Ten Commandments, the context most amenable to a discussion of contractual doctrine was theft. His sprawling account of theft takes into account anything connected with property, from the ownership of bees to the real contracts. It is in the latter context, '*de peccatis circa contractus, et primo circa depositum*', that *culpa* is discussed.[22] Unlike Soto, he was comfortable framing *culpa* in Roman terms, identifying it as the middle ground between *dolus* and *casus*, and subcategorising it into *culpa lata*, *levis* and *levissima*. And, despite his comfort using the language of Roman law, his goal was consistently to support his position through references both to jurists and Aquinas. He begins by arguing that these variations of *culpa* taken together act as the gateway to contractual sin.[23] So far as Roman authority is concerned, he needs to do nothing more than point towards the real contracts as a whole. For Thomist authority, he relies on two passages. The first justifies the use of *dolus*, and is familiar: a reference to the article in the *prima secundae* that establishes that praise and blame are only merited where a person acts voluntarily, thereby providing a Thomist basis for considerations of fault.[24] The second brings *culpa* into the equation. For this, he relies on a passage from the *prima* in which *culpa* and *poena* are differentiated.[25] Aquinas describes *culpa* as voluntarily causing evil (*malum*).[26]

19 Ibid., 5.1.9: '*peccatum non est nisi quatenus voluntarius*'; '*nemo dans opera res licitae, neque sinistra habens intentione, dum modo debita adhibuerit diligentia ne noceat quia ex actione sua sequatur homicidiu, reatu illius incurrit*'.

20 E.g. Soto, *De Iustitia et Iure*, 5.1.9.

21 Navarrus, *Enchiridion*, 17.177.

22 Ibid., 17.177–181.

23 Ibid., 17, 177.

24 ST, I-II, q.21.a.2.

25 ST, I, q.48.a.5.

26 ST, I, q.48.a.5: '*Malum autem quod consistit in subtractione debitae operationis in rebus voluntariis, habet rationem culpae. Hoc enim imputatur alicui in culpam, cum deficit a perfecta*

Theologically tenuous, the association of *culpa* with voluntariness (and, by extension, *dolus*) was sufficient to embark on a discussion of principle.

The first standard to be considered is *dolus*. Navarrus notes that both Aquinas and the jurists recognise that *dolus* has two forms. Within Thomism, *dolus* is split into *fallacia* and *fraus*.[27] The former is *dolus* manifested in words, the latter in deeds.[28] The civilians divided *dolus* according to whether it was *verus* or *praesumptus*.[29] He argues that the *dolus praesumptus* of the civilians is not actually *dolus* at all. Rather, it is *culpa lata*. There is a great deal of support for such a position, though he does not rely on it, as *dolus* and *culpa lata* had been equated for centuries.

Thus the *dolus verus* of the civilians aligns with the bifurcated *dolus* of the Thomists. Navarrus then moves on to *culpa*:

> Lata est, quam regulariter omnes communiter vitant; qualis est eius, qui extra domum, aut scamno librum sibi commodatum relinquit. Levis vero, quam regulariter homines diligentes suae professionis evitant; qualis est eius, qui librum aliquem in suo cubiculo, ostio tamen aperto, relinquit. Levissima, quam homines diligentissimi vitare solent; qualis est eius, qui librum commodatum intra cubiculum relinquit, quod clave observavit, non tamen manu, an bene obseratum esset tentavit, iuxta commune opinionem ...[30]

Culpa lata retains its association with *dolus*, but it still needs content. If it is not the same as positive intent, what is it? Navarrus defines *culpa lata* as (implicitly a failure to abide by) the standards of ordinary people. This is the language typically used to define *culpa levis*. *Culpa levis* is instead conceptualised as a standard of professional care. *Culpa levissima* retains its usual definition as the standard of extremely diligent people. Tellingly, there are no references

---

actione, cuius dominus est secundum voluntatem. Sic igitur omne malum in rebus voluntariis consideratum vel est poena vel culpa'.

27 Navarrus, *Enchiridion*, 17, 177.

28 *Fraus*: ST, I-II, q.77; *fallacia*: ST, II-II, q.118.a.8.

29 Navarrus, *Enchiridion*, 17.177, with a generic citation of Bartolus.

30 Ibid., 17.178: '*Lata* refers to those standards by which everyone ordinarily lives; consider he who, when out of the house, leaves a book he has been loaned on a bench. *Levis* is the standard that careful men regularly show in their professions; like he who leaves another's book in his own room, but leaves the door to the room open. *Levissima* is the standard by which the most careful of men live their lives; like he who leaves the loaned book in his room, which he locks, then tests with his hand to ensure it is locked, according to common opinion ...'

to Aquinas in support of these positions. This is simply because they do not exist: Navarrus is advancing a slightly distorted but largely orthodox account of contractual fault in the civil law.

Finally, he deals with *casus*. The basic rule, to which there are three exceptions, is that nobody can be held responsible for loss caused through chance accident.[31] The exceptions are predictable. Firstly, where the accident was brought about by prior fault. If you ride a borrowed horse into a gang of thieves and they steal the horse, you can't tell the owner that it was a chance accident. It is straightforwardly blameworthy to put borrowed property in a position where it is likely to be stolen. Secondly, where the Roman rules on *mora* apply. Thirdly, where there is an agreement to abide by a higher standard of care. Again, in formulating these rules Navarrus relies on strictly Civilian sources.

Taken as a whole, Navarrus is clearly trying to bring Thomism into line with civilian learning. The sole concept akin to fault in Thomist ethics, voluntariness, is reformulated in the Roman language of *dolus*. Where there is no Thomist concept, the gaps are filled by simply importing Roman concepts. However, the way in which Navarrus deals with *dolus praesumptus* shows that his overall concern is for Thomist doctrine. The problem was simple: both traditions said that *dolus* had two forms, but disagreed as to what they were. Moreover, their substance made it impossible to say that the two traditions simply had different names for the same ideas. As such, Navarrus argues that the civilians had mistakenly identified *culpa lata* as a type of *dolus*, and in so doing advances the Thomist model of voluntariness as *dolus* as a more sophisticated analysis of the civilian *dolus verus*. And, though the context is contractual, parts of his analysis are couched in language that could easily be transplanted into a discussion about loss caused by other means. An example of this is the claim that nobody can be liable for loss caused by chance unless it is possible to identify pre-existing fault or an obligation to prevent such loss.[32] It is these aspects of Navarrus' treatment of *culpa* that were carried forward by Lessius.

Put simply, by the turn of the seventeenth century there was no clear approach to the relationship between *restitutio* and fault, nor the language that ought to be used to describe fault in this context. By far the most lucid attempt at solving these problems is provided by Lessius, who in advancing his own theory dealt with all the individual solutions outlined above. He begins by adopting the language of *culpa* alone, rather than the threefold model of *dolus*, *culpa* and *casus* favoured by civilians and Thomists such as Navarrus. Lessius

31 Ibid., 17.179.

32 Ibid., 17.178.

considers *culpa* and its relationship with *restitutio* in three stages: firstly, can the obligation to restore ever arise in the absence of culpa? Secondly, can the obligation to restore ever arise in response to *culpa levis* or *levissima*? Thirdly, can the obligation to restore be triggered by ignorance?[33] He begins by equating the Roman *culpa* with the theological *peccatum,* and offering a fivefold classification of *culpa*: *lata, latior, latissimus, levis*, and *levissimum*:[34]

> Culpa latissimus est dolus apertus: latior, est dolus praesumptus. Est autem dolus quaevis calliditas, fallacia et machinatio ad circumveniendum, fallendum, et decipiendum adhibita. Calliditas fit tacendo, fallacia mentiendo, machinatio arte verborum ... Culpa lata est omissio eius diligentiae et circumspectionis, quam passim homines eiusdem conditionis adhibere solent: ut si quis librum commodatum relinquat foris ante ostium. Culpa levis est omissio eius diligentiae et circumspectionis, quam solent diligentiores illius artis vel professionis adhibere. Culpa levissima est omissio diligentiae, quam diligentissimi et prudentissimi adhibent.[35]

Lessius' definitions of *culpa levis* and *levissima* are straightforwardly civilian, requiring progressively more onerous versions of the adjective *diligens*. Less familiar are the terms in which *culpa latissimus* and *latior* are described, which allude to the manner in which *dolus* was analysed in the *mos italicus*. This can be seen most clearly in the writings of Baldus on *dolus*, in which the concept is divided into *apertus* and *praesumptus*.[36] This effectively eliminates the need to talk about voluntariness, with the Thomist standard completely enveloped in the language of *culpa*. With *dolus* now associated with the loftier *culpa*

33 Lessius, *De Iustitia et Iure*, 2.7.6–9.

34 Ibid., 2.7.6.

35 Ibid., 2.7.6 '*Culpa latissimus* is the same as *dolus apertus*; *latior* is the same as *dolus praesumptus*. This is any callidity, deception or machination designed to deceive. Callidity is keeping silent, deception is lying, and machination is done by words ... *Culpa lata* is a failure of diligence in the circumstances, that standard which the same sort of men are used to living by; for instance, leaving a loaned book outside the house. *Culpa levis* is a failure of diligence in the circumstances, that standard which more careful men adhere to in their professional practice. *Culpa levissima* is a failure of diligence, the standard or the most careful and prudent men'.

36 On *dolus praesumptus* in Baldus, see Alexander Löffler, *Die Schuldformen des Strafrechts: In vergleichend-historischer und dogmatische Darstellung* (Leipzig: Hirschfeld, 1895), 156; on *dolus apertus* in Baldus, see Franco Cordero, *Criminalia: nascita dei sistemi penali* (Rome: Biblioteca universale Laterza, 1986), 268; see generally Gian P. Demuro, *Il Dolo. I. Svolgimento storico del concetto* (Milan: Giuffrè, 2007).

latissimus and *latior*, a new definition would have to be found for *culpa lata*. Following Navarrus, this is found in the standard of the reasonable man, or ordinary diligence.

It is this standard of ordinary diligence that Lessius associates with *restitutio*. His reasoning is refreshingly straightforward:

> Quia nemo tenetur adhibere maiorem diligentiam in suis operibus, ne alteri noceat, quam eiusdem conditionis homines passim in similibus adhibere solent (nemo enim tenetur esse prudentior et circumspectior hominibus suae sortis) ergo damnum eveniens non debet illi imputari, sed censebitur involuntarium.[37]

The logic is appealing: in the absence of any other factor, we cannot expect individuals to take greater care with regards to others than they take towards themselves. The reference to involuntariness adds nothing to the substance of his argument, and is likely a reassuring reference to the Thomist framework for analysing such scenarios for the benefit of his reader. He bolsters his position by reference to the position in the law of contract. The innocent seller of defective goods is not liable in the absence of *culpa*, so why should the rules governing other aspects of everyday life be any different? This is an appeal to legal doctrine over theological principle that is typical of Lessius. Any loss caused through *culpa* less than *culpa lata* is to be treated as accidental unless there was a duty (whether contractual or *ex officio*) to exercise greater care.[38]

The gap between Lessius and his intellectual foundations can be seen by comparing a problem used to illustrate issues of voluntariness since Aristotle and beyond: what happens when a storm forces a sailor to throw wares belonging to another overboard? Is that a wrong that ought to be compensated? The Aristotle of the *Nicomachean Ethics* would call it a voluntary wrong, as the harm caused still flowed from a choice internal to the wrongdoer.[39] The Aristotle of the *Eudemian Ethics* would disagree.[40] Aquinas would have agreed with the position in the *Nicomachean Ethics*, and for the same reasons.[41] An act

37 Lessius, *De Iustitia et Iure*, 2.7.6: 'For no one can be held to a higher standard of care in his acts, lest he harm another, than is expected or men in similar conditions (no one is held to be more careful and circumspect than his peers), and so any loss caused ought not to be imputed to him, but rather treated as involuntarily caused'.

38 Ibid., 2.7.6.

39 Aristotle, *Nicomachean Ethics*, 3.1.

40 Aristotle, *Eudemian Ethics*, 1225a.

41 ST, I-II, q.6.a.1.

is voluntary when it proceeds from the will. The simple presence of a choice is sufficient for these purposes. Thus our sailor, though compelled by the circumstances in which he found himself, voluntarily caused the owner of the goods to have less than his due. He committed the sin of *iniustitia*, a sin against justice, and so must restore that loss in full.

Lessius' solution is quite different, relying not on Thomist doctrine but a variation of the *lex Rhodia*:

> Ratio est quia cum etiam propriae merces cooperentur ad navis depressionem, iniquum est totum onus conferre in merces alterius. Imo hoc casu, omnes tenetur pro sua parte, qui ibidem merces habent ... Dico secundo, si is qui alienas eiicit, nullas habeat, non tenetur ad ullam restitutionem.[42]

Responsibility lies not with the sailor who took action, but with the merchants and traders who first placed the ship in danger by overburdening it. The sailor is only bound to make *restitutio* if he too had wares on the ship, and even then only in part. This is an analysis that can only be reached through inquiries into *culpa* instead of voluntariness. The solution according to voluntariness is easy: the sailor intentionally caused loss to another when he chose to throw his wares overboard. Voluntariness cares not one wit for questions of blameworthiness. Lessius uses an argument founded on self-defence to explain why the sailor isn't liable, claiming he was acting to protect his life and the lives of others. But this does not explain why the other owners of the ship's cargo are responsible, nor why the sailor would be liable if he did have cargo aboard the ship. It seems that he is relying wholly on the *lex Rhodia*'s solution, and trying to find a justification for that position.

So much for how Thomist doctrine adapted to questions of individual wrongdoing. The final aspect of Thomist doctrine that needs to be examined is how, if at all, Aquinas' notion of participation in wrongdoing was adapted in the sixteenth century. Aquinas' proffered an expansive approach to responsibility

42 Lessius, *De Iustitia et Iure*, 2.12.20: 'The reason for this is that everyone reaps the reward of the jettison, and so it seems unfair to place the entire burden on the other mechants. I think that in this case everyone ought to be bound to their part, relative to their wares ... Secondly, if anyone throws anothers goods overboard, who has none himself, he is not held to make restitution to the other'. On the *lex Rhodia*, see D.14.2. The rule formulated in D.14.2.1 is '*Lege Rodia cavetur, ut si levandae navis gratia iactus mercium factus est, omnium contributione sarciatur quod pro omnibus datum est*'. Lessius' solution is a slight variant on this, apportioning responsibility for damages not *pro omnibus* but according to who had wares (*merces*) aboard the vessel.

couched in the language of causation. Not only was the person who 'did' the harm bound to make *restitutio*, so too was anyone who commanded, consented to, assisted or participated in the sin. All of these possible actors were viewed by Aquinas as being causally identical. A second tier of causal factors, including those who failed to prevent the commission of a sin, could also be bound to make *restitutio* if it could be proven that they were causally significant. Should this be shown, once again no effort was made to differentiate between types of causes.

This is an area in which the Thomists were reluctant to depart from the *Summa*. Soto justified Aquinas' position by arguing that '*quicunque causa est iniuste acceptionis, ad restitutionem tenetur ratione eiusdem acceptionis*' before running through the different modes of involvement discussed in the *Summa*.[43] Occasional stabs were made at reclassification. For example, Navarrus linked the failure to prevent what one is bound by duty to prevent to the Roman categories of quasi-delict.[44] But such lines of inquiry represent only the briefest flirtations with taking the Thomist doctrine in a new direction. Navarrus confines the comparison with quasi-delict to just one of the nine forms of involvement ('*non impediendo*') and provides eight others that are familiarly Thomist: '*consentiendo, vel iubendo, consulendo, laudando, recipiendo, particpando, tacendo, non impediendo aut non manifestando*'.[45]

By Lessius these problems had been recognised as issues that required a dedicated analysis. Though their chapter in his treatise is entitled '*De cooperantibus ad furtum vel damnum*', the reference to *furtum* is quickly elided.[46] The very first *dubitatio* is '*Quot modis censeatur quis mediate cooperari ad damnum alterius*'.[47] But the content is once again faithful to Aquinas: '*Respondeo … novem modos numerari, qui continentur hisce versibus: iussio, consilium, consensus, palpo, recursus, participans, mutus, non obstans, non manifestans*'.[48] The terms given to the modes of participation differ between Navarrus and Lessius. This is simply due to an inconsistency within the *Summa Theologiae*, where one article uses a variety of terms for the same basic ideas:

43 Soto, *De Iustitia et Iure*, 4.7.3: 'Anyone who is the cause of an unjust taking is held to make restitution by reason of that taking'.

44 Navarrus, *Enchiridion*, 17.17.

45 Navarrus, *Enchiridion*, 17.17: 'By consenting, commanding, advising, praising, receiving, participating, remaining silent, failing to intervene and failing to reveal [to authorities]'.

46 Lessius, *De Iustitia et Iure*, 2.13.

47 Ibid., 2.13.1.

48 Ibid., 2.13.1.

> Et ideo quicumque est causa iniustae acceptionis tenetur ad restitutionem quod quidem contingit dupliciter, directe scilicet, et indirecte. Directe quidem, quando inducit aliquis alium ad accipiendum. Et hoc quidem tripliciter. Primo quidem, movendo ad ipsam acceptionem, quod quidem fit **praecipiendo, consulendo, consentiendo** expresse, et **laudando** aliquem quasi strenuum de hoc quod aliena accipit. Alio modo, ex parte ipsius accipientis, quia scilicet eum **receptat**, vel qualitercumque ei auxilium fert. Tertio modo, ex parte rei acceptae, quia scilicet est **particeps** furti vel rapinae, quasi socius maleficii. Indirecte vero, quando aliquis non **impedit**, cum possit et debeat impedire, vel quia subtrahit praeceptum sive consilium impediens furtum sive rapinam; vel quia **subtrahit** suum auxilium, quo posset obsistere; vel quia **occultat post factum**. Quae his versibus comprehenduntur, IUSSIO, CONSILIUM, CONSENSUS, PALPO, RECURSUS, PARTICIPANS, MUTUS, NON OBSTANS, NON MANIFESTANS.[49]

Lessius clearly lifted his definition verbatim from the last sentence of this passage, whereas Navarrus extracted his ideas from the preceding detail. Aquinas must have intended for the two sets of terminology to align, and there is no reason to believe Navarrus intended to depart from this ninefold analysis, even where he uses language without a basis in the *Summa*.

In Lessius' analysis the first six modes are grouped together as '*positive cooperari*', the latter three as '*privative cooperari*'. Under Lessius' approach, those who positively contribute to the harm suffered are normally bound to make *restitutio*.[50] The reason is once again familiar: those who positively contribute are to be seen as the engine of the wrong, without which it would not have occurred. As such, the obligation to restore will not arise if it can be shown

49 ST, II-II, q.62.a.7. Underlined passages denote Navarrus' authority; capitalised passages denote Lessius' authority: 'So then whoever is a cause of the unjust taking is bound to make restitution. He may be a cause directly or indirectly. Directly, when he moves another to the injustice. And this in three ways. First, with respect to the taking, by impelling him with express command, or advice, or consent, or by praising him for his hardihood. Second, with respect to the taker, by giving him shelter or any other kind of help. Third, with respect to the thing taken, by sharing in the theft or robbery as an accomplice in the wrongdoing. Then indirectly he may be a cause when he does not stop the wrongdoer when he could and should; either he omits the effective command or advice which would have prevented the injustice or he denies the help which would have halted it or he covers it up when committed. All these nine factors are comprised in the following lines: command, advice, consent, flattery, shelter, taking part, keeping dumb, not preventing, not revealing'.

50 Lessius, *De Iustitia et Iure*, 2.13.2.

that the same harm would have occurred anyway. This takes the way in which Aquinas analysed flattery, asking whether or not it was an effective cause, and applies it wholesale.[51] To make this point, Lessius uses the language of supervening causes: '*si executor absque illo consilio* [...] *aeque bene et eodem modo damnum erat illaturus, quamvis nulla alia similis causa esset superventura; tunc illi non tenentur ad restitutionem*'.[52] While Aquinas sought to identify all possible causes of the harm, Lessius is trying to find the main cause. All those who positively cooperated *can* be liable, but only where they were an effective cause of the loss. Such assumptions cannot be made automatically. For example, an order is an effective cause only if it is followed, and its issuer failed to withdraw the order before it was acted upon.[53]

Those who positively contribute to the wrong, along with the actual wrongdoer, are liable *in solidum*.[54] There is, however, a natural order in which the debt ought to be repaid. In cases of theft, liability first falls at the feet of the person who has the property, who is compelled to return it by *restitutio ratione rei*.[55] Despite marginalising this form of *restitutio* so as to push *restitutio ratione acceptionis* to the fore, he still views it as the primary obligation. Where the property no longer exists, or for wrongs other than theft, the ball is passed to the wrongdoer '*quatenus est executor*'.[56] He is followed by anyone who positively contributed to the wrongdoing. The difficulty clearly lies in calculating *quatenus est executor*. Damages representing the extent to which he is *not* the wrongdoer will have to be reallocated to other actors who positively contributed to the wrongdoing. In this context, and for the first time, Lessius refers to positive contributors other than the *executor* as '*secundarias causas*'.[57] The *executor* is then referred to as the *principalis*.[58] This language is grafted onto the Thomist approach to these issues, and does not appear to have held any significance to Lessius other than providing a helpful shorthand.

Turning to the category of *privative cooperari*, the question is not under what circumstances the obligation to restore arises, but whether the obligation can arise at all. In all three cases—*mutus, non obstans* and *non manifestans*—there can only be a question of causal significance if the person in question was

51 Ibid., 2.13.2; ST, II-II, q.62.a.7.
52 Ibid., 2.13.2.
53 Ibid., 2.13.3.
54 Ibid., 2.13.4.
55 Ibid., 2.13.5.
56 Ibid., 2.13.5.
57 Ibid., 2.13.6.
58 Ibid., 2.13.7.

under a duty to act.[59] These duties to act arise in the same way as in relation to *culpa*. The primary example in this context is where one's position (e.g. as a magistrate) ought to have forced them into action, typically because of the public responsibility such a position entails. In the absence of such a duty there can be no obligation to make *restitutio* because a failure to act does not constitute a wrong against justice.[60] It may well be an affront to charity, but charity has no mechanism akin to *restitutio*. Where there was a duty to act to prevent wrongdoing, responsibility only arises where it was breached *ex culpa grava*.[61] Lessius was clearly reluctant to recognise a legal duty arising from omissions in the absence of serious blameworthiness.

By Lessius responsibility was being analysed as the confluence of two factors: fault and causation. Both were present to some degree in the *Summa Theologiae*, but in different forms. Fault was masked behind voluntariness, and causation was a concern dealt with under the aegis of *restitutio*. The contribution of the Thomists was to turn both of these into independent ingredients of liability. The transition from voluntariness to fault occurred far earlier than most of the developments studied here, with clear roots in the fourteenth century. And from this early point there was a marked influence of canon (and, by extension, civil) conceptions of fault on Thomist doctrine. This trend was not universal, with the likes of Soto clearly rejecting the assimilation in favour of a strictly Thomist approach to responsibility. But the results are plain to see in the treatises of Navarrus and Lessius: a clearly civilian model of fault supplanting the previous Thomist notion of voluntariness. The isolation of causation as a distinct ingredient of liability came much later, and is far more faithful to the *Summa*. The only difference is structural: in the *Summa*, causation is a tangential issue dealt with under *restitutio*, while in Lessius' *De Iustitia et Iure* is it a distinct topic worthy of its own *distinctio*. Within his account, Lessius still quotes verbatim from the *Summa*.

A Syncretic Legal Culture?

The indelible influence of Roman law on the Thomist approach to fault and responsibility is plainly visible. But to what degree is this indicative of a broader syncretic culture that sought to assimilate Roman law and Thomism? At a doctrinal level the answer varies significantly depending on the topic under

59 Ibid., 2.13.9.
60 Ibid., 2.13.10.
61 Ibid., 2.13.10.

examination. The concept of *restitutio* bears virtually no trace of a Roman law influence, with developments being made through the manipulation of its internal mechanisms—the triggers by which it is invoked—rather than the introduction of external influences. More significant civilian influences can be seen in individual forms of wrongdoing. The Thomist notion of *furtum* was at least partially displaced by a Roman law definition in several treatises.[62] The Roman notion of *contumelia* was also conjoined to the Thomist sin of the same name, evident in even the most loyal Thomists.[63] But in other sins, there is nary a trace of Roman law: *homicidia*, *mutilatio*, sexual wrongdoing and *detractio* all look distinctly Thomist.

The three main areas within the Thomist theory of delict that rely on Roman law are fault, *furtum* and *contumelia*. Each of these is an area in which Aquinas' formulation was impractical or otherwise problematic. The problems with using voluntariness as a fault standard have already been discussed.[64] In *furtum*, Aquinas's definition of the wrong as 'secretly taking another's property' was insufficient. Secrecy as a criterion for liability is uninformative, and seems to suggest a gap in the scope of liability where a thief is brazen but does not resort to violence. Taking is similarly narrow, especially when compared to the *contrectatio* of Roman law. Aquinas' definition was simply too impractical to be adopted by an increasingly pragmatic formulation of Thomist delict.

The same problems arise in relation to *contumelia*. The interest protected—*honor*—was of paramount importance within Aristotelian ethics. It was the badge of virtue, a possible contender for the purpose behind all human endeavours. While ethically important, this is a difficult idea to translate into a legal right capable of protection and valuation. Within the Spanish context in particular *honor* had become a twisted form of the original Aristotelian concept. *Honor* was used in the same way Thomists used *fama*, as a person's reputation and good name.[65] So what was to be done with *contumelia*, a seemingly redundant sin? It was provided with a fresh coat of paint through its association with the Roman delict of *iniuria*, which itself was built around the idea of *contumelia*. This would prove to be only a temporary remedy, with successive Thomist authors reducing the relevance of the sin ever further.

In each of these instances Roman law is being used to patch the Thomist theory of delict where the foundations provided by the *Summa* are insufficient.

62 Cajetan, *Secunda Secundae Summae Theologiae cum Commentariis*, ad q.66.a.3; Navarrus, *Enchiridion*, 2.17.1.

63 Soto, *De Iustitia et Iure*, 5.9.2.

64 Above, pages 209–211.

65 See the treatment of *deshonras* in Siete Partidas, 7.9.1.

This is not syncretism, which would suggest a blend of the two traditions. This is absorption, with the necessary strands of civilian learning being used to fill in the gaps in the Thomist doctrine. The ideas once absorbed lose their Roman character and context. There is, however, an argument to be made that individual Thomists were influenced by the methodologies of the civilians. The willingness to restructure an authoritative source for the sake of presenting a more cogent argument is considered to be the hallmark of legal humanism, and Donellus' greatest contribution to the development of private law was his systematisation of the *Corpus Iuris Civilis*.[66] Precisely the same methods underpin Lessius' *De Iustitia et Iure* and Navarrus' *Enchiridion*, both of which restructure their source material to provide a more cohesive treatment of private law. But this is more likely than not a reflection of the humanist zeitgeist that can be seen shaping academia across Europe through the sixteenth century rather than any assimilation of civilian and Thomist learning.

66 Peter Stein 'Systematisation of private law in the sixteenth and seventeenth centuries' *Die Entwicklung der Methodenlehre in Rechtswissenschaft und Philosophie vom 16. bis zum 18. Jahrhundert*, ed. Jan Schröder (Stuttgart: F. Steiner, 1998).

PART IV

Conclusion

CHAPTER 11

The Historical Foundations of Grotius' Analysis of Delict

We are now in a position to examine Grotius' delictual doctrines in detail, and to evaluate their intellectual origins. This chapter will proceed by examining three elements of Grotius' delictual theory: remediation, responsibility and interests. In the first two of these it is possible to treat *De Jure Belli ac Pacis* and the *Inleidinge tot de Hollandse Rechtsgeleerdheid* together. The treatment of both remediation and responsibility in both works is focused and broadly consonant, and so their intellectual origins can be unravelled as one.[1] And, in both these contexts, it will be argued that Grotius' approach is a near perfect replication of Thomist doctrine as developed by Lessius. The various rights and wrongs advanced in each work prove to be more of a problem. The three ideas of rights, responsibility and remediation taken together provide Grotius' model of delict with its skeleton, and to this degree there is a significant degree of overlap between the two treatises. But the treatment of individual wrongs differs significantly, with the *Inleidinge* referring to many more specific scenarios and drawing more heavily on both Roman and local laws.

It will be argued that this reflects the different purposes of the two works. *De Jure Belli ac Pacis*, a treatise on natural law, was a work of legal theory. The rules presented are idealised as a rational system of law, without any necessary connection to the real world. The *Inleidinge* had a far more difficult task: it had to take the same model of delict and show that it could be used to explain contemporary law. It is for this reason that Grotius gives his natural law theory a *ius proprium* veneer in the *Inleidinge*. The overall structure of delict is the same in both works, but in order to sell his theory as viable to Dutch lawyers it was necessary to show how common scenarios from both the *Corpus Iuris Civilis* and local statutes could be dealt with within the Thomist framework. The references to such sources in the *Inleidinge* are evidence not of authority, but accommodation.

1 See above, chapter two.

 | DOI 10.1163/9789004344372_012

Remediation

In both his natural and Dutch law treatments of delict Grotius presents a remedy that is restorative in nature.[2] The goal is to restore what the victim has lost so far as it is physically possible, and not necessarily through monetary compensation. This is seen most clearly in the remediation of defamation, where the best course of action is to undo the harm caused to the victim's reputation by singing his praises and taking back the vituperative comments.[3] In both works the remedy stands apart from any particular type of wrongdoing, a mechanism of general applicability that binds together the rest of wrongdoing. This unifying power of the remedy is reflected in the location of its treatment: at the very outset of both of Grotius' delictual inquiries.[4]

In all of these respects Grotius' delictual remedies are closely paralleled by the Thomist *restitutio*. The Roman law of delicts retained its fragmentary focus on the forms of actions through to Donellus. Even if these were reduced to just two, the *actio legis Aquiliae* and the *actio iniuriarum*, each action awarded damages according to different calculations.[5] Moreover, the civil law of delict rarely awarded damages in direct proportion to the harm suffered. The penal nature of delict justified mechanisms such as *lis crescens* that doubled the possible award of damages, and for multiple recovery in cases with multiple wrongdoers.[6] This fragmentary and punitive approach to damages is far removed from the corrective approach found across Grotius' works. This is one area in which there can be no doubt as to Grotius' influences.

Responsibility

Grotius' theory of delict divides responsibility into two parts: fault and causation. This in itself is indicative of a Thomist influence, with Roman law

2 *Restitutio*: DJBAP, 2.17.1; *Weder-evening*: *Inleidinge*, 3.32.

3 DJBAP, 2.17.22; *Inleidinge*, 3.32.17–18.

4 DJBAP, 2.17.1; *Inleidinge*, 3.32.

5 And even within the *lex Aquilia* the calculation of damages differed according to the harm, with *servi corrupti* resulting in double damages: Donellus, *Commentariorum de Jure Civili*, 15.27.6.

6 Though it is unclear whether these penal mechanisms applied within Donellus' general action.

relying solely on the notion of *culpa*.[7] From whence the language of *culpa* was lifted by Grotius is extremely difficult to determine. By the seventeenth century the Thomist approach to delict had already incorporated the language of Roman law. Though slight variations would inevitably exist between individual civilian and Thomist authors, both traditions were drawing from the same well. The only evidence indicative of one tradition in particular—in this case Thomism—is the universal nature of the adopted fault standard. There is no delineation between *dolus* and *culpa*, a distinction that prevented Donellus from unifying *iniuria* and *damnum iniuria datum* to create a generalised model of delict. Although it hardly matters from which tradition Grotius extracted his notion of *culpa*, given their shared heritage, the sheer scope of its operation is indicative of a Thomist origin.

Grotius' account of causation rests on two distinctions: firstly, between acts and omissions and secondly, within both categories, between primary and secondary causes, both of which are seen as accessories to the principal wrongdoer. These can be reordered as follows:

TABLE 11.1 *Grotius' taxonomy of causal contributions*

Act	Primary[8]	By commanding (*iubet*)
		By consenting (*consensum adhibet*)
		By assisting (*adiuvat*)
		By sheltering (*receptum praestat*)
		By participating (*participat*)
	Secondary[9]	By advising (*consilium dat*)
		By praising (*laudat*)
		By assent (*assentatur*)
Omission	Primary[10]	When under a duty to intervene
	Secondary[11]	When one ought to intervene, but is not bound by duty to do so

7 Donellus. *Commentariorum de Jure Civili*, 15.27.2. *Culpa* had been used to resolve questions of causation within delict since antiquity.

8 DJBAP, 2.17.6.

9 Ibid., 2.17.7.

10 Ibid., 2.17.8.

11 Ibid., 2.17.9.

TABLE 11.2 *Grotius' taxonomy of causal contributions*

Positive cooperari	By ordering (*iussio*)
	By advising (*consilium*)
	By consenting (*consensus*)
	By flattery (*palpo*)
	By sheltering (*recursus*)
	By participating (*participans*)
Privative cooperari	By silence (*mutus*)
	By failing to obstruct (*non obstans*)
	By failing to report (*non manifestans*)

These ten forms of agency align closely with Lessius' ninefold analysis, with the obvious exception of a tenth variety:[12]

Structurally Grotius has reorganised the Thomist categories, but the substance is broadly consistent. A handful of the labels have changed, but the ideas behind them are the same. Flattery is described as *palpo* by Lessius, but *assentatur* by Grotius. Similarly Lessius' *recursus* and Grotius' *receptum praestat* correspond. The sole exception to this is *laudat*, the tenth variety without a synonym in Lessius' analysis. This is the only verb in the three passages cited above for which Grotius provides a reference, unexpectedly to the Digest.[13] The verb was also used by Aquinas, but fell out of use among the later Thomists.[14] One can only speculate as to why Grotius brought *laudare* back, or why he sought to justify it through a reference to Roman law when an equally convincing basis for its inclusion was provided in the *Summa*. It may just be one more aspect of the assimilation of Roman law and Thomism, a means of showing his reader that although much of his analysis was founded in Thomism it was still compatible with the Civil Law. The language of *primario* and *secundario*, along with the rules governing the order in which *restitutio* must be made when there are multiple parties responsible for the loss, are all directly lifted from Lessius.[15]

Fault and responsibility are united in a conclusory paragraph explaining how they are to be balanced. If you encourage a madman to go on a rampage, are you to be considered a cause of whatever harm he causes if it can be shown that he would have acted in an identical fashion even if he had never met you?

12 Lessius, *De Iustitia et Iure*, 2.13.1.

13 D.11.3.1.4 (Ulpian).

14 ST, II-II, q.62.a.7; though it did not disappear entirely: Navarrus, *Enchiridion*, 17.17.

15 Lessius, *De Iustitia et Iure*, 2.13.7.

Grotius thinks that you are in the clear, for you cannot be said to be a 'real' cause of the harm. The sorts of considerations found in civilian analyses are absent. Who, a civilian might ask, was to blame for the harm? Lunatics typically lack culpability for their own actions, and so it is entirely plausible that liability would exist for encouraging him. The absence of any such considerations founded on *culpa* casts doubt on whether Grotius is channelling the civil law in this passage. Rather this, like his formulation of the ways in which a person can be treated as a primary or secondary accessorial cause of harm, is soundly Thomist in nature.

Taken as a whole Grotius' account of responsibility seems to have been lifted entirely from Thomist sources, though as has already been acknowledged the Thomist formulation of fault in particular owed a sizable debt to the civil law tradition. One final scenario pertinent to questions of responsibility is dealt with in *De Iure Belli ac Pacis*:

> Illud quoque notandum est, ut mancipium aut animal quod damnum, aut pauperiem fecit, noxae dedatur, itidem ex iure civili esse. nam dominus, qui in culpa non est, natura ad nihil tenetur. ut nec is cuius navis sine ipsius culpa navi alterius damnum dedit; quanquam multorum populorum legibus, ut et nostra, damnum tale dividi solet ob culpae probandae difficultatem.[16]

The scenario under discussion includes references to noxal liability and pauperies, scenarios specific to Roman law that are not dealt with by Thomist authors. This seems inconsistent with the rest of Grotius' account of responsibility: why include something that is expressly not Thomist if it is from those authors that he is taking his concept of responsibility? The answer lies in how noxal liability and the *actio de pauperie* are treated in the text. Liability exists only where there is fault on the part of the owner—where this is not the case, '*natura ad nihil tenetur*'. This is a conscious departure from Roman law, in which liability arises strictly in both doctrines. Grotius includes it precisely because the Thomist authors did not, in order to show that his (and, by extension, the Thomist) idea of responsibility is capable of dealing with any scenario that arises under the civil law.

16 DJBAP, 2.17.21: 'It must be noted that the civil law also makes an owner accountable for the loss caused by his animal. For the owner, who is not to blame, naturally ought not to be bound to offer any remedy. Neither is the person whose ship, at no fault of his own, causes loss to the ship of another. But according the laws of many peoples, including our own, such loss is to be divded between them because proving fault is difficult'.

Loss and Harm

Grotius' gateway to discussing the harm that results in delictual liability is *damnum*. This simply means the lessening of what a person has whether by natural or civil right. Each natural right is presented in the abstract in the opening paragraphs of Grotius' treatment. On first appearances, any diminution whatsoever of *vita, corpus, membra, fama, honor* or *actiones propriae* ought to ground a delictual claim. The truth is more complicated, as each natural right is explored further through associated forms of wrongdoing. Both the language of natural rights and the forms of wrongdoing through which they are given content will need to be examined.

Damnum

The language of *damnum* has clear roots in both the civil law and Thomist traditions. Its association with delict is strongly Roman, where it acts as the damage word in chapter three of the *lex Aquilia*. However, by the seventeenth century the term was equally familiar to Thomists, with Lessius using the term to describe the imbalance addressed by *restitutio* throughout his discussion of wrongdoing.[17] Some of these usages connect *damnum* to non-patrimonial loss.[18] This is a departure from the civil law, which had consistently linked *damnum* to financial harm.[19] It also comes closer to capturing Grotius' use of the word, wherein any reduction in a right a person has, no matter what that right is, can be called *damnum*. This can be contrasted with Donellus, who even though he recognised natural rights sought to protect them through the delict of *iniuria*, keeping them far removed from the *damnum* remedied under the *lex Aquilia*.

A more definitive link to Thomism can be seen in Grotius' analysis of hypothetical losses:

> Sed et spes lucri ex nostro aestimabitur, non ut illud ipsum, sed secundum propinquitatem ad actum, ut in semente spes messis.[20]

17 E.g. Lessius, *De Iustitia et Iure*, 2.7.6–9, 2.9.16–18, 2.9.22, 2.10.6, 2.11.9, 2.11.19, 2.12, 2.12.9, 2.12.18–20, 2.13.1–3, 2.13.7–10.

18 Homicide: Lessius, *De Iustitia et Iure*, 2.9.16–18; *detractio* and *fama*: Lessius, *De Iustitia et Iure*, 2.11.19.

19 An association apparent in Donellus, who divided all delictual liability into two categories based on whether it addressed patrimonial or non-patrimonial harm.

20 DJBAP, 2.17.5: 'But we value our hopes of making a gain not according to the actual gain, but according to the likelihood of realisation, e.g. by the season in case of crops'.

Both the rule and the illustrative scenario are ripped straight from the *Summa Theologiae*.[21] The scenario proved to be a recurring point of discussion among the Thomists, as has already been seen.[22] While the civil law of delict was familiar with allowing damages for hypothetical losses to some degree, the rule was simply that they were recoverable up to a point.[23] Instead of drawing this link, Grotius opted for to draw a parallel with the Digest' treatment of the value of an unsatisfied conditional debt within the law of inheritance.[24] Again, this seems to be little more than showing how such matters could be dealt with under a Thomist model. Given the near total parallels between Grotius and the Thomist on the recoverability of hypothetical losses there can be little doubt as to his influences.

Rights

Both Grotius' analyses rely on the language of rights to show the scope of delict. Both the precise terminology and the enumeration of rights differ across natural law and Dutch law. In natural law rights are categorised according to whether they arise naturally or through a human institution. The latter category of positive rights contains most of private law: proprietary rights, contractual rights and statutory rights.[25] The natural rights are sixfold: *vita, corpus, membra, fama, honor* and *actiones propriae*. In the *Inleidinge* these are replaced with 'inalienable' rights: *leven* (life), *lichaam* (body), *vryheid* (autonomy or freedom) and *eer* (reputation).[26] The phrase '*ander niet zouden konnen toebehooren*' ('which cannot belong to another') becomes the Latin '*inalienabiles*' in the margin.[27] When this list of rights resurfaces in a delictual context, property (*goederen*) is added to the list, though this is obviously not an inalienable right.[28]

The differences between the two lists are plain to see: natural law recognises two rights that Dutch law does not: *membra* and *honor*. But this does not seem to affect the overall scope of delict. Neither right has a distinct form of wrongdoing. Both are packaged with a similar right: *corpus* in the case of *membrum* and *fama* for *honor*, and wrongdoing against these interests is discussed at a general level. If one overlooks these two seemingly superfluous rights and

21 ST, II-II, q.62.a.4.

22 Above, pages 178–179; Gordley, *The Jurists*, 87.

23 D.9.2.27.3.

24 D.35.2.73.1.

25 DJBAP, 2.17.2.

26 *Inleidinge*, 2.1.42.

27 Ibid., 2.1.42.

28 Ibid., 3.33.1.

focuses on the four found in the *Inleidinge* – *vita*, *corpus*, *fama* and *actiones propriae*—the claim that Grotius was influenced by Donellus becomes more readily understandable.[29] Donellus also provided four natural rights: *vita*, *incolumitas corporis*, *libertas* and *existimatio*.[30] The right to life is later omitted from the scope of delict, paralleling Grotius' refusal to grant a delictual action for a homicide except for the recovery of consequential financial harm. Moreover, one ought not to have to look very far for Grotius' influences in this respect, as the use of protected interests within a model of delict was still relatively revolutionary in the early seventeenth century. Donellus, who also used this form of analysis, seems like a likely source of influence.

However, there is a shift in language between the two models that needs to be explained. Firstly, is it justifiable to equate *libertas* with *actiones propriae* and *vryheid*? It appears that all three terms are exploring the same idea. In the *Inleidinge*, *vryheid* is defined as '*des mensches vrije macht over sijne daden*' (someone's free control of his own actions).[31] That *actiones propriae* represents a similar idea can be seen both through its very name, and the context in which it is further explored: fraud and deceit that removes a person's capacity for free choice. What of *libertas*? This too had a long tradition of being associated with a person's inherent capacity for self-determination.[32] The correspondence of these three interests seems to be justifiable.

By contrast, it is less easy to show that the terms *existimatio*, *fama* and *eer* are similar. Within *De Jure Belli ac Pacis*, '*fama*' is left undefined, as is '*existimatio*' in Donellus' corpus. In the *Inleidinge*, '*eer*' is said to be a composite of the opinions others hold about us. Given the absence of definition, it is difficult to say how similar the three are. It might be sufficient to note that all three are personality interests, and so the scope of Donellus' and Grotius' natural rights are the same. But this does not explain why Grotius would abandon the terminology of Donellus' analysis. Moreover, even though they do not add appear to add anything to the scope of Grotius' natural law model of delict, the inclusion of '*honor*' and '*membra*' cannot be brushed aside.

The only Thomist to use a rights-based analysis of delict was Lessius. Unlike Grotius and Donellus, he did not provide a list of rights. Rather, it must

29 Feenstra, 'Grotius' doctrine of negligence', 143.

30 Donellus, *Commentariorum de Jure Civili*, 2.8.3.

31 *Inleidinge*, 3.1.12.

32 Gustaaf van Nifterik, 'Hugo Grotius on "slavery"' in *Grotius and the Stoa*, eds Hans W. Blom and Laurens C. Winkel (Assen: Van Gorcum, 2004), 235 n.10, citing D.1.5.4 and Eltji J.H. Schrage, *Libertas est facultas naturalis: Menselijke vrijheid in een tekst van de Romeinse jurist Florentinus* (Leiden: Universitaire Pers, 1975).

be extracted from his discussion of wrongdoing. Wrongs are divided into four basic groups based on the interests harmed: *bona spiritualia*, *corpus*, *fama* and *honor*, and *fortuna*.[33] This is the same hierarchy of *bona* found in the *Summa Theologiae*. Within *corpus*, two further interests are discussed: *vita* and *membra*.[34] A man is said not to own his own life and limbs, but to be entrusted with their protection. As they fall outside the scope of *dominium*, they cannot be valued nor restored. As in Grotius and Donellus, the only compensation owed in the wake of a homicide (or any other wrong to *corpus*) is to address the financial consequences of the death.

Lessius' analysis of rights includes a pair of personality interests, again an aspect of Thomism with roots stretching back for centuries. Thus in Lessius we find parallels for five of Grotius' six natural rights: *vita*, *corpus*, *membra*, *fama* and *honor*. The only omission is *actiones propriae*. However, there is nothing in Lessius' analysis that resembles this idea. The wrongs against *actiones propriae* in Grotius' analysis, fraud and deceit, are identified as aspects of the law of contract by Lessius, and so are isolated from his treatment of delict.[35] Given Thomism's silence on such a right, and the close correspondence between Grotius and Donellus on the nature of that right, it seems safe to conclude that *actiones propriae* entered Grotius' delictual thought through the civil law. Thus while there are aspects of Grotius' enumeration of rights that are distinctly Thomist, principally the duality of rights found in *corpus* and *membra*, and *fama* and *honor*, there are aspects that must have their origin in the civil law tradition. The only ambiguity is *vita*, which is dealt with in much the same way by Grotius, Lessius and Donellus.

Homicidia and mutilatio

In 1959 Professor Robert Feenstra, when looking at the inclusion of *vita* as the basis of a claim for damages brought by the deceased's dependents in *De Jure Belli ac Pacis* 2.17.13, argued that it was clear evidence of the influence of Thomist learning on Grotius' natural law.[36] His argument rested partially on the absence of any parallel provision in contemporary civilian writings. This aspect of his argument was seized upon thirty years later by Professor

33 Lessius, *De Iustitia et Iure*, 2.8, 2.9–10, 2.11, 2.12.

34 Ibid., 2.4.10. The three terms (*corpus*, *membrum* and *vita*) had been associated within Thomist thought since Aquinas.

35 Ibid., 2.17.5–6.

36 Robert Feenstra, '*Théories sur la responsabilité civile en cas d'homicide et en case de lesion corporelle avant Grotius*' in *Etudes d'histoire du droit privé offertes à Pierre Petot* (Paris: Librairie Générale de Droit et de Jurisprundence, 1959), 151.

Edwin Rabbie, who showed that not only did contemporary civilian authors have such a notion, derived principally from the throwaway text in the *Collatio* discussed earlier,[37] but that Grotius relied on these authors when writing about damages for homicide in a different context.[38] When he returned to the topic, Feenstra appeared doubtful as to Rabbie's claims.[39] Nevertheless, when writing about the origins of Grotius' list of natural rights, Feenstra had no qualms in ascribing all influence to Donellus and the civilians.[40]

Feenstra's first instincts were likely accurate. As a preliminary matter, it should not be ignored that Grotius' own identification of authority is to Lessius. However, we cannot ignore Rabbie's advice that it is best to take Grotius' attribution of sources with a pinch of salt.[41] The best that we can do is to look at the detail of Grotius' account and see to which tradition it most closely conforms. In allowing claims to be brought by the wives, children and parents of the deceased there is a similarity in terminology between Grotius and the Thomists that suggests their influence on his thought. Grotius restricted claims to those whom the deceased was under an obligation to maintain (*alere ex officio*), namely wives, parents and children.[42] This is the same language found in Lessius' treatment of claimants when drawing a distinction between ordinary creditors and family members.[43] Distancing himself from claims founded on natural equity, Lessius argues that *restitutio* must be made to family members because, when considered in terms of assets, they are essentially the same person as the deceased. By the same logic, there is no obligation to make *restitutio* to those whom the deceased '*alebat ex liberalitate*'.[44] This insight is a fortunate by-product of the novelty of remedial considerations in Thomist thought. Their novelty, combined with the scholastic method's attention to detail, meant that any new insight had to be justified in full. It may well be that the concept of maintenance underpinned the civilian list of claimants, but it is far easier to say '*Ulpianus dicto loco*' than provide a justification *ab initio*. In the absence of any evidence of the basis of the civilian position, it is difficult to overlook the strong correspondence between the substance of Grotius' and Lessius' analyses, not to mention Grotius' own attribution of Lessius as a source.

---

37 Above, 58.

38 Edwin Rabbie, 'Grotius on damages in case of homicide: *De Iure Belli Ac Pacis* 2,17,13 and *De Satisfactione* 2,9', (1989) 57 Tijdschrift voor Rechtsgeschiedenis 109, 111–116.

39 Feenstra *'Das Deliktsrecht bei Grotius'*, 429, 436–439.

40 Feenstra, 'Grotius' doctrine of liability for negligence', 143.

41 Rabbie, 'Grotius on damages in case of homicide', 116.

42 DJBAP, 2.17.13.

43 Lessius, *De Iustitia et Iure*, 2.9.26.

44 Ibid., 2.9.26.

The *Inleidinge*'s analysis of homicide is similarly reliant on Thomist ideas, though it has the expected veneer of civil law authority. On the topic of funeral expenses, a reference is provided to the Customs of Antwerp, stating simply that a person responsible for the death of another must cover the family's expenses.[45] It has already been shown that the compilers of the Customs relied heavily on Lessius' treatise.[46] So why not rely on a Thomist author directly? Grotius was concerned to root his treatment of Dutch law in positive law and civilian learning. Given the choice between a treatise and actual laws that gave the same rule, of course he would choose the source with legal authority. The same concerns can be seen behind his usage of Roman law in relation to homicide. When stating that a killer ought to give the family of his victim reconciliation money if they are poor, he relied on D.9.2.11.1.[47] This anomalous reference is used to support a point that is only made in the *Collatio*, and only as an exceptional case. So far as his treatment of Dutch law was concerned, Grotius was more concerned with a Roman appearance than Roman content.

The principal form of wrongdoing affecting the body—*mutilatio*—is a variation on *homicidia*. Under natural law, the mutilator is bound to cover any medical expenses and lost income stemming from the wound.[48] The wound itself is beyond valuation, because the body cannot be valued. The same approach is found in the *Inleidinge*, although a sum for pain and suffering might also be included despite the impossibility of valuing the body.[49] This is rooted in a text in the Digest discussing the recoverability of medical expenses where the value of the slave itself was unaffected by the injury.[50] Such expenses are recoverable on the *lex Aquilia* despite the absence of any measurable decrease in the slave's value. This reasoning is simply carried over to the injuries to free men: as in the case of the slave, there is no measurable injury to the body, simply because the body's value cannot be estimated. So all the claim can stand for is the expenses incurred in repairing the injury.

The same rule formulated in a natural law context carries a reference to the examination of homicide in Navarrus' *Enchiridion*.[51] This passage not only

45 *Inleidinge*, 3.33.2.

46 Bram Van Hofstraeten, *Juridisch humanisme en costumiere acculturatie, Inhoudsen vormbepalende factoren van de Antwerpse Consuetudines compilatae (1608) en het Gelderse Land- en Stadtsrecht (1620)* (Maastricht: Universitaire Pers Maastricht, 2008).

47 *Inleidinge*, 3.33.3.

48 DJBAP, 2.17.14.

49 *Inleidinge*, 3.34.2.

50 D.9.2.27.17.

51 DJBAP, 2.17.14, referencing Navarrus, *Enchiridion*, 15.22.

gives the orthodox Thomist response that the body is beyond valuation, it addresses the difficulties in assessing damages under chapter one of the *lex Aquilia*. Ownership of even a slave's body is vested in God alone, so chapter one ought to be incompatible with Thomism. It is in this passage that Navarrus shows his frustration with Thomist doctrine, commenting on how '*esse stultum putare, eum, qui bovem proximi necat, teneri ad restitutionem: non autem, qui proximum ipsum occidit*'.[52] Nevertheless he stands by Thomist doctrine, and allows a remedy only for medical expenses and lost income. This is the same rule found in the *Inleidinge*, but Grotius' choice of authority is interesting. The core stance found in Navarrus can be found in any other Thomist author. It is only in his attack on the Roman principles behind the calculation of damages that Navarrus differed from his peers, and it seems to be for this reason that Grotius chose to adopt Navarrus' views as his own.

Sexual Wrongdoing

The treatment of sexual wrongdoing in *De Jure Belli ac Pacis* is unusual. It is located at the end of a series of three texts on wrongs to the body, the first two of which have just been explored. It is followed by theft, and then by wrongs to *actiones propriae*. Substantively, two distinct forms of sexual wrongdoing are discussed. The first is adultery, and the impact it has on a family's finances when it results in a child. The second is the forceful or fraudulent deflowering of a virgin, and the consequent remedy to repair her damaged marriage prospects. The latter's focus on decision making and autonomy shows that, despite its location, it is an affront to *actiones propriae*, and so will be discussed in that section, leaving only adultery. The rule is straightforward: the adulterous pair must ensure that the costs of raising their progeny doesn't fall on the cuckolded husband, and restore any harm caused to the inheritance of legitimate children.[53] This is precisely the same rule as found in Lessius.[54]

Wrongs to fama *and* honor

In the very last paragraph of his natural law formulation of delict Grotius returns to wrongs against *fama* and *honor*:

52 Ibid., 15.22.

53 DJBAP, 2.17.15: '*Sic adulter et adultera tenentur non tantum indemnem praestare maritum ab alenda prole, sed et legitimis liberis rependere siquod damnum patiuntur ex concursu ita susceptae sobolis ad hereditatem*'.

54 Lessius, *De Iustitia et Iure*, 2.10.6.

> Sed damnum, ut diximus, etiam adversus honorem et famam datur, puta verberibus, contumeliis, maledictis, calumniis, irrisu, aliisque similibus modis. In quibus non minus quam in furto atque aliis criminibus vitiositas actus ab effectu discernenda est. Nam illi poena respondet, huic damni reparatio quae sit culpae confessione, exhibitione honoris, testimonio innocentiae, et per ea quae his similia sunt: quanquam et pecunia tale damnum rependi poterit, si laesus velit, quia pecunia communis est rerum utilium mensura.[55]

Unlike the list of interests in 2.17.2, which is unsupported by references, here Grotius indicates that he has relied on the works of Lessius and Soto in constructing this paragraph. Yet the content of this paragraph is not so straightforward that the scholastics can be credited as his sole influence in this area. The language used is a hodgepodge of Roman and scholastic terminology. *Verberibus* is distinctively Roman, appearing early in the list of forms *iniuria* can take in Justinian's *Institutes*.[56] *Contumelia* is an extremely common term in both civilian and scholastic texts. *Maledictio* and *irrisu* are characteristic of the Thomist tradition.

That Grotius relied principally on the scholastic tradition as the basis for this blend is quite clear. The very language of *fama* and *honor* is distinctively scholastic. Grotius discusses the possibility of restoring a damaged *fama* through oaths, confessions of fault and displays of reverence, which are lifted directly from Navarrus and Lessius.[57] The list of forms harm to *fama* and *honor* might take are populated primarily by sins: *detractio, maledictio, irrisu* and *contumelia*. However, there are also signs that Grotius was trying to force together scholasticism and Roman law. The most telling hint is the inclusion of *verberibus* in the forms of harm to *honor* and *fama*, which has no precedent in the scholastic tradition. There is also the problem of the inclusion of *honor* as a second interest. By the time of Lessius it was an irrelevance. However, in Soto it is presented as an analogue for *existimatio*. It is conceivable that Grotius

55 DJBAP, 2.17.22: 'But loss, as we have said, can be caused even as against honour and reputation, such as through blows, contumelies, curses, slander, mockery, and similar methods. The effects of these wrongs must be discerned, no less than in theft and other such vicious crimes. Such loss can be repaired by confessing to the wrong, by displays of honour, by attesting to the wronged party's innocence, and through similar methods; and in some situations such loss can be restored monetarily, at the wronged party's election, since money is the common measure of all things'.

56 J.4.4.1.

57 DJBAP, 2.17.22; Lessius, *De Iustitia et Iure*, 2.11.20.

continued in Soto's footsteps, essentially treating the Roman *iniuria* and the scholastic *contumelia* as one.

Wrongs to actiones propriae

In both natural law and Dutch law a person's capacity to make decisions for themselves is protected as a natural or inalienable right. In *De Jure Belli ac Pacis* this right is discussed through fraud and deceit. It is clear enough how such trickery or duress affects a person's to make a choice. In the *Inleidinge*, the consequences of rape are used instead.[58] The link between such wrongdoing and the capacity for free choice is perhaps less obvious. Grotius focuses on the victim's marriage prospects. Simply put, to the seventeenth-century mind a victim of rape did not have the same range of options open to her—she was a less attractive match. As a consequence of the rape, her options in the marriage were narrowed.

Treating fraud and duress as bases for a restorative remedy has foundations in both Thomism and the civil law; indeed, it is one of the few contexts where the language of *restitutio* is used in the civil law, in relation to the discretionary remedy *restitutio in integrum*. A restorative remedy founded on harm to marriage prospects is more distinctly Thomist. It parallels the consequences of *struprum*. By Lessius, this meant the deflowering of a virgin whose will was overwhelmed through force or trickery, a wrong clearly mirrored in the *Inleidinge*.[59] The harm to be restored is the diminution in the victim's marriage prospects, to be remedied by marrying the wrongdoer to his victim.[60] All of these aspects are mirrored in the treatment of sexual wrongdoing in *De Jure Belli ac Pacis* as well as the *Inleidinge*'s analysis of wrongs to *vryheid*.[61] Though one might have doubts about whether Grotius' natural law conception of wrongs to autonomy insofar as they related to contractual wrongdoing was drawing from the civil law or Thomism, both his natural law and Dutch law treatments of the same issues when stemming from sexual wrongdoing points to a clear Thomist foundation. The twist comes in the treatment of such wrongs, classified as wrongs to the body in the Thomist hierarchy, as harming an interest unrecognised in Thomism: autonomy.

---

58 The same scenario is discussed in *DJBAP*, 2.17.15. Its location is curious—wrongs to *actiones propriae* are discussed later in 2.17.17. Between these two passages stands theft. 2.17.15 completes a series of three texts on wrongs to the body, suggesting that is the proper context for this wrong.

59 Lessius, *De Iustitia et Iure*, 2.10.2.

60 Ibid., 2.10.2.

61 DJBAP, 2.17.15.

Theft and Associated Wrongs

The sole form of wrongdoing discussed in a natural law context that does not affect a natural right is *furtum*. As has already been seen, this heading is used to consider a disparate range of wrongdoing: *furtum*, *rapina*, failing to pay taxes and injuries caused through unjust sentences, false accusations and false testimony.[62] The first mystery is why Grotius should care about theft at all in a natural law treatise. Property rights, as the subject matter of individual legal systems, cannot be protected in the abstract. Two explanations present themselves: firstly, even though property rights are not protected naturally, their infringement is naturally wrongful. Thus theft can be an affront to natural law. Secondly, and assuming a strongly Thomist basis for Grotius' natural law model of delict, it could be that Grotius wanted to completely accommodate the Thomist model of delict. Both theft and injuries inflicted in the courtroom number among the original sins against justice dealt with in the *Summa*, and recur (albeit with decreasing significance in the case of the courtroom wrongs) throughout the Thomist commentaries and treatises on justice. Despite their want of an infringed natural rights, they are sins—natural forms of wrongdoing—that need to be addressed.

This explanation depends upon a strongly Thomist basis for Grotius' natural theory of delict. This is borne out in relation to *furtum* by the focus of his treatment of the wrong. No definition is given for it. Instead, he concentrates on the remedy: the thief is bound to restore the property, its fruits, and to indemnify the owner for any failure to make a gain. If the property has been destroyed, he must restore its value according to a '*mediam aestimationem*'.[63] The focus of this remedy is once again directly restorative, a far cry from the multiplied damages of the civil law. Moreover, the same remedy is proposed by Lessius.[64] The assumption of a Thomist foundation seems well founded.

Conclusion

Grotius' natural law model of delict is drawn primarily from Thomist sources. In some areas this influence is overwhelming. The clearest case of this is the remedy, *restitutio*, which is authentically Thomist with nary a trace of civilian or local learning. The manner in which questions of responsibility are approached is also distinctively Thomist. Despite its reliance on the language

62 Above, page 24.

63 DJBAP, 2.17.16.

64 Lessius, *De Iustitia et Iure*, 2.12.17.

of *culpa*, Grotius' analysis of delict only deals with fault at a superficial level. Responsibility for wrongdoing and its remediation is established through a systematised model of causation that is ripped from the pages of Thomist treatises. The influence of Roman law can still be felt. The status of autonomy as a natural right has a distinctly Roman flavour, and lacks any parallel in the Thomist tradition. But even this novel introduction to an otherwise Thomist theory serves only to group together wrongs which were uncomfortable within the Thomist taxonomy. Roman law is used only to fill in what few gaps remained in the Thomist model of delict, and there is very little that is distinctly civilian.

The *Inleidinge*'s origins prove more problematic. The footnotes of *De Jure Belli ac Pacis* are generally honest, attributing Thomist ideas to Thomist authors.[65] The sources provided in Grotius' guide to Dutch law are more deceitful. Ideas that are clearly not civilian, such as the restorative remedy *wederevening*, are grounded in references to the *lex Aquilia*. These references are often unconvincing, leading to texts that deal with similar fact patterns but divergent rules. As has already been suggested, this reflects the differing purposes of the two works. As a quasi-jurisprudential work, *De Jure Belli ac Pacis* had the freedom to be true to its origins. By Lessius, the Thomist model of delict had been shorn of any necessary theological beliefs. Grotius could simply import Lessius' approach and, with a few tweaks, present it as the ideal model of delict for a system of natural law. The *Inleidinge*, on the other hand, was by necessity grounded in positive law. Though Grotius could and did systematise and reconceptualise the extant law, he still had to present something that was recognisably Dutch. And this was achieved primarily through authority, by linking Thomist rules to civilian and local sources. This subterfuge allowed him to advance a model of delict in both the natural and local spheres that was heavily reliant on a theological analysis of wrongdoing, thereby introducing a multitude of new ideas into delictual scholarship. The influence of Grotius' adoption of Thomist doctrine can still be felt in many modern delictual regimes.

65 Though the work is not short of humanist flourishes, typically seen through the citation of classical authors.

Bibliography

1 Ancient Primary Sources

Aristotle (tr. Inwood, B.), *Eudemian Ethics* (Cambridge: Cambridge University Press, 2012)

Aristotle (tr. Ross, D.), *The Nicomachean Ethics* (Oxford: Oxford University Press, 2009)

Crawford, M.H. (ed.), *Roman Statutes* (London: Institute of Classical Studies, 1996)

Festus (ed. Thewrewk, A.), *De Verborum Significatu* (Budapest: Academiae Literrarum Hungaricae, 1889)

Gaius (tr. Gordon, W.M. and Robinson, O.F.), *The Institutes of Gaius* (London: Duckworth, 1988)

Hyamson, M. (ed.), *Mosaicarum et Romanarum Legum Collatio: With Introduction, Facsimile and Transcription of the Berlin Codex, Translation and Appendices* (Oxford: Oxford University Press, 1913)

Justinian (ed. Watson, A.), *The Digest of Justinian* (4 vols; Philadelphia: University of Pennsylvania Press, 1998)

Justinian (tr. Blume, F.), *Annotated Justinian Code* (consulted: http://www.uwyo.edu/lawlib/blume-justinian/ajc-edition-2/)

Justinian (tr. Birks, P. and McLeod, G.), *Justinian's Institutes* (London: Duckworth, 1987)

Pliny the Elder (ed. Whalley, J.I.), *Historia Naturalis* (London: Sidgwick and Jackson, 1982)

Riccobono, S., *Fontes Iuris Romani Antejustiniani* (Florence: Barbèra, 1941)

2 Medieval and Early Modern Primary Sources

Peter Abelard (ed. Luscombe, D.), *Peter Abelard's Ethics* (Oxford: Clarendon, 1971)

Accursius, *Corpus Iuris Civilis Iustinianei cum Commentariis* (Lyon, 1527)

Adrian of Utrecht (Adriaan Boeyens, Pope Adrian VI), *Quaestiones in Quartum Sententiarum ubi Sacramentorum Materia Exactissime Tractatur* (Paris, 1530)

Aegidus de Lessinia, *De Usuris in Communi* (http://www.corpusthomisticum.org/xtu.html)

Giovanni Albani, *Lucubrationes in Bartolum in Quibus Pene Omnia, Quae ad Iuris Interpretationem, et ad Iustitiam Administrandam Attinent, Novo, et Perutili Quodam Ordine Feliciter Explicantur* (Venice, 1571)

Albertus Magnus (eds Siedler, D, Kubel, W, and Vogels, H.G.), *Summa Theologiae, Sive, de Mirabili Scientia Die Libri 1 pars 1* (Aschendorff: Monasterii Westfalorum, 1978)

Andreas Alciatus, *De Verborum Significatione Libri Quatuor: Eiusdem in Tractatum Eius Argumenti Veterum Iure-consultorum, Commentaria* (Lyon, 1540)

Andreas Alciatus, Andreas, *In Digestorum Sive Pandectarum Libri* XII (Basel, 1537)

Andreas Alciatus, *Opera Omnia in Quatuor Tomos Legitime Digesta, Nativo Suo Decori Restituta, Indice Locupletissimo Adaucta* (Frankfurt, 1617)

Alfonso X (tr. Scott, S.P and ed. Burns, R.I.), *Las Siete Partidas* (Philadelphia: University of Pennsylvania Press, 2001)

Thomas Aquinas (ed. Gilby, T.), *Summa Theologiae* (61 vols; Cambridge: Cambridge University Press, 2006)

Azo of Bologna, *Summa Codicis et Institutionum* (Venice, 1489)

Baldus de Ubaldis, *Lectura Super Institutionibus* (Milan, 1493)

Éguinaire Baron, *Commentariorum ad Varios Digestorum Iuris Civilis Titulos* (Paris, 1572)

Éguinaire Baron, *Institutionum seu Elementorum Iustiniani Libri Quattor* (Paris, 1562)

Bartolusde Saxoferrato, *In Primam Digesti Veteris Partem Commentaria* (Basel, 1562)

Bartolus de Saxoferrato, *Lectura Super Prima et Secunda Parte Digesti Novi* (Venice, 1490)

Bartolus de Saxoferrato, *Lectura Super Prima et Secunda Parte Digesti Veteris* (Venice, 1488)

Stephani Bodei, *In Quatuor Institutionum Imperialum Libros Commentarii* (Paris, 1555)

Guillelmus Budaeus, *Annotationes in* XXIV *Libros* (Cologne, 1527)

Guillelmus Budeaus, *Opera Omnia* (Basel, 1557)

Bulgarus, *Ad Digestorum Titulum de Diversis Regulis Iuris Antiqui Commentarius* (Bonn, 1856)

Thomas Cajetan, *Secunda Secundae Summae Sacrosanctae Theologiae Sancti Thomae Aquinatis cum Commentariis* (Antwerp, 1567)

Alfonso de Castro, *Adversus Omnes Haereses Libri* XIII, *in Quibus Recensentur et Reuincuntur Omnes Hareses, Quarum Memoria Extat, Quae ad Apostolorum Tempore ad hoc usque Seculum in Ecclesia Ortae Sunt* (Cologne, 1543)

Guilio Claro, *Opera Omnia* (Frankfurt, 1576)

Diego de Covarruvias, *Opera Omnia* (Geneva, 1724)

Iacobus Cujas, *Opera, Quae de Jure Fecit Libros* IV (Geneva, 1609)

Angelo Carletti di Chivasso, *Summa de Angelica* (Nuremberg, 1492)

Hugo Donellus, *Commentariorum de Jure Civili libri* XII (Florence, 1840)

Hugo Donellus, *Opuscula Posthuma* (Hannover, 1604)

Guillelmus Durandus, *Speculum Iudiciale* (Paris, 1499)

Ioannis Faber, *In Quatuor Libros Institutionum Eruditissima Commentaria* (Venice, 1572)

Prospero Farinacci, *Praxis et Theoricae Criminalis Libro Duo in Quinque Titulus Distributi* (Frankfurt, 1597)

Angelus de Gambiglionibus, *Tractatus de Maleficiis* (Venice, 1494)

Albertus de Gandino, *Tractatus Maleficiorum* (Venice, 1578)

Gregory XIII, *Corpus Iuris Canonici Emendatum et Notis Iusstratum; Iussu Editum Gregorii* XIII. *Pont. Max.* (Lyon, 1605)

Hugo Grotius (eds Kanter-van Hettinga Tromp, B.J.A., Feenstra, R. and Persenaire, C.E.), *De Iure Bello ac Pacis Libri Tres in Quibis Ius Naturae et Gentium Item Iuris Publici Praecipua Explicantur* (Aalen: Scientia Verlag, 1993)

Hugo Grotius, *Inleiding tot de Hollandsche rechts-geleertheyd* (Leiden: Leiden University Press, 1952)

Hugo Grotius (tr. Lee), *The Jurisprudence of Holland* (Oxford: Clarendon, 1926–36)

Hugo Grotius (ed. Tuck), *The Rights of War and Peace* (Indianapolis: Liberty Fund, 2005)

Leonardus Lessius, *De Iustitia et Iure Caeterisque Virtutibus Cardinalibus Libri Quatuor: Ad Secundam Secundae D. Thomae, a Quaest. 47, usque at Quaest. 171* (Paris, 1618)

Caspar Manz, *Commentarius Ratio-regularis in Quatuor Libros Institutionum Imperialium* (Nuremberg, 1701)

Guillelmus Maran, *Opera Omnia seu Paratitla Digestorum et Varii Tractatus Iuris Civilis* (Utrecht, 1741)

Juan de Medina, *De Poenitentia, Restitutione et Contractibus Tractatus* (Ingolstadt, 1581)

Martín de Azpilcueta (Navarrus), *Enchiridion, sive Manuale Confessariorum et Poenitentium* (Rome, 1588)

Petrarch (ed. Bishop, M.), *Letters from Petrarch* (Indiana: Indiana University Press, 1966)

Placentinus, *In Summam Institutionum Libri IV Eiusdem de Varietate Actionum Libri* VI (Lyon, 1536)

Giovanni Porporato, *In Quatuor Institutionum Iustiniani Libros Commentaria* (Venice, 1609)

Robert Pothier, *Traité des obligations* (Paris, 1768)

Johann Schneidewein, *In Quatuor Institutionum Imperialium Iustiniani Libros Commentarii* (Strasbourg, 1586)

Domingo de Soto, *De Iustitia et Iure Libri Decem* (Salamanca, 1569)

Nicolaus Vigelius, *Digestorum Pars Sexta: De Obligationibus et Actionibus ex Delicto Descendentibus* (Basel, 1571)

Bonifacio Vitalini, *Super Maleficiis* (Cadomum, 1550)

Matteus Wesenbeck, *Paratitla in Pandectarum Iuris Civilis Libros Quinquaginta* (Basil, 1563)

Ulrich Zasius, *Operum Omnium* (Frankfurt, 1590)

Ulrich Zasius, *Singulares Intellectus et Novi in Nonnulla Loca Iuris Civilis* (Lyon, 1530)

Hendrik Zoesius, *Commentarius ad Digestorum seu Pandectarum Juris Civilis Libri L* (Cologne, 1745)

3 Secondary Literature

Allison, J.W.F., *A Continental Distinction in the Common Law: A Historical and Comparative Perspective on English Public Law* (Oxford: Oxford University Press, 2000)

Auzary-Schmaltz, N., 'Liability in tort in France before the Code civil' in Schrage, E.J.H. (ed.), *Negligence: The Comparative Legal History of the Law of Torts* (Berlin: Duncker & Humblot, 2001)

Barton, J., 'The *lex Aquilia* and decretal actions' in Watson, A. (ed.), *Daube Noster: Essays in Legal History for David Daube* (Edinburgh: Scottish Academic Press, 1974)

Bellomo, M. (tr. Cochrane, L.G.), *The Common Legal Past of Europe 1000–1800* (Washington DC: Catholic University of America Press, 1995)

Bettetini, A., '*La 'restitutio in integrum' processuale nel diritto canonico*' (Padua: CEDAM, 1994)

Buckland, W.W., '*Contrectatio*' (1941) 57 LQR 467

Buckland, W.W., *A Textbook of Roman Law* (3rd edn ed. Stein, P.; Cambridge: Cambridge University Press, 1963)

Cerami, P., '*La responsabilità extracontrattuale dalla compilazione di Giustiniano ad Ugo Grozio*' in Vacca, L. (ed.), *La responsabilità civile da atto illecito nella prospettiva storico-comparatistica* (Turin: G. Giappichelli, 1995)

Cloud, D., '*Leges de sicariis: the first chapter of Sulla's lex de sicariis*' (2009) ZSS 114

Coleman, J., 'Property and poverty' in Burns, J.H. (ed.), *The Cambridge History of Medieval Political Thought c.350-1450* (Cambridge: Cambridge University Press, 1988)

Cordero, F., *Criminalia: nascita dei sistemi penali* (Rome: Biblioteca universale Laterza, 1986)

Cursi, M.F., *Iniuria cum damno* (Milan: Giuffrè, 2002)

Cursi, M.F., '*What did occidere iniuria in the lex Aquilia actually mean?*' (2011) 7 Roman Legal Tradition 16

Dahm, G., 'On the reception of Roman and Italian law in Germany' in Strauss, E. (ed.), *Pre-Reformation Germany* (London: Macmillan, 1972)

Daube, D., '*Furtum probium* and *furtum improbium*' (1936–1938) 6 CLJ 217

Daube, D., 'The influence of interpretation on writing' (1970) 20 Buffalo Law Review 41

Daube, D., 'On the third chapter of the Lex Aquilia' (1936) 52 LQR 253

Daube, D., 'On the use of the term *damnum*' in *Studi in Onore di Siro Solazzi* (Naples: E. Jovene, 1948)

Daube, D., *Roman Law: Linguistic, Social and Philosophical Aspects* (Edinburgh: Edinburgh University Press, 1969)

Dawson, J., *The Oracles of the Law* (Westport, Conn.: Greenwood Press, 1978, 1968)

Dean, T., *Crime and Justice in Late Medieval Italy* (Cambridge: Cambridge University Press, 2007)

Decock, W., *Theologians and Contract Law: The Moral Transformation of the Ius Commune (ca.1500–1650)* (Leiden: Brill, 2013)

Demuro, G.P., *Il Dolo. I. Svolgimento storico del concetto* (Milan: Giuffrè, 2007)

Descheemaeker, E., *The Division of Wrongs: A Historical Comparative Study* (Oxford: Oxford University Press, 2009)

Dolezalek, G., 'The moral theologian's doctrine of restitution and its juridification in the sixteenth and seventeenth centuries' (1992) ACTA JURIDICA 104

Dondorp, H., 'Crime and punishment' in Schrage, E.J.H. (ed.), *Negligence: The Comparative Legal History of the Law of Torts* (Berlin: Duncker & Humblot, 2001)

Epstein, S.A., *The Medieval Discovery of Nature* (Cambridge: Cambridge University Press, 2012)

Feenstra, R., '*Das Deliktsrecht bei Grotius, insbesondere der Schadenseratz bei Tötung und Körperverletzung*' in Feenstra, R. & Zimmermann, R. (eds), *Das römisch-holländische Recht* (Berlin: Duncker & Humblot, 1992)

Feenstra, R., 'Die Glossatoren und die actio legis Aquiliae utilis bei Tötung eines freien Menschen' in Schrage, E.J.H. (ed.), *Das römische Recht im Mittelalter* (Darmstadt: Wissenschaftliche Buchgesellschaft, 1987)

Feenstra, R., 'Grotius' doctrine of liability for negligence: its origin and its influence in Civil Law countries until modern codifications' in Schrage, E.J.H. (ed.), *Negligence: The Comparative Legal History of the Law of Torts* (Berlin: Duncker & Humblot, 2001)

Feenstra, R., '*Hugues Doneau et les juristes néerlandais du* XVIIe *siècle: L'influence de son système sur l'évolution du droit privé avant le pandectisme*' in Schmidlin, B. and Dufour, A. (eds), *Jacques Godefroy (1587–1652) et l'Humanisme juridique à Genève* (Basel: Helbing & Lichtenhahn, 1991)

Feenstra, R., '*L'influence de la scolastique espagnole sur Grotius en droit privé: quelques expériences dans des questions de fond et de forme, concernant notamment les doctrines de l'erreur et de l'enrichissement sans cause*', in Grossi, P. (ed.), *La Seconda Scolastica nella Formazione del Diritto Privato Moderno* (Milan: Giuffrè, 1973)

Feenstra, R. '*Théories sur la responsabilité civile en cas d'homicide et en cas de lésion corporelle avant Grotius', in Etudes d'histoire du droit privé offertes á Pierre Petot* (Paris: Librairie Générale de Droit et de Jurisprundence, 1959)

Franklin, J.H., *Jean Bodin and the Sixteenth-Century Revolution in the Methodology of Law and History* (New York: Columbia University Press, 1963)

Gordley, J., *Foundations of Private Law: Property, Tort, Contract, Unjust Enrichment* (Oxford: Oxford University Press, 2006)

Gordley, J., *The Jurists: A Critical History* (Oxford: Oxford University Press, 2013)

Gordley, J., *The Philosophical Origins of Modern Contract Doctrine* (Oxford: Oxford University Press, 1991)

Gordley, J., 'Tort law in the Aristotelian tradition' in Owens, D.G. (ed.), *Philosophical Foundations of Tort Law* (Oxford: Oxford University Press, 1995)

Grant, E., *The Foundations of Modern Science in the Middle Ages: their religious, institutional and intellectual contexts* (Cambridge: Cambridge University Press, 1997)

Grant, E. (ed.), *A Source Book in Medieval Science* (Cambridge, Mass.: Harvard University Press, 1974)

Hallebeek, J., *The Concept of Unjust Enrichment in Late Scholasticism* (Nijmegen: GNL, 1996)

Hallebeek, J., 'Negligence in Roman law' in Schrage, E.J.H. (ed.), *Negligence: The Comparative Legal History of the Law of Torts* (Berlin: Duncker & Humblot, 2001)

Helmholz, R.H., *The Spirit of Classical Canon Law* (Athens, GA.: University of Georgi Press, 1996)

Honoré, A.M. 'Linguistic and social context of the *lex Aquilia*' (1972) Irish Jurist 138

Höpfl, H., *Jesuit Political Thought: The Society of Jesus and the State, c.1540–1630* (Cambridge: Cambridge University Press, 2004),

Humphreys, M.T.G., *Law, Power and Imperial Ideology in the Iconoclast Era* (Oxford: Oxford University Press, 2014)

Huvelin, P., *Etudes sur le furtum dans le très ancien droit romain* (Lyon: A Rey, 1915)

Ibbetson, D.J., 'The danger of definition: *contrectatio* and appropriation' in Ibbetson, D.J. and Lewis, A.D.E. (eds), *The Roman Law Tradition* (Cambridge: Cambridge University PRess, 1994)

Ibbetson, D.J., 'The dating of the Lex Aquilia' in Burrows, A.S., Johnston, D. and Zimmermann R. (eds), *Judge and Jurist: Essays in Memory of Lord Rodger of Earlsferry* (Oxford: Oxford University Press, 2013)

Ibbetson, D.J., 'How the Romans did for us: ancient roots of the tort of neglignece' (2003) University of New South Wales Law Journal 475

Ibbetson, D.J., '*Iniuria*, Roman and English', in Descheemaker, E. and Scott, H. (eds), *Iniuria and the Common Law* (Oxford: Hart, 2014)

Jansen, N., 'Duties and rights in negligence: a comparative and historical perspective on the European law of extracontractual liability' (2004) 24 OJLS 443

Jansen, N., 'The idea of legal responsibility' (2014) 34 OJLS 221

Jansen, N., *Theologie, Philosophie und Jurisprudenz in der spätscholastischen Lehre von der Restitution* (Tübingen: Mohr Siebeck, 2013)

Jolowicz, H.F., 'The original scope of the *lex Aquilia* and the question of damages' (1922) 38 LQR 220

Kantorowicz, A., *Albertus Gandinus und das Strafrecht der Scholastik* (2 vols; Berlin: J Guttentag, 1907–1926)

Kantorowicz, A., 'Baldus de Ubaldis and the subjective theory of guilt' (1934) 1 Social Research 358

Kantorowicz, A. & Buckland, W.W., *Studies in the Glossators of the Roman Law* (Cambridge: Cambridge University Press, 1938)

Kelley, D.R., 'The rise of legal history in the renaissance' (1970) 9 History and Theory 174

Kuehn, T., '*Fama* as a legal status in renaissance Florence' in Fenster, T. and Smail, D.L. (eds), *Fama:* The Politics of Talk and Reputation in Medieval Europe (Ithaca, NY: Cornell University Press, 2003)

Kuttner, S., *Kanonistische schuldlehre von Gratian bis auf die Dekretalen Gregors* IX (Vatican: Biblioteca Apostolica Vaticana, 1935)

Landau, P., 'The development of law' in Luscombe, D. and Riley-Smith, J. (eds), *The New Cambridge Medieval History Volume 4: c.1024-c.1198* (Cambridge: Cambridge University Press, 2004)

Lanza, L. and Toste, M., 'The *Sentences* in sixteenth-century Iberian scholasticism' in Roseman, P.W. (ed.), *Medieval Commentaries on the Sentences of Peter Lombard* (3 vols; Leiden: Brill, 2001–2015)

Lawson, F.H. & Markesinis, B.S., *Tortious Liability for Unintentional Harm* (2 vols; Cambridge: Cambridge University Press, 1982)

Löffler, A., *Die Schuldformen des Strafrechts: In vergleichend-historischer und dogmatische Darstellung* (Leipzig: Hirschfeld, 1895)

Loomis, W.T., 'The nature of premeditation in Athenian homicide law' (1972) 92 Journal of Hellenic Studies 86

MacDowell, D.M., *Athenian Homicide Law in the Age of the Orators* (Manchester: Manchester University Press, 1999)

Madden, M.R., *Political Theory and Law in Medieval Spain* (New York: Fordham University Press, 1930)

Mäkinen, V. and Pihlajamäki, H., 'The individualization of crime in medieval canon law' (2004) 65 Journal of the History of Ideas 525

Meyer, S.S., *Aristotle on Moral Responsibility: Character and Cause* (Oxford: Oxford University Press, 2011)

Migliorino, F., *Fama e infamia* (Catania: Editrice Giannotta, 1985)

Müller, J., 'Agency and responsibility in Aristotle's *Eudemian Ethics*' (2015) 60 *Phronesis* 206

Nifterik, G., 'Hugo Grotius on "slavery"' in Blom, H.W. and Winkel, L.C. (eds), *Grotius and the Stoa* (Assen: Van Gorcum, 2004)

Nörr, D., *Causa Mortis: Auf den Spuren einer Redewendung* (Munich: Beck, 1986)

Nörr, D., '*Causam mortis praebere*' in MacCormick, N. and Birks, P. (eds), *The Legal Mind: Essays for Tony Honoré* (Oxford: Oxford University Press, 1986)

Nufer, G., *Über die Restitutionslehre der spanischen Spätscholastiker und ihre Ausstrahlung auf die Folgzeit* (privately published Munich, 1969)

Owens, J., 'Aristotle and Aquinas' in Kretzmann, N. and Stump, E. (eds), *The Cambridge Companion to Aquinas* (Cambridge: Cambridge University Press, 1993)

Pagden, A.R.D., 'The diffusion of Aristotle's moral philosophy in Spain, ca.1400–1600' (1975) 31 Traditio 287

Petit, C., '*Derecho común y derecho castellano: notas de literatura juridica para su estudio (siglos XV-XVII)*' (1982) 50 Tijdschrift voor Rechtsgeschiedenis 157

Rabbie, E., 'Grotius on damages in case of homicide: *De Iure Belli Ac Pacis* 2,17,13 and *De Satisfactione* 2,9', (1989) 57 Tijdschrift voor Rechtsgeschiedenis 109

Radding, C.M. and Ciaralli, A., *The Corpus Iuris Civilis in the Middle Ages* (Leiden: Brill, 2007)

Robinson, O.F., *The Criminal Law of Ancient Rome* (London: Duckworth, 1995)

Rodger, A. 'Damages for the loss of an inheritance' in Watson, A. (ed.), *Daube Noster: Essays in Legal History for David Daube* (Edinburgh: Scottish Academic Press, 1974)

Rodger, A., 'Labeo and the fraudulent slave' in Ibbetson, D.J. and Lewis, A.D.E. (eds), *The Roman Law Tradition* (Cambridge: Cambridge University Press, 1994)

Rotondi, G., '*Dalla* lex Aquilia *all'art. 1151 Cod. Civ: ricerche storico-dogmatiche*' in Rotondi, G., *Scritti Giuridici* (Pavia: Tipografia e legatoria cooperativa, 1922)

Ruggiero, G., 'Excusable murder: insanity and reason in early Renaissance Venice' (1982) 16 Journal of Social History 16

Schipani, S., *Responsabilitá 'ex lege Aquilia'* (Turin: G. Giappichelli, 1969)

Schofield, M., 'Aristotelian mistakes' (1973) 19 Proceedings of the Cambridge Philological Society 66

Schrage, E.J.H., *Libertas est facultas naturalis: Menselijke vrijheid in een tekst van de Romeinse jurist Florentinus* (Leiden: Universitaire Pers, 1975)

Schulz, F., '*Die Lehre vom erzwungenen Rechtsgeschäft im antiken römischen Recht*' (1922) 43 Zeitschrift der Savigny-Stiftung 171

Scott, T.J., 'Passive transmissibility of delictual actions in old canon law' (1978) Acta Juridica 17

Shalgi, M., 'Aristotle's concept of responsibility and its reflection in Roman jurisprudence' (1971) 6 Israel Law Review 39

Stein, P., 'Donellus and the origins of the modern civil law' in Ankum, J.A., Cannata, C.A., Feenstra, R., Le Roy, Y., Spruit, J.E. and Weimar, P. (eds), *Melanges Felix Wubbe* (Freiberg: Editions universitaires, 1993)

Stein, P., 'Legal Humanism and Legal Science' (1986) 54 Tijdschrift voor Rechtsgeschiedenis 297

Stein, P., *Regulae Iuris* (Edinburgh: Edinburgh University Press, 1966)

Stein, P., *Roman Law in European History* (Cambridge: Cambridge University Press, 1999)

Stein, P. 'Systematisation of private law in the sixteenth and seventeenth centuries' in Scröder, J., *Die Entwicklung der Methodenlehre in Rechtswissenschaft und Philosophie vom 16. bis zum 18. Jahrhundert* (Stuttgart: F. Steiner, 1998)

Thieme, H., '*Qu'est ce-que nous, les juristes, devons á la seconde scolastique espagnole?*' in Grossi , P. (ed.), *La Seconda Scolastica nella Formazione del Diritto Privato Moderno* (Milan: Giuffrè, 1973)

Thireau, J., '*Hughes Doneau et les fondements de la codification moderne*' (1997) 26 Droits: revue française de théorie, de philosophie et de culture juridiques 81

Thomas, J.A.C., '*Contrectatio*, complicity and *furtum*' (1962) 13 IURA 70

Thomas, J.A.C., *Textbook on Roman Law* (Amsterdam: North-Holland Publishing Company, 1976; 2013 reprint)

Tierney, B., *The Idea of Natural Rights* (Atlanta, Ga.: Scholars Press, 1997)

Valiente, F.T., *Manual de historia del derecho Español* (Madrid: Tecnos, 1983)

Van Dongen, E., *Contributory Negligence: A Historical and Comparative Study* (Leiden: Brill, 2014)

Van Hofstraeten, B., *Juridisch humanisme en costumiere acculturatie, Inhoudsen vormbepalende factoren van de Antwerpse Consuetudines compilatae (1608) en het Gelderse Land- en Stadtsrecht (1620)* (Maastricht: Universitaire Pers Maastricht, 2008)

Van Ittersum, M., 'The working methods of Hugo Grotius: which sources did he use and how did he use them in his early writings on natural law theory?' in Du Plessis, P. & Cairns, J. (eds), *Reassessing Legal Humanism and its Claims* (Edinburgh: Edinburgh University Press, 2015),

Visser, D. and Whitty, N.R., 'The structure of the law of delict in historical perspective' in Reid, K. and Zimmermann, R. (eds), *A History of Private Law in Scotland* (Oxford: Oxford University Press, 2001)

Von Mehren, A. and Gordley, J., *The Civil Law System: An Introduction to the Comparative Study of Law* (Boston: Little, Brown & Co., 1977)

Watson, A., '*Contrectatio* again' in Watson, A., *Studies in Roman Private Law* (London, 1991)

Watson, A. '*Contrectatio* as an essential of *furtum*' (1961) 77 LQR 526

Watson, A. 'D.7.1.13.2: The *lex Aquilia* and decretal actions' in Watson, A., *Studies in Roman Private Law* (London: Hambledon Press, 1991)

Weinrib, A., *The Idea of Private Law* (Cambridge, Mass.: Harvard University Press, 1995)

Weinrib, A., 'Liberty, community and corrective justice' (1988) 1 Canadian Journal of Law and Jurisprudence 3

Weinrib, E., 'The special morality of tort law' (1989) 34 McGill Law Journal 403

Weinzierl, K., *Die Restitutionslehre der Frühscholastik* (Munich: Verlag Max Hueber, 1936)

Willoweit, D. (ed.), *Die Entstehung des öffentlichen Strafrechts* (Cologne: Böhlau Verlag, 1999)

Zimmermann, R., *The Law of Obligations: Roman Foundations of the Civilian Tradition* (Oxford: Oxford University Press, 1990)

Index

Printed in the United States
By Bookmasters